Nicholas Kulish and **Souad Mekhennet**

THE ETERNAL NAZI

Nicholas Kulish is a correspondent for *The New York Times*. He was the paper's Berlin bureau chief from 2007 to 2013.

Souad Mekhennet is a journalist and reports for *The Washington Post* and ZDF German television. She is an associate at the Weatherhead Center for International Affairs at Harvard University and a fellow at Johns Hopkins School of Advanced International Studies, and she previously worked for *The New York Times*.

ALSO BY NICHOLAS KULISH

Last One In

ALSO BY SOUAD MEKHENNET

Die Kinder des Dschihad: Die neue Generation des islamistischen Terrors in Europa (with Michael Hanfeld and Claudia Sautter)
Islam (with Michael Hanfeld)

THE ETERNAL NAZI

THE ETERNAL NAZI

FROM MAUTHAUSEN TO CAIRO, THE RELENTLESS
PURSUIT OF SS DOCTOR ARIBERT HEIM

NICHOLAS KULISH AND SOUAD MEKHENNET

VINTAGE BOOKS
A DIVISION OF RANDOM HOUSE LLC
NEW YORK

FIRST VINTAGE BOOKS EDITION, DECEMBER 2014

Copyright © 2014 by Nicholas Kulish and Souad Mekhennet

All rights reserved. Published in the United States by Vintage Books, a division of
Random House LLC, New York, and in Canada by Random House of Canada
Limited, Toronto, Penguin Random House companies.
Originally published in hardcover in the United States by Doubleday,
a division of Random House LLC, New York, in 2014.

Vintage and colophon are registered trademarks of Random House LLC.

The Library of Congress has cataloged the Doubleday edition as follows:
Kulish, Nicholas.
The eternal Nazi : from Mauthausen to Cairo, the relentless pursuit of
SS doctor Aribert Heim / Nicholas Kulish and Souad Mekhennet.— First Edition.
p cm
1. Heim, Aribert, 1914–1992. 2. War Criminals—Germany—Biography.
3. Physicians—Germany—Biography. 4. Mauthausen (Concentration camp).
5. Human experimentation in medicine—Germany—History—20th century.
6. World War, 1939–1945—Atrocities. 7. Fugitives from justice—Germany.
8. Fugitives from justice—Egypt. I. Mekhennet, Souad. II. Title.
DD247.H3543K85 2014 943.086092—DC23 [B] 2013034604

Vintage Trade Paperback ISBN: 978-0-307-47521-3
eBook ISBN: 978-0-385-53244-0

Kulish author photograph © Tyler Hicks
Mekhennet author photograph © Ben Kilb

www.vintagebooks.com

146122990

CONTENTS

THE ETERNAL NAZI ■ 1

ACKNOWLEDGMENTS ■ 247

NOTES ■ 251

BIBLIOGRAPHY ■ 275

INDEX ■ 283

THE ETERNAL NAZI

The black-and-white photograph is crossed with lines from two days of folding and unfolding. It has turned gray around the edges from the perspiration on the hands of the vendors who looked at it. Dozens grasped the picture, pulled it closer to examine the face of the middle-aged European man staring into the camera with a hint of a smile. The photograph so far has earned mostly puzzled looks and the same probing question. "Why," they ask, pointing at the enlargement of an old passport picture, "why are you looking for him?"

No one on the streets of Cairo recognized him, but Egyptians love a good story almost as much as they love a good joke. They have long exported their soap operas around the Middle East and beyond because they know a good adventure, romance, or mystery when they see one. Maybe, they say, it is a search for a lost father or more likely someone who has failed to pay a debt. Perhaps it is even trouble with the law. This is Cairo in 2008, and there are plainclothes security officers on most every block.

The picture came with a tip, to look for a hotel in the neighborhood of al-Azhar, but at a dozen small hotels managers and clerks give the same answer. "We don't know him." Finally, one man, after a question or two, has an idea. "There is a place that used to be a hotel that sometimes put up foreigners. It's on Port Said Street, not far from the overpass."

The neighborhood is named after al-Azhar mosque, built in the tenth century and one of the preeminent centers of Islamic learning in the world. With its five minarets the mosque may reflect the glories of heaven, but the air on Port Said Street is acrid from burning garbage and the tangy scent of meat hung a little too long in front of butcher shops. A postwar block of concrete rises nine stories, a dull tan color except for green or blue shutters dotting it here and there, failing entirely to cheer up its appearance. Though no longer in business, the Kasr el-Madina Hotel still announces itself with large letters, but one arm of the *K* in "Kasr" has broken off, as has half of the *H* in "Hotel."

Two men in the dark former lobby are deep in conversation, but they stop to answer the stranger's question. One of them, Abu Ahmad, says he knows the owners of the hotel. "I have been here for many years and used to help out in the hotel from time to time," he says. He takes the black-and-white portrait. "I know this man," he says. Tears start to fill his eyes. "This is the foreigner who used to live upstairs. This is Mr. Tarek," he says. "Tarek Hussein Farid."

Abu Ahmad gladly tells what he knows of the foreigner's story but insists that Mahmoud Doma, the son of the hotel's former proprietor, knows far more. After a quick series of calls he has Doma's number. "Hello?" a deep voice answers the phone. "I am Mahmoud, yes. What do you want?" he asks. When he hears the name Tarek Hussein Farid, he says, "Amu," Arabic for uncle.

A few days later, the incessant noise of Cairo traffic infiltrates a women's clothing shop run by the Doma family. Mahmoud Doma's brother opens up an old attaché case. The leather of the briefcase is coated with dust. The clasps are rusted almost completely shut. It is stuffed full of documents, some important records and others just the magazine clippings of an avid reader. There are letters in German, English, and French written in blue ink on yellowish paper. There are applications for residency in Egypt and transfer slips from the National Bank of Egypt. There is also a copy of a last will and testament dividing property between two sons.

Many of the news clips are about Hitler and Nazism, as well as a great deal on Israel. Near the bottom of the case are several copies of a photograph showing rows and rows of white crosses outside a concentration camp. Impassioned handwritten pages describe and then refute accusations of the most brutal crimes committed at the camp, claims of execution, vivisection, and decapitation. Several names are mentioned again and again: Kaufmann, Sommer, Lotter, Kohl, and Simon Wiesenthal, who gained fame in the 1960s for his pursuit of Nazi war criminals.

A Ferdinand Heim or an Aribert Ferdinand Heim has signed much of the correspondence. It is this name, Aribert Ferdinand Heim, that resonates in much of the world as Tarek Hussein Farid does not. Aribert Heim is not just the name of a convert to Islam living out his days quietly in an inexpensive hotel, playing games with children, reading books, and taking long walks around the city. Heim was a physician with Hitler's elite Waffen-SS, a concentration camp doctor, and an accused murderer. He is a phantom, a man sought by investigators for war crimes since 1946.

At the close of the war, investigators barely knew who Aribert Heim was. At most he was considered a small fish, not one of the architects of the Holocaust like Adolf Eichmann or a leading practitioner of deadly Nazi pseudoscience like Josef Mengele, just one of tens of thousands who worked in the concentration camps and death camps overseen by the SS. Yet somehow over the course of decades, as those men went to the gallows, repented, or died undiscovered, Heim grew in stature, at last becoming the world's most wanted Nazi war criminal.

Heim was an Olympic-caliber athlete, a former member of Austria's national ice hockey team. He was a physician, one of the legions of SS doctors who perverted the science of healing into the science of death. In one of the only two photographs investigators had of Heim, the handsome doctor was wearing a tuxedo. His last known residence was the sparkling casino town of Baden-Baden, where he lived in a magnificent white villa. Law enforcement discovered that he had left behind a fortune worth more than $1 million in a bank account in Berlin.

In 2007 a retired colonel of the Israel Defense Forces, Danny Baz, claimed to have been a member of a secret cell of Nazi hunters known as the Owl that tracked down the elusive Heim, who, he claimed, was the leader of a shadowy, powerful organization of former SS officers. After a firefight in upstate New York, Baz said, he recovered a waterproof briefcase containing guns, banknotes, diamonds, and fake passports. "In the inner compartment, a splendid Luger; the grip is made of ivory and the middle, encrusted with gold and silver, is engraved with a swastika with, underneath it, the name of the gun's owner: Aribert Heim."

This tall tale of Nazi hunting was eventually proved untrue. But stories like these helped make Heim into a powerful symbol whose pursuit was a matter of principle, a debt to six million victims, object of the rallying cry "They're still out there." Germany is often lauded as unique among countries for the way it has dealt with its violent past. Its dedication to accepting responsibility for past wrongs, paying compensation, and prosecuting war criminals up to the present day has been held up as an example to other nations from Japan to Turkey to Rwanda. The pursuit of Nazi war criminals helped lay the groundwork for the ongoing experiment of the International Criminal Court.

Yet Germany's path was neither linear nor inevitable. In the postwar years the search for war criminals was left to the occupying Allied forces, whom the local public accused of implementing an arbitrary and punitive form of victors' justice. Then the Allies' focus shifted from the punishment of Germans to the escalating tensions between the United States and the Soviet Union. The Americans, more focused on the next conflict than the last, employed former Nazis to spy on the Soviets.

If the Americans were willing to ignore the past, the Germans were happy to oblige. During the period of rapid rebuilding in the 1950s known as the economic miracle, most Germans simply wanted to forget what had happened under the Nazi regime. The burden of grappling with the country's history fell on the shoulders of a small number of men and women: police officers, prosecutors, and politicians with a conscience and a sense of duty to the victims. For years their pursuit of justice earned them not plaudits but insults. They were taunted as traitors. Criminal cases were ignored, sidetracked, and even sabotaged by former Nazis in high positions in law enforcement and the courts and all the way up to the chancellery in Bonn.

Even decades later, after the mood in Germany shifted toward penitence for the crimes of the Holocaust, society often diffused responsibility into a broad collective guilt rather than individual culpability. Nazi Germany had committed heinous acts, the thinking went, but fathers, sons, brothers, and friends were only following orders. So many murderers went unpunished that any prosecution could seem arbitrary, especially when it was directed decades after the war against seemingly model citizens. In the popular imagination, groups of former Nazis such as the infamous Odessa financed life on the run for comrades-in-arms. Instead of shadowy organizations, it was the support of family and friends that made it possible for people like Heim to elude justice for so long.

The last papers found in the briefcase are in the painstaking handwriting of children. There are drawings of tanks and soldiers, promises of kisses, and announcements of good grades. In one letter, a boy named Rü describes his recent bicycle accident. It is written on a stained piece of graph paper, folded many more times than the copy of the photograph of his father that led to the discovery of the briefcase. He was riding with a friend when their bicycles collided, sending Rü sprawling to the ground, cut and bleeding. "The scars have once again healed well. But during these incidents one notices indeed how much we miss you," he writes to his father. The family thinks about him daily and hopes to see him soon.

"And then at last we will have peace," writes his son. "So we will not despair but instead just wait a bit."

CHAPTER 1

They called it zero hour. Six years of conflict culminated with incendiary bombing raids, artillery shelling, tanks rolling through the countryside. Cities were reduced to rubble. The death and destruction Nazi Germany had visited upon the rest of Europe came home to the Reich with a vengeance. The Allies had won, but the Continent was near chaos. Europe was full of desperate souls on the move. There were caravans of displaced persons clogging the roads in every direction: forced laborers returning to Poland; prisoners of war returning to France and Britain; nearly twelve million ethnic Germans expelled from Poland, Czechoslovakia, Yugoslavia, and elsewhere, seeking refuge in Germany and Austria. Most haunting by far were the survivors of the concentration camps, who emerged from their imprisonment like walking skeletons. Soon the world realized that the crimes committed in the name of Nazi Germany went far beyond ordinary violations of the rules of war.

The Supreme Headquarters, Allied Expeditionary Force, prepared a comprehensive list of suspected war criminals. It was known as the Central Registry of War Criminals and Security Suspects, or CROWCASS. The first version of the list contained 70,000 names. By some estimates 160,000 people should have been included. The question facing the Allies was how to find and punish even those 70,000 perpetrators in the chaos of the months after Nazi capitulation. The Americans alone had to deal with some 7.7 million German military personnel in custody, including regular Wehrmacht soldiers; members of the paramilitary wing of the Nazi Party, the Sturmabteilung, or SA, which had played a key role in Hitler's rise to power; high members of government who had enacted deadly policies; and members of Hitler's dreaded vanguard, the Schutzstaffel, better known as the SS. Separating them proved difficult.

One clue as to who was who came from a mandatory blood-type tattoo under the left arm of all SS members. Captured soldiers were lined up and inspected for the telltale mark. But the method was not always effective. Two of the most notorious Nazi war criminals, Adolf Eichmann and Josef Mengele, were not detected. Seventeen people named Josef Mengele served in the German armed forces, and when captured, the Auschwitz doctor gave his last name as Memling, a famous Bavarian painter. He did not have the SS tattoo and claimed to be a regular doctor with the Wehrmacht. He ultimately fled custody, as did Eichmann. Neither was forced to stand in the dock for the postwar trials that began in Nuremberg.

The pursuit of war criminals was just one of the Allies' responsibilities and not necessarily the most urgent. Germany was reeling from a total defeat rather than a negotiated surrender. People were starving, crops needed harvesting, and millions of POWs without jobs were released within months. The U.S. Third Army had released more than half a million prisoners by June 8; the Twelfth Army group freed an average of 30,000 prisoners a day. Meanwhile, the British sent home some 300,000 Germans as part of Operation Barleycorn, specifically so that they could save the harvest. That number grew to more than a million by August 1945 so that former soldiers could also work in mining and transport. There were untold tons of rubble to clear, bridges to rebuild, unexploded bombs to remove. The telecommunication network, postal service, highways, railways, and even local public transport systems had to be rebuilt.

On June 29, 1945, the Allied Supreme Headquarters issued Disbandment Directive No. 5, which authorized a general discharge of German prisoners not in "automatic arrest categories" such as SS members and war criminals. Captured soldiers were simply looked over by a doctor and given a questionnaire to fill out. Interviews were brief. If a soldier was discharged, he received half a loaf of black bread and roughly a pound of lard as rations for the journey home. With such speed and great numbers it was unavoidable that some war criminals would be among those set free.

One of the men kept in custody was Hauptsturmführer Aribert Ferdinand Heim, an Austrian doctor with the Waffen-SS, the military wing of the SS that had grown into a parallel German army. Though a prisoner, he continued to serve as a doctor, treating wounded Germans at the 8279th General Hospital, near Carentan, France, about twenty miles away from Normandy's Omaha Beach. The hospital was actually a giant tent complex, previously an American field hospital before the United States handed it over to the Germans. When the Red Cross visited in May 1945, there were 1,417 wounded or sick soldiers there. The Red Cross inspector found the conditions to be "excellent" and said that German soldiers had even volunteered that the treatment there was better than it had been on the German side in the last few years of the war.

The tents could be hot during the day and frigid at night, but there were operating rooms, X-ray machines, and a laboratory. The facility was well stocked with surgical equipment and medicine, according to the Red Cross observer. In essence, the German doctors themselves ran the hospital, with four American officers overseeing their work. "On a professional level," the Red Cross assessor wrote, "the cooperation between the American and the German doctors is good." That included Heim. His American superiors were impressed with his skill and dependability. In a recommendation, the American captain Edward S. Jones wrote that Heim's work in the surgical section "had been excellent and essential for the care of the POW patients."

Heim struck up friendly acquaintanceships with fellow doctors and even a German pastor, Werner Ernst Linz. The pastor observed how Heim "practiced his medicinal arts in a very responsible manner for the well-being of the soldiers entrusted to him." Dr. Heim was particularly "self-sacrificing" in treating sexually transmitted diseases, doing everything he could to help his patients, Linz wrote in a letter of recommendation.

Though he traveled widely during the war, Heim ended up right where he had begun, in France. After Germany annexed Austria in 1938, Austrians had the same duty to serve as their new compatriots. Heim insisted under questioning that he had been drafted into the Waffen-SS against his will. His first assignment after earning his medical degree in Vienna at the age of twenty-five had been as a driver during the German invasion of France in 1940. Heim assisted in the resettlement of ethnic Germans in Yugoslavia and worked on earthquake relief in Romania. He had served at the frigid northern reaches of the eastern front in Norway and Finland and been wounded in action.

Just eight days after the first American soldier crossed the Rhine on March 7, 1945, Heim's unit was captured at Buchholz in western Germany. Heim was fortunate to find himself a prisoner of war on the American side, rather than facing a trip to Siberia courtesy of the Soviets. He was sent to the prisoner-of-war camp in France.

He was not on the CROWCASS list of wanted war criminals, but as a former member of the Waffen-SS he was in the Allied automatic arrest category, and it was not easy to secure release. Arrest and prosecution would have been certain but for an omission. For all the places Heim went over the course of the war, one post was missing from his file—through oversight or intentional removal, it was unclear—a small town in Austria called Mauthausen.

CHAPTER 2

Less than nine months after he was liberated from six years in concentration camps in Germany and Austria, Dr. Arthur A. Becker was in Vienna working as a special investigator for the U.S. Army's War Crimes Investigating Team 6836. He was a slender, brown-eyed fifty-five-year-old, with noticeable gaps between his teeth, born in the northern German town of Prenzlau. A writer by profession, Becker had studied pharmacology and had been living in Stuttgart when he was arrested. During his incarceration he wore the green triangle of the common criminal, but as he told the American authorities once he was freed, one of his grandfathers was Jewish. He had been arrested for making critical statements about the SS after Kristallnacht.

American war-crimes investigators struggled to build their cases quickly for trials they planned throughout their zones of occupation; they were drastically understaffed. Manpower was shifted first to the Pacific theater, where the United States was still fighting the Japanese. After the Japanese surrender, GIs were sent home as quickly as possible. Those soldiers kept to investigate war crimes were "mostly shell-shocked tank officers who were sent to this new unit as a form of recreation and rehabilitation," one prosecutor recalled. "They sat around with no idea what to do." The enormity of the task, as well as the language barrier, required the help of locals, and the ranks of former inmates provided enthusiastic volunteers like Becker.

On the morning of Friday, January 18, 1946, Becker had appointments in Vienna to interview other former inmates—a man named Josef Kohl in the morning and one named August Kamhuber in the afternoon—about the killings of Allied military personnel in violation of the Geneva Convention. Like Berlin, the Austrian capital was a divided city at the time, occupied by British, French, American, and Soviet troops, all with their own zones plus a jointly administered international zone in the first district. The investigative team Becker worked for was headquartered in Salzburg, but even the simple task of bringing witnesses from the Soviet sector required a special settlement between the increasingly mistrustful wartime allies. The Russians deemed the movement of witnesses from their zone to be "kidnapping."

Much of Vienna's former grandeur was still obscured by wartime damage. Between the bombing raids and the final Red Army offensive to take the city, large swaths of the old first district had been demolished. In all, some eighty thousand homes had been destroyed or damaged. Displaced persons from all over Europe, including camp survivors and former slave laborers, sought refuge, adding to the housing crisis. Gas, electricity, and telephone services were disrupted, and the Viennese received permission from their occupiers to chop down many of the trees lining the city's once-lovely boulevards to fend off the cold of the hard postwar winter.

The shortages and rationing were nothing out of the ordinary for Josef Kohl, who had grown up poor and often gone hungry as a child. As an adult, he was bald with a tight-lipped, self-conscious smile, possibly to hide his large and slightly crooked teeth. The Austrian Communist looked more like the trained accountant he was than the street fighter he had become. Kohl took to the barricades in 1934 to fight for the Austrian republic against the fascist takeover and was shot in the chest, the bullet passing through his lung. After the Nazis absorbed Austria into the growing Third Reich, the Gestapo arrested Kohl. Following several months in the Gestapo jail at Morzinplatz in downtown Vienna, he was transferred to the infamous Dachau concentration camp on the outskirts of Munich.

One year later, in September 1939, Kohl was transferred again, this time to a year-old camp in Upper Austria. Heinrich Himmler chose the site for economic exploitation so that inmates could be used as slave labor to cut granite from the Wiener Graben stone quarry. The camp was named for the nearby town of Mauthausen. The inmates at the camp were forced, under threat of violence and even summary execution, to carry heavy stones up 186 steep stone steps carved into the hillside. Many simply died from the exertion. The inmates eventually built their own prison, unique in appearance among the concentration camps with its high stone wall and guard towers, giving their camp the look of a medieval castle.

Before the Nazis opened extermination camps in Poland, Mauthausen stood as the only Class III concentration camp in a three-tiered system. That meant that, according to the Nazis' own rating, it was the harshest in the whole network of camps, even worse than Dachau, Buchenwald, or Auschwitz, designed for "Vernichtung durch Arbeit," or extermination through work. That year more than half of the nearly sixteen thousand inmates at Mauthausen died or were killed. Kohl remained there for the entire war, almost six years in all, until liberation came in the waning days of the conflict. Now he was free, living again with his wife, Agnes, and working as the head of the branch of Volkssolidarität, or the People's Solidarity, an organization of former camp inmates.

Becker's interview with Kohl began at 10:55 a.m., with the witness giving his biographical information, his address on Endergasse in the Hetzendorf neighborhood south of the city center in Vienna, and his account of how he came to be held at Mauthausen. These formalities taken care of, Becker asked, "What do you know about the abuse and murder of English or alternatively Anglo-American prisoners of war?"

"The first English prisoners, who jumped with parachutes into France and there procured civilian clothes for themselves, were brought to Mauthausen in 1940 and there were shot as spies," Kohl answered. How did Kohl know that they were English? Kohl explained that he spoke English and had talked to the men before they were executed. He went on to describe the mistreatment of the Allied pilots in July 1944, the kicks, the heads slammed against walls, and he named the members of the SS responsible.

Becker wanted to know what Kohl could tell him about the mistreatment and killing of prisoners. "I was a clerk in the sick quarters from

April 1940 to June 1941," Kohl said. "As a result I was present as an eye-witness at the first killings by syringe injections."

"What sorts of prisoners were killed?" Becker asked.

"First and foremost it was those unfit for work, the weak, and the sick."

"Are you aware of any other atrocities committed by SS camp doctors?" Becker asked.

"Yes. Camp physician Dr. Heim had the habit of looking in the mouths of inmates to determine whether their teeth were in flawless condition. If this was the case, then he would kill the inmate by injection, cut off the head, and let it cook for hours in the crematorium until the naked skull was bared of all flesh and this skull prepared for him or his friends as decoration for their desks."

"What else can you say about this Dr. Heim?" Becker asked.

"If he selected an inmate for his experiments, he took care first to question him thoroughly, in particular about the state of his family, whether they were provided for in the event that he was gone. Once he had established that, he performed operations on healthy people. He convinced them through figures of speech that it was just a small, harmless operation and that once they were recovered they would immediately be let go. Then he performed the most difficult, complicated operations such as stomach, liver—even heart operations—on these people that had to lead to their deaths. These people were entirely healthy human beings, and the operations were for experimental purposes," Kohl concluded.

"Do you know whether Dr. Heim is still alive?" Becker asked.

"I cannot provide any specific information about that," Kohl said. "It cannot be ruled out that he is in hiding."

CHAPTER 3

A new sign hung over the entryway at the brick barracks at Dachau, reading, "War Crimes Branch, Judge Advocate Sections, H.Q. Third United States Army." Where SS power had once been absolute, uniformed American military officers now sat in judgment, a giant Stars and Stripes hanging behind them. On March 29, 1946, American MPs escorted sixty-one defendants from the Mauthausen concentration camp into the courtroom. Originally, it was supposed to be sixty, but one of the most murderous guards from the stone quarry, Hans Spatzenegger, had his name added into the typed indictment by hand.

By the end of the war, the camp headquarters alone employed more than 350 people. Mauthausen and its forty-nine sub-camps strewn across the Austrian countryside combined had nearly ten thousand guards. There were also more than fifty SS doctors. *U.S. v. Hans Altfuldisch et al.* was the first important trial of Mauthausen personnel. The defendants ranged from Nazi Party leaders to simple guards. One U.S. intelligence officer criticized the inclusion of certain individuals among the sixty-one as "a throw of the dice or a spin of the roulette wheel."

The men on trial were not chosen at random, but neither were they selected because they had committed the most serious crimes. The lead prosecutor, Lieutenant Colonel William Denson, wanted to establish precedents that would make convictions in subsequent trials easier to achieve. He wanted as broad a cross section of camp life as possible. Ultimately, Denson chose defendants who "ranged in age from twenty-one to sixty-two, and included forty-two Germans, twelve Austrians, three Czechs, two Yugoslavians, one Romanian, and one Hungarian," and who had "served at more than fifteen sub-camps, as well as the Hartheim euthanasia facility." There was a civilian employee of the SS firm that ran the quarries. A total of eight of those indicted were medical personnel.

On the second day of the trial, the director of the Innsbruck gas-works, Ernst Martin, took the stand. During his time as inmate number 3148 at Mauthausen, Martin seemed a disinterested paper pusher, a model prisoner-clerk. When he was ordered in April 1945 to burn all the documents in the office of the chief physician concerning the prisoners as well as those dealing with SS personnel, he set about incinerating papers, a process that took more than a week. "The material was so large because it concerned approximately 72,000 deaths and you had a single file for each one that we were burning without interruption for eight days," Martin told the court. "And because it was such a long procedure, there was such a tremendous amount, and it took such a long time, I was able to save and hide these death books."

Martin was concealing the most incriminating materials in the basement of the prisoners' sick quarters, in a cupboard filled with old surgical equipment. If the SS had realized what he was doing, they would have executed him on the spot. The books comprised thirteen heavy volumes registering the 71,856 official deaths at the camp. Martin testified that the causes of death were routinely falsified and that many of those killed by lethal injection were not included at all.

He had also preserved the operation book, Prosecution's Exhibit 15, which recorded the surgical procedures at the camp. Under the surgeries from the fall of 1941, the name Heim was scrawled along the margin of the page. The *H* was written with a distinctive double loop that looked almost like an infinity symbol tilted at an angle. Officially—for much happened off the books at Mauthausen—Heim had operated 263 times while he was at the camp. All eleven of the Jewish inmates he operated on were listed as having died within a few weeks. But Heim was not seated in the five rows of defendants listening to the testimony against them.

Mauthausen's former chief physician, Dr. Eduard Krebsbach, was among those who did stand trial. He had admitted to selecting roughly two hundred tuberculosis patients for lethal injections and later, on orders of the camp commandant, choosing another two thousand prisoners for the gas chamber. At his trial, under intense questioning, Dr. Krebsbach maintained that he was only following orders in euthanizing the "hopelessly ill," referring to the Nazi doctrine that sanctioned such killings. "It is the same with people as it is with animals," Dr. Krebsbach said. "Animals that come into the world crippled or otherwise nonviable are killed immediately after birth . . . It is the right of every state to defend itself against asocial elements, and that also includes those unfit to live."

The most detailed information about the medical murders came from several Czech physicians held as inmates and forced to assist the SS doctors. Dr. Josef Podlaha stated that he had reported almost immediately to the American Counter Intelligence Corps (known as the CIC) on what he called the SS doctors' "degenerate and perverse practices." Podlaha also testified about being forced by one of the defendants, Dr. Hans Richter, to help him operate on living people "for different diseases which they were not suffering from, for instance, stomach ulcers, stomach resections, gallbladders, kidneys, and also brain operations," all so Richter could improve his skills as a surgeon.

Another witness was Josef Kohl, who returned to the concentration camp at Dachau, where he had once been imprisoned, to confront his former captors. Kohl testified against a capo who beat prisoners, pointing him out from among the defendants sitting in the dock. The capo had a piece of paper hanging around his neck with the number 21 printed in black on it. Kohl picked out another guard as number 29 and a functionary from the political department as number 37. But the prosecutor asked Kohl no questions about Dr. Heim, nor was the doctor sitting among the accused, waiting to be identified. There was no sign of the man alleged to have murdered prisoners to take skulls as trophies. Nor had Heim's name been on the list of around one hundred SS officers, guards, and others provided to the Americans by camp survivors shortly after liberation. The verdicts in the Mauthausen trial were read on May 13, 1946. All sixty-one defendants were convicted, and of them all but three were sentenced to death by hanging. Although Heim was not among them, neither was he forgotten.

Three days later, a little over a hundred miles away across the Austrian border in Salzburg, a new play about the concentration camp, written by one of its inmates, made its debut at the State Theater. For *The Road into Life,* the playwright, Arthur Becker, drew not only on his own experiences but also on the testimony he gathered as a war-crimes investigator from other survivors, including Josef Kohl. "Officially, there is no murder here," says one of the characters in the play, Hermann, a capo described as a "small-time crook but otherwise a good person." Hermann continues, "One dies from pneumonia, weakness, or some other harmless illness, and the crematorium makes sure that no one discovers your cause of death.

"We have a doctor—doctor?—no, a headhunter," Hermann says. "Do you know how many people, healthy people, with sets of teeth in flawless condition he has killed because their prepared skulls made wonderful desk ornaments for him and these SS bandits?" The SS *Obersturmführer* insinuates that Heim will decapitate a new inmate. "Someone should introduce him to the camp doctor. Perhaps he has a use for his skull!" The SS officer yells to an underling, "Speak with Dr. Heim. He should see him, and today."

CHAPTER 4

The Jewish Historical Documentation Center in Linz was a tiny office filled with underpaid workers. They scribbled down notes about some of the worst crimes humanity had witnessed onto tiny index cards in the belief that the little pieces of evidence would be assembled over time into a larger picture. Thirty volunteers, most of them fed and sheltered in displaced-persons camps like the one in Bindermichl, collected testimony about Nazi war criminals from their surviving victims. The rent and basic expenses of the office at Goethestrasse 63 came to about $50 a month and were paid by Abraham Silberschein, an affluent Jew and former Polish parliamentarian living in Geneva. But the whole operation would never have existed were it not for the determination and tenacity of the center's mastermind, Simon Wiesenthal.

In 1947, Wiesenthal was thirty-eight years old, reunited with his wife, Cyla, and living with their baby daughter, born just the year before. Wiesenthal had studied architectural engineering and might have made a good middle-class existence for himself whether there in Austria, in the United States, where some family members urged him to emigrate, or in Palestine, where many survivors were moving in the hopes of founding a Jewish state. After the chaotic life he had experienced even before the camps, it would have been more than understandable for him to want to leave Europe behind. Instead, he had founded the documentation center.

Wiesenthal was born on New Year's Eve in 1908 in Buczacz, which was then part of the Austro-Hungarian Empire. His father died in 1915 fighting in World War I. Young Simon himself barely survived a pogrom by Cossacks. His homeland ended up as part of the Second Polish Republic. He studied architectural engineering in Prague and then settled in Lvov with his wife. Under the 1939 Molotov-Ribbentrop Pact, in which Hitler and Stalin agreed to divide Poland between them, Wiesenthal found himself a citizen of the Soviet Union. Less than two years later Hitler broke the deal, and Wiesenthal, like the majority of European Jewry, found himself at the mercy of the Nazis. He secured false papers for Cyla that spared her from the death camps but could not escape himself.

Four years later he emerged from Mauthausen weighing less than a hundred pounds. He had fended off consignment to the gas chambers. He narrowly escaped execution on numerous occasions and finally, barely surviving the death marches of prisoners as the Nazis retreated, ended up in a Mauthausen barrack reserved chiefly for the dead and the dying. When the U.S. Army liberated the camp, Wiesenthal had no interest in a long convalescence. He wanted those responsible brought to account. Less than three weeks after being rescued, he addressed a letter to Colonel Richard Seibel, the American officer in charge of the camp, offering his services in hunting for war criminals. In addition to a curriculum vitae he provided a list of ninety-one Nazis, describing in the most detail he could their crimes and physical appearances. The Americans accepted his letter and told him to come back when he had regained some fraction of his strength.

Wiesenthal kept coming back, and his persistence soon paid off. He began working for the War Crimes Unit of the American Counter Intelligence Corps. He was so weak when he went to make his first solo arrest that he barely made it up the stairs to the ex-Nazi's apartment. He was so light-headed on the way back down that the man he apprehended had to help him down the stairs to the waiting jeep.

At first Wiesenthal lived in a displaced-persons camp set up at the local school in Leonding near Linz, where as a boy Adolf Hitler attended primary school. Wiesenthal could look out the window and see the small house where Hitler's parents had lived, and he knew they were buried in the nearby cemetery. He quickly moved to Landstrasse 40 in Linz. There,

Wiesenthal lived just a few doors down from the father and stepmother of Adolf Eichmann. As Hungarian survivors told him about Eichmann and his meticulous orchestration of the mass deportations in Hungary, finding the man responsible for so much slaughter became an obsession for Wiesenthal. In the meantime, he worked with the Briha, which funneled survivors to Palestine. Some forty thousand of the nearly quarter million displaced Jews lived in Austria. Wiesenthal helped refugees make contact with living family members or, more often, find out how they died.

At that point he still believed his own wife had been killed in Warsaw during the war. In fact she had been forced to work in an ammunition factory in Germany. Cyla in turn believed Simon was dead. By coincidence she met a common acquaintance in Krakow who had just received a letter from Wiesenthal, and they were reunited. By Wiesenthal's count a combined eighty-nine members of his family and his wife's family had been killed in the Holocaust. On September 5, 1946, Simon and Cyla added to their depleted ranks with the birth of their daughter, Pauline Rosa.

The public in Germany and the United States was absorbed by the Nuremberg Major War Criminals Trial, which played out between November 20, 1945, and October 1, 1946, in the city's Palace of Justice before the International Military Tribunal. Many German citizens, struggling with deprivation and occupation, blamed the upper echelon of the Nazi leadership for their own suffering at the end of the war and were happy to see them brought to account. Others grumbled about victors' justice, a complaint that would grow with each new trial.

The desire to hunt down war criminals was quickly fading on the Allied side. The soldiers who had witnessed the inhumanities at the liberated concentration camps rotated back home. Wiesenthal perceived a lack of drive among many of the U.S. officers. There were a few anti-Semitic comments that rang in the Holocaust survivor's ears, making it that much harder to deal with the growing apathy on the part of his associates.

The focus of American enmity was rapidly shifting away from the defeated Nazis and toward the Soviets and Joseph Stalin's rising ambitions in Europe. The division of the Continent deepened, with Eastern

Europe slipping into the Communist camp and Western Europe gravitating toward the Americans. The rivalry between the United States and the Soviet Union, former allies and budding superpowers, meant that both sides hoped to win the gathering battle for German public opinion. The defeated power in the heart of Europe could prove decisive in a struggle between east and west. The German people might have tolerated seeing Nazi leadership in the dock, but they wanted their privates, sergeants, and lieutenants home, whether they served in the Wehrmacht or the Waffen-SS.

Wiesenthal wanted to keep looking for perpetrators but decided he was better going out on his own than working with the increasingly distracted Americans. Wiesenthal started the Jewish Historical Documentation Center in 1947 with the help of like-minded survivors, whom he called fellow "desperadoes."

Any refugee was a witness. Name, appearance, age, where did he work? What was his rank? What had he—or she—done? Before computers Wiesenthal had to meticulously organize by card file the perpetrators, the witnesses, and the locations of the crimes. He was not the only one assembling evidence. In Vienna another survivor, named Tuviah Friedman, had set up his own Jewish Historical Documentation Center and worked for the Haganah, the paramilitary group that would become the Israel Defense Forces.

Friedman was an avenger with a relish for brutal retaliation. He was from Radom, Poland, and only he and his sister survived the Holocaust out of his immediate family. He escaped one camp just before the inmates were sent to Auschwitz. He was recaptured but got hold of a bayonet, crept up to his sleeping guard, and felt "the sensation of ripping his flesh" as he "plunged the bayonet into his neck." In the immediate postwar days Friedman quite literally hunted Nazis "with burning enthusiasm" and, when he caught them, by his own account, whipped, tortured, and even killed them.

Friedman and Wiesenthal exchanged nearly two hundred letters in 1947, swapping information about war criminals and survivor testimony from their files. It felt at times like a losing battle. More and more of the refugees received emigration visas or left the displaced-persons camps and restarted their lives. The Allies had other priorities, and the German and Austrian authorities, to the extent that they wanted to deal with Nazi crimes at all, focused on the regime's persecution of its own people or the euthanasia program, the systematic murder of mentally and physically disabled Germans, not the mechanized slaughter of Jews in the east.

In 1947, Wiesenthal published a book about the Grand Mufti of Jerusalem, Haj Amin al-Husseini, who had worked with the Nazis and even visited concentration camps. Wiesenthal was interested in the collaboration between the Nazis and their Arab allies. But his real passion was Eichmann, who as a member of the Reich Security Central Office played a fundamental role in the attempted extermination of the European Jews. Wiesenthal had found purpose after the war in part by focusing on the killers, listening to the stories of refugees in the faint hope that someday they would aid in bringing men like Heim to justice. The nightmare was over, and most people went back to the closest thing they could find to their old lives. Wiesenthal could not let go, could not forget.

CHAPTER 5

Alfred Aedtner never had any intention of hunting Nazi war criminals for a living. Then again, the young Wehrmacht veteran did not have any real plans for the future after the war ended. If there was any group for whom the rapid collapse of the Thousand-Year Reich was particularly difficult to comprehend, it was young men like Aedtner. Born in 1925, he was barely seven years old when Adolf Hitler came to power in 1933. Nazi propaganda served as the foundation of his schooling.

He was born in Alt-Seidenberg in Silesia, at the old Three Kings' Corner, where the Austro-Hungarian Empire, Prussia, and Saxony once met. Like the other boys, young Fredi, as he was known, wore the brown shirt and black shorts of the Hitler Youth, a dagger in his belt and a swastika armband on his upper arm. He was good-looking, a bit vain about his clothes, always wanting to be perfectly dressed, but a well-behaved teenager. He led the younger boys in their calisthenic exercises, serving as a *Fähnleinführer,* little flag leader, a position of responsibility in the top-to-bottom hierarchy of the Reich.

Growing up in a newly built settlement on the edge of town, Aedtner did not want to go to the town's largest employer, the Seidenberger Tonwerke, the factory where his father worked and, when Fredi was just sixteen, died of a heart attack. Fredi was a cadet at a military school. With his military haircut buzzed short on the sides, his ears stuck out, making him look younger than his years, but he still kept his cadet's cap tilted just so. He looked forward to a career as an army officer. While many were drafted, Aedtner volunteered for the Wehrmacht on January 3, 1944, shortly after his eighteenth birthday. A private in a grenadier regiment, he was stationed on the western front.

The fact that Nazi Germany was going to lose the war had been apparent to many Germans for some time, from the high command down to the gossips on the street. The information machine so carefully tended by Minister of Public Enlightenment and Propaganda Joseph Goebbels could not explain away the costly defeat at Stalingrad. The letters announcing the deaths of sons, husbands, and brothers added up to a different narrative from the official version of events, one that could be no more easily ignored than the nearing echo of booming artillery just on the other side of the Rhine or the streams of refugees fleeing the Red Army from the east.

Aedtner continued to believe what his superiors told him. During what would be his final visit home in the autumn of that year, he told the family friends and next-door neighbors, the Montags, that the *Endsieg*, the final victory promised by the Führer, was coming. "We won't lose the war," he told them. "Whoever believes that has a loose screw."

Aedtner returned to the front and in December 1944 faced French forces near Cernay, where an Allied offensive aimed to retake the town. They retook Thann, just to the west, on December 10. They seized Aspach-le-Bas and Aspach-le-Haut to the south on December 11, soldiers from the 6e Régiment de Chasseurs d'Afrique destroying a machine-gun position and capturing twenty German soldiers. The following day the French pressed to gain control of Cernay, but German troops had dug in at an SS training facility and fought back. A grenade exploded, wounding Private Aedtner and killing the man beside him. Aedtner had shrapnel in his right eye. He was carried from a first-aid station to a field hospital before eventually landing in a military hospital in Singen, a peaceful corner of Germany near Lake Constance, not far from the border with Switzerland.

At the hospital Aedtner made friends with another wounded veteran his age named Fritz Haag. Both wore the gray uniform of the Wehrmacht as eighteen-year-olds, and both had been wounded less than a year into their military service, suffering shrapnel injuries to the face.

Haag, from the southwest region of Baden, had been in combat on the eastern front, near Minsk. Though an avid athlete, in a black-and-white photograph young Haag hardly looked big enough to carry the oversized pack strapped to his back. He still managed to win an Iron Cross, First Class, for bravery. A shell had exploded near him, severing an artery in his neck and nearly killing him. He survived the explosion but lost both of his eyes.

When he was physically strong enough, with Aedtner's help, at least he got to go home. Aedtner had been declared fit for military service again, but rather than returning to the front, he first escorted his friend home. They traveled together from Singen almost a hundred miles through the Black Forest. Haag was born and raised on the edge of the famous woods, in Oberschopfheim, a village between the foothills of the mountainous forest and the flat valley of the Rhine River, not far from Strasbourg and the region known as Alsace. The territory had traded hands between Germany and France several times, a violent process playing out once again at that very moment.

It was February 1945, and the war was nearly over. These two blond, baby-faced young veterans moved through a landscape of defeat. Fate had proved capricious in its treatment of the towns and cities along their way; one stood pristine, untouched by conflict, while the next lay in smoking ruins from the Allied air raids. Often the only difference was a railway switching station or a small factory producing ball bearings, the sort needed for armaments.

Haag's hometown of Oberschopfheim was one of the lucky places that were spared the aerial bombardment. Landmarks like the church tower, the local inn, the *Gasthaus zur Linde,* the stately older houses with the wooden beams, and even the Haag family home on Meiersmatt- strasse were still standing. It was still more than a month before French forces took the town in April 1945.

It was a dangerous time for Aedtner, fit for military service but not with a combat unit. Overzealous SS officers summarily executed desert- ers with growing frequency as the certainty of defeat loomed larger. Some twenty-two thousand German soldiers were killed in all. It was not just soldiers but the boys drafted to fire the antiaircraft guns, the so- called *Flakhelfer,* and the middle-aged men of the Volkssturm auxiliary forces charged with defending their cities, towns, and villages to their last breaths. Bodies hung from lampposts in the final spasm of violence that was the bloody end of a murderous regime.

In Oberschopfheim the local residents knew that defending their homes was best accomplished by surrendering before they were destroyed by Allied artillery. When French forces arrived outside neighboring Niederschopfheim that April, a few men from the local Volkssturm took down the defensive barricades in the dark of night. Residents hung white sheets out the windows, and children waved white handkerchiefs as French soldiers, many of them Moroccans from the North African protectorate, marched into town. The German surrender followed the next month, on May 7, 1945.

With the capitulation, everything young men like Alfred Aedtner knew was gone. Adolf Hitler had been not just the chancellor or the president but the Führer, the totalitarian leader in every way. He had led Germans not into lasting victory and world domination but into total defeat. When Hitler committed suicide in his bunker in Berlin, his entire worldview died with him.

Even after the war ended, Aedtner still could not go home. The Soviets controlled his family home in Seidenberg. For a German Wehrmacht veteran to travel into the Soviet zone would mean risking detention by the Red Army and deportation to a prisoner-of-war camp in Siberia. Aedtner had no work, nothing to do but hang around in the front yard of the Haag house, gently kicking a soccer ball back and forth with Fritz. He was like a sleepwalker awakened from a dream that had lasted a dozen years.

One of the punishments the victors inflicted was a loss of territory, a border redrawn on a map for most but a very personal loss for Aedtner. Stalin claimed Polish territory in the east for the Soviet Union and compensated Poland with German lands in the west, including Aedtner's home in Seidenberg. Görlitz, about a half hour's drive away, was divided into two parts, a German city on the west bank and a Polish city on the east. In Oberschopfheim, almost at the French border, Aedtner was about as far from home as he could get and still be in Germany.

Aedtner continued to help Haag, taking his friend to doctors' appointments. They went to the eye clinic in Freiburg and to training courses to help Haag learn braille and make other practical adjustments to the loss of his sight. Haag wore a yellow armband with black dots to alert drivers and passersby to the presence of a blind person. Aedtner kept busy doing odd jobs like painting houses, maybe baling a little hay. No one went hungry in the village. The Haags kept pigs and a milk cow in the barn next to the house and had potato fields; others grew grapes, corn, and tobacco.

When the war ended, Aedtner had nothing but the uniform on his back. For a born clotheshorse that was an unacceptable state of affairs. If he could not afford a new suit, he could at least ask the local tailor, Johannes Ackermann, for alterations to make the trousers and jacket look a little more civilian—perhaps a bit more fashionable if that was remotely possible. Ackermann was friends with Fritz's father, Johann Haag, and the two had served in World War I together. They lived down the block on Meiersmattstrasse. Ackermann's daughter Eleonore quickly caught Aedtner's eye. As it did for men and women across war-torn Germany, zero hour began to recede for the young man, and the possibility of a future, however different, began to take shape.

CHAPTER 6

The Americans transferred Heim into German custody in December 1946. As a former member of the SS, he was transferred from detention camp to detention camp. He was briefly held in the hilltop stone fortress in southwest Germany known as Hohenasperg, which had been used as a prison for centuries, holding poets and deserters, students who had fought illegal duels, and regime opponents in the years after Hitler came to power. From there he went to Lager 74, the former Flakkaserne, the antiaircraft barracks in the town of Ludwigsburg. The Flakkaserne had been a symbol of the Nazis' decision to flout the conditions of the Versailles Treaty and remilitarize Germany once they took power. Construction began in late 1935, the year before Heim and his brother visited Berlin for Hitler's Olympics. By the time Heim got there a decade later, it was under the control of the U.S. Seventh Army.

There was a twenty-foot-high watchtower and ten-foot barbed-wire fencing. The men slept in crowded dormitory rooms with three-tiered bunk beds. For their edification and reeducation, there were concerts and theater performances. One photograph from the time shows a basketball game in which the ball handler and the opponent defending him had only one arm each. Men worked at the shoemaker, watchmaker, or bookbinder, at the motor pool or the blacksmith shop, where a sign over the anvil read "We want to go home to wife and child!" Finally, Heim found himself at the state-owned salt mine that had been the concentration camp Kochendorf, used for defense production during the final year of the war. He worked there hauling salt and awaiting a final judgment in his case.

Aribert Ferdinand Heim was born in the Austrian town of Radkersburg on June 28, 1914. For the family it was a day of personal tragedy. His twin brother, Peter, was stillborn. For the world it was the disastrous, historic day when the assassin Gavrilo Princip shot and killed Archduke Franz Ferdinand, along with his wife, Sophie, Duchess of Hohenberg, plunging the Continent into the devastating conflict known as the Great War. The Treaty of Saint-Germain-en-Laye in 1919, when Aribert was barely five years old, dismantled the Habsburg Empire and divided Radkersburg along the line of the Mur River. The part of town south of the river joined the new state of Yugoslavia.

In 1929, while Aribert was attending the Marien Institute secondary school in Graz, the family suffered a terrible setback when his father, Josef Ferdinand Heim, a gendarmerie commander, passed away from a heart condition. His mother, Anna Heim, was left with four children and only a modest widow's pension to support them. She, her elder son, Josef, and her younger daughter, Herta, the baby of the family, were high-spirited and enjoyed playing the accordion and laughing. The elder daughter, Hilda, and younger son, Aribert, had inherited their father's more contemplative manner. Hilda promised her father just before he died that she would take care of her mother so the other children could study medicine.

Aribert Heim moved to Vienna in the fall of 1931, when he was just seventeen years old, to begin studying Latin at the university with the help of a stipend from the state of 250 Austrian schillings per semester. He rented a room at Alserstrasse 22, in the student quarter to the west of the city center known as Josefstadt. Heim worked as a tutor to earn extra money and also played professional ice hockey for the Eissport Klub Engelmann with increasing success. Sports were his passion. He was also serious about competing in track and field but eventually gave it up as hockey took more and more of his time. Heim was invited to join the Austrian national ice hockey team as well. The *Sport-Tagblatt* of January 15, 1936, wrote about an upcoming test match for the Austrian national team, listing excellent young players, "most notably the young, talented defenseman Heim."

Aribert's older brother, Josef, was brave but impetuous, once saving a drowning man at risk to his own life. His impulsiveness also carried him headlong into the dangerous politics of the times, as fascists and Communists vied for control of Austria just as they were doing to the north in Germany. Josef took part in the failed Nazi coup in Austria in 1934 and had to flee the country. The government charged him with high treason and stripped him of his citizenship when he refused to appear in court. Josef lived first in Varazdin, which was then in Yugoslavia and is today in Croatia, before arriving in Germany that December. There he underwent military training as part of Hitler's Austrian Legion.

Black-and-white photographs show Aribert and Josef visiting Berlin together during the 1936 Olympic Games, a pair of young men dressed up in their best suits attending the biggest sporting event in the world, which became a significant showcase for the resurgence of Germany and the pageantry of Nazism three years into Hitler's reign. The following year Aribert moved to Rostock in the German Reich, a city with a booming armaments industry that was flush with new contracts from the military. It was there that he, like his brother, joined the party. Back in Vienna, the zealous Nazi anatomist Eduard Pernkopf, who lectured in his SA uniform, was one of his professors and signed his diploma.

After Nazi Germany absorbed Austria in the Anschluss on March 12, 1938, Josef was able to return home. Under the Nazi regime his participation in the failed coup and the Austrian Legion was now a mark of distinction. According to family stories, he wanted to volunteer for the military without finishing his medical studies first. "The Führer is not going to give you your doctorate," Aribert told his brother. "You can always join later." Aribert himself requested deferments twice so that he could complete his studies, in 1938 and 1939, the latter on the eve of the invasion of Poland, which would mark the start of World War II. He was drafted immediately after finishing his medical degree at the University of Vienna in 1940.

After graduation Josef volunteered to join the paratroopers. On May 20, 1941, the young assistant doctor was among the first to parachute into Crete as part of the ill-fated Nazi invasion. With the help of intelligence intercepts, Allied forces were waiting for the landing, and the invasion, though ultimately successful, turned into a bloodbath for the Nazi forces. Josef Heim was among those killed near Chania, in the northwestern part of the island. The official cause of death was infantry fire. When a comrade later came to visit Anna Heim in Radkersburg, he told the grieving mother that her son had volunteered to parachute in with the first wave, saying it was his duty as he had neither wife nor children for whom he had to provide. The comrade went on to tell how Josef had been not just killed but butchered alive by soldiers from New Zealand who were defending the island as part of the British Commonwealth forces. They tore off Josef's fingernails, jabbed out his eyes, and smashed the teeth from his mouth, the paratrooper said.

The family feared for Aribert until the very end of the war before learning that he had survived, though he would not be coming home right away. The postwar years were times of deprivation. A colleague warned Heim of the terrible conditions on the outside in a letter in December 1947, saying, "Freedom in destroyed Germany looks quite sad. There are more than enough doctors, and even I, despite good connections and without a political burden, have been unable to find a proper position."

The colleague had been working in the tuberculosis station at a displaced-persons hospital near Kassel, where he saw "sad images, poor people without homelands, or those who do not dare return to their homelands, lying here with the gravest pulmonary tuberculosis, most hopeless cases." He signed off by saying, "I still hope that someday the gateway to the world opens for us too and one can start life again in another part of the world."

Many of the remaining prisoners were finally freed at the end of 1947 in what was known as the Christmas Amnesty of 1947, which also spelled the end to Aribert Heim's detention. Captain John D. Austin signed and stamped Heim's release papers on December 14, 1947, and eight days later he was allowed to leave after nearly three years in custody. In the same month, the Dachau court ended its work and disbanded, after judging fifteen hundred German defendants and sentencing some four hundred of them to death.

Heim was allowed to travel the more than 150 miles north to the town of Fritzlar near Kassel to see his sister Herta. He arrived to find a brother-in-law, Georg Barth, he had never met and a baby niece he did not know who was about to be christened. According to family lore, Aribert turned up at the celebration by accident, uninvited but very welcome. He was emotionally overwhelmed seeing the family and the bounteous feast and broke down in tears. But he could not stay for long. For the time being, Heim had to report back to the saltworks and would ultimately have to face a hearing to determine how involved he really had been in Nazi war crimes. He was furloughed, on parole essentially, but not yet truly free.

What Ford was to cars or Hershey to chocolate in America, Persil was to laundry detergent in Germany. The product was introduced to the market in 1907 but captured the popular imagination with the introduction in 1922 of a woman clad in a long, spotless white dress and a wide-brimmed white Florentine straw hat, known as the White Lady. She was soon plastered everywhere from packaging to billboards, an elegant symbol of cleanliness to an entire nation.

In postwar Germany a certificate of denazification quickly acquired the nickname of a Persilschein. To remove the brown stain of Nazism, to wash yourself clean of your Nazi past, you needed a Persilschein. The fact that *schein* could mean not only certificate but also "in appearance only" or even "phony" made the word all the more fitting. There was no small cynicism in German public opinion about the effectiveness of Allied justice, which could seem capricious to the public and was all the more complicated by the different approaches taken in the different zones of occupation.

After the war the Allies had carved Germany into four zones. The Soviets ruled in the east, the British in the north, and the Americans in the south. Stalin initially did not want to give the French their own German territory to administer, but ultimately they received the smallest zone of the four in the west along their border. The entire German population, in the meantime, was divided into five categories based on their complicity in the Nazi regime: Major Offenders, Offenders, Lesser Offenders, Followers, and Persons Exonerated. The problem facing the Allies was figuring out who was a clean as the White Lady and who bore that brown stain.

The three states that made up the American occupation zone—Baden-Württemberg, Bavaria, and Hesse—passed the Law for Liberation from National Socialism and Militarism on March 5, 1946. Those found to have played a significant role in the Nazi regime or its crimes faced punishments of up to ten years in work camps as well as fines, confiscations of property, and bans from certain forms of employment. Rooting out the influence of the Nazi Party while building a new, functioning German state proved nearly impossible without making exceptions for some members of the former government. The process was like a strike zone, judgment calls that varied from person to person and place to place.

The umpires in the American zone were known as *Spruchkammern,* civil courts, each of which was made up of a panel of three judges. The chairman of each panel was part of the *Spruchkammern*'s professional staff, and the other two members were nominated by the approved political parties: the Social Democrats, the Communist Party, the Christian Democrats, and the Democratic People's Party. All were supposedly drawn from the ranks of the upstanding, certifiably non-fascist citizenry.

In Neckarsulm, where Aribert Heim awaited denazification, members included a brewer, a carpenter, a pharmacist, and a baker. They were checked out with the American military government before they could sit in judgment over their fellow citizens. Officials sent each candidate's questionnaire to the military government in Heilbronn and a copy to the inspection division of the Ministry for Political Liberation. The pharmacist was rejected for not listing his membership in the Nazi Party for eight months.

The authorities had their work cut out for them. The local *Spruchkammer* that would handle Heim's case was so busy that it was forced to leave its offices in Kochendorf in the summer of 1947 after work came "to a complete standstill as a result of a lack of space," a member of the body wrote to the building authority in Heilbronn. The very same people charged with determining the Nazi past of Aribert Heim and others were also trying to secure tar paper, roof tiles, and parquet for their new offices in the bombed-out courthouse in Neckarsulm. The staff arrived at their new offices in July, only to find that there were no lights. When they held a morale-building get-together in May 1947 at a local tavern, they were each told to bring ration cards for fifty grams of meat and five grams of fat. "Everything else," the invitation promised, "including the ride home, is taken care of."

By the time Heim's case came up in March 1948, the Spruchkammer Heilbronn-Neckarsulm had thirty-three employees, near its peak of thirty-five employees the previous October, including prosecutors, investigators, and clerical staff. The prosecutors and investigators prepared the cases against the potential offenders, who could retain their own defense counsel to represent them before the three-member panel that would ultimately rule on their level of involvement. After twelve years of Nazi rule and six years of total war, few could claim to have had no interaction with the regime. Accordingly, the net was cast wide.

Every German over the age of eighteen in the American zone was required to fill out a survey with 131 questions—known as the *Fragebogen*. Some thirteen million people reported the details of their party membership, voting record, and military service, their writings and speeches, their income and assets, their travel and residence abroad, both military and civilian, even a honeymoon weekend in Paris. Heim wrote a brief description of his life by hand. He began by telling the German authorities who had taken custody of him after his period as an American prisoner of war had ended, that he was born in Austria but was "the son of German parents." Heim traced his education from primary school through his postgraduate medical course in jaw surgery. He explained that he reported at the beginning of January 1940 to the Luftwaffe but "was drafted into the Waffen-SS against my will and there pursued a medical career." When he joined the group, Heim said, "I was unaware of the criminal intentions and goals of the SS. Further I declare that I at no time participated in actions that violated human rights or international law."

He moved quickly from his education to his military service, listing wartime service in Russia, Finland, Norway, and France as well as every rank he had held, ending with his final promotion in 1944 to *Hauptsturmführer,* or captain. He viewed himself as a victim of circumstance, held back by the course of history. "As a result of the events of war I did not have the opportunity to marry," Heim wrote. "I have no property or other wealth. I was solely dependent on the earnings of a troop doctor for the necessities of life."

Heim gathered, with the help of his sister, testimonials to his political reliability. He referred to his internship before the war in the booming northern German port city of Rostock in 1937. It was the first time he lived in Germany. "He dedicated himself to his medical training and in his free time did a lot of sports, so that he could earn additional income for his studies," wrote Herta Weinaug, a widow in whose home Heim had lived as a boarder. It was true, she acknowledged, that Heim had applied for membership in the Nazi Party but only "after he was advised to do so at the clinic."

Otherwise he exhibited, according to Mrs. Weinaug, little interest in party or politics. "His behavior from that point on never gave the appearance that he in any way whatsoever was bound to the party," she wrote. "He did not promote the party or enthuse about it. The block leader never came to see him. I assumed for that reason that nothing came of his membership application." Mrs. Weinaug affirmed the truth of her statement and that she had never been a member of the Nazi Party, just "a simple member of the NSV," the Nazis' social welfare organization.

Her daughter, too, attested to Heim's good character. The medical student had "spent a great deal of time with our family," Ursula Kraft wrote. She also got to know him while he was stationed in Berlin during the war. "Aribert Heim always carried himself impeccably, courteously, politely and never harmed anyone for political, racial, religious, or other such reasons," wrote Kraft. "He demonstrated no interest in politics and never exhibited objectionable or harsh behavior."

His letter of recommendation from Captain Jones of the U.S. Army was included in his file, as was the one from Pastor Werner Ernst Linz. Linz did his best to impress upon the Allies that Heim might have fought for the Waffen-SS but he deplored its cause. "I learned through conversations with Dr. Heim that he was a convinced opponent of euthanasia and the National Socialist racial theories," Linz wrote of his friend at the POW hospital. "It would be gratifying if Dr. Heim could once again resume his medical practice."

The prosecutor handling the case before the panel was not so sure. "The investigations undertaken did not yield a satisfying result," he wrote. As a member of the Waffen-SS, Heim "has to prove that he did not participate in the criminal objectives of this organization and in particular that he did not take part in war crimes." It was Heim's job, in other words, to prove his innocence. Prosecutors had at their disposal the personnel files of millions of former party and SS members, including Aribert Heim. And something did not add up.

—————

The central card catalog of the National Socialist German Workers' Party had been kept in fireproof cabinets at the party administrative headquarters in Munich. The cards, some 14 million in all, were supposed to be incinerated at the end of the war. However, only around 3 million could be destroyed before the 10.7 million remaining fell into the hands of the U.S. military. The surviving files represented a valuable trove of information for the Allied effort to identify and root out high-ranking Nazis. The catalog was moved to Berlin for safekeeping.

Much of the German capital had been destroyed in the invasion, but an underground complex in the Zehlendorf district was largely undamaged. The reinforced bunker had been built as a surveillance post for Hermann Göring. The neighborhood along with the bunker had briefly fallen under Soviet control in the war's chaotic conclusion before officially ending up in the American zone. Watchful residents in October 1945 saw truck after truck delivering government files for safekeeping. It was the birth of the Berlin Document Center, a central repository for information on Nazis, from the rank and file to the top of the leadership.

As other documents were discovered, they were also sent to the bunker in Berlin. The personnel files of the Reich Justice Ministry, for instance, were found in Kassel and sent along to the growing Nazi archive. The document center contained files that had been used in the Nuremberg trials, as well as party correspondence, records from the race and resettlement office, paperwork from the chamber of culture, and personnel records of members of the SA and the SS.

Heim's file showed that he had joined the party on May 1, 1938, receiving the membership number 6,116,098. He joined the SS a few months later, on October 1, 1938, shortly before Kristallnacht. In 1940 he joined the Waffen-SS, the military wing of the organization, and worked his way up the ranks, first as an *Untersturmführer* and then as an *Obersturmführer*. On Hitler's next-to-last birthday, April 20, 1944, Heim was promoted for the final time to *Hauptsturmführer*.

Most of that was in his questionnaire. But the denazification investigators found information that he had neglected to include on his *Fragebogen*. Two entries had been left out of his postings. The file prepared by the Berlin Document Center, dated October 14, 1947, said that from April 10 to June 19, 1941, Heim worked as a concentration camp inspector. And from June 19 to July 14 of the same year he was at the concentration camp Buchenwald. The prosecutor found no mention of Mauthausen.

Heim's lawyer, Dr. Hans Frank from the Swabian town of Aalen, argued in a brief that his client was a healer, a saver of lives, who through a series of coincidences and no fault of his own ended up in the Waffen-SS. Heim's relationship with the Nazi Party consisted of a "purely nominal membership, for he was in no way politically active and limited his duties to the payment of his dues," which were a mere 1.50 reichsmarks a month. His membership was, and the lawyer underlined his next words, "against his will," that is, "f o r c i b l e"—here the lawyer inserted a space between each letter for even clearer emphasis—his induction was part of "an attempt to solve the shortage of doctors under which it suffered at the time through forced recruitment."

Dr. Frank stressed the contrast between Dr. Heim's nominal crime of serving in the Waffen-SS and his regular duties saving lives as a troop doctor. The statements in support of Heim demonstrated how he "kept himself clear of any objectionable or criminal behavior with his entire being." He was free from "political blindness, intolerance, and chauvinistic hate."

But the most significant testimonials on his behalf pertained to his behavior during fierce fighting in France in January and February 1945, shortly before he was taken prisoner. The mayor of Offwiller, France, north of Strasbourg, where Heim was stationed at the time, wrote a letter in support of him, saying, "The civilian populace embraced him. During the hostilities he voluntarily placed himself at the disposal of the civilian wounded and administered first aid."

His superior officer, Dr. Franz Niedner, supported the story. Writing from detention at Hohenasperg, the former fortress where Heim had also been held, Niedner wrote that "because the populace had remained in these places, Dr. Heim undertook their entire medical care, despite the fact that during the fighting he was deeply engaged in his duties as doctor to the troops, administering first aid to wounded civilians and ensuring their orderly evacuation to the division medical teams in the rear."

A French civilian, Friedrich Schauly, with whom Dr. Heim was quartered in Offwiller, substantiated the story, adding, "The entire community can confirm it." Heim took "the greatest care and gave the wounded civilians emergency dressings." Mr. Schauly told of a farmer who had committed a political offense and after he was injured in an accident came to the aid station for treatment. The police wanted to arrest him, but Dr. Heim ordered him sent back home instead. Were it not for Dr. Heim, Schauly wrote, the farmer "never would have come back."

The defense attorney kept the court focused on the commendations by the Americans and the French. He pointed out that those letters demonstrated "what esteem the person concerned enjoyed, even among his enemies." Still, after six years of war and two and a half years of internment, Heim found it difficult to locate the people who would testify to his many actions "that would document his humane conduct since his acquaintances have been scattered to the four winds."

Heim's hearing on March 20, 1948, began the same day that the Soviet representative Marshal Vasily Sokolovsky walked out on the Allied Control Council in Berlin for good. The slow breakdown of cooperation among the Allies became official. The Cold War had begun in earnest. Both the Americans and the Soviets wanted the Germans on their side. Already, the Allies were using former Nazis to spy against the Russians. In America, the public perception of who was the enemy was shifting from the defeated Nazis to the alarmingly powerful Soviets. The intelligence units in Europe responded accordingly.

The prosecution of war criminals only alienated the very Germans the Allies needed on their side. Almost a year before Heim's case came up, the U.S. military government had commanded "the swiftest possible conclusion to the entire denazification proceedings by mandatory decree and has already made clear that it would use direct orders to implement the necessary measures," the head of the chamber in Neckarsulm wrote in May 1947. The Soviet Military Administration in Germany, known by the acronym SMAD, issued order number 35, ending denazification in the Soviet zone as of March 10, 1948. The Western Allies would not be far behind.

With all the political pressure favoring a speedy resolution, a doctor who saved the lives of French civilians faced relatively little scrutiny. On one of the three questionnaires Heim filled out, he was asked in question number 13 in which group he believed that he belonged. Dr. Heim answered group 4, *Mitläufer*, follower or fellow traveler in German. The three-judge panel issued its ruling on March 22, 1948.

> The person concerned has credibly proved that he was forcibly drafted into the Waffen-SS, which through its establishment in the then Ostmark had a shortage of doctors. The person concerned was a doctor and as such promoted at regular intervals. His occupation as a doctor with the Waffen-SS can, due to Art. 39 III, not be imputed as incriminating. The investigations undertaken have resulted in absolutely no facts under Art. 7-9. The person concerned has credibly proved that he took part in no activities directed against humanity and against international law.
>
> As such, the person concerned belongs to the circle of follower.

The chamber did not address the conflicts between his file in Berlin and Heim's own description of his service; indeed, there was not a single comment written on the Berlin Document Center file.

The Spruchkammer Neckarsulm office closed its doors for good in July 1948, forwarding all outstanding questions, issues, and requests to Heilbronn. A letter went out to the committee members inviting them to a party. This time it did not ask them to bring their own meat rations. The chairman noted that in a year and a half, the Spruchkammer Neckarsulm had processed over thirty-six thousand questionnaires, out of which it prosecuted thirty-four hundred cases, or less than 10 percent. The majority of those were handled, like Heim's case, without oral arguments. The Spruchkammer Neckarsulm found 1,145 fellow travelers, 485 lesser offenders, and 21 offenders. There were no major offenders to be found in its jurisdiction. The tallies suggest an extremely lenient, forgiving approach to denazification.

"The chamber hopes and wishes that through your work the necessary requirements for the new creation of a free, democratic state have been accomplished," the chairman wrote to the members.

In the meantime, requests for information on Heim were incomplete; the official channels were overwhelmed. The Office of Military Government for Germany in Heilbronn had continued researching Heim's case at the request of the *Spruchkammer* investigators. An official noted that Dr. Heim's involvement with the Nazi movement went back further than it appeared. His SS card said that he had been a member of the Sturmabteilung, or SA, from January 1, 1935, until October 1, 1938, the day that he joined the SS. The form was dated February 6, 1948, at the top but marked March 30 at the bottom. It was not stamped as received by the Spruchkammer Neckarsulm until May 13, 1948. By that time, Aribert Heim was already free.

CHAPTER 9

"Pardon me for my sincere inquiry," wrote Karl Kaufmann, a clerk at the Linz Iron and Steelworks, on February 2, 1948, to the Austrian Ice Hockey Association in Vienna. "It deals with a man who during the war belonged to your organization, whose name was Dr. Heim, by profession a physician."

Kaufmann's letter was brief but included a disturbing list of accusations. In it, he described what he called "terrible barbarities" visited upon inmates by Dr. Heim. A former prisoner who worked as an orderly in the camp sick bay, he said he had seen the physician kill "countless people with gasoline to the heart, and all of this he did with a cynical smiling expression." Heim's residence "is to date unknown. Is there no member of the association who knows where Dr. Heim is located?" He signed the letter: "Karl Kaufmann, former antifascist inmate 1463. Concentration Camp Mauthausen."

The hockey association forwarded the letter to the prosecutor's office in Vienna on February 24, 1948. The association staffer included a note saying that Dr. Heim had been registered with Eissport Klub Engelmann during the period in question. The court in Vienna turned to Heim's old hockey club in the hopes of locating him. Kaufmann had achieved his goal. The Austrian authorities had begun searching for Heim.

On March 1, 1948, the trains to the historic health resort of Bad Nauheim were stuffed "as full as sausage casings," with visitors arriving from miles around to watch SC Riessersee from Bavaria take on the upstart Red Devils of Bad Nauheim. Crowds filled the aisles, some even climbing the trees outside to get a view of the game. The hockey rink officially only had room for four thousand, but estimates of the attendance that day ran as high as fourteen thousand people. The American Military Police had to pull intrepid climbers down from the roof of the stadium for fear it would cave in.

The Red Devils kept pace in the fast-moving game. The core of the team that held Riessersee to a 2–2 tie was made up of men expelled from the far eastern reaches of Prussia, which was now part of Poland. Their ranks included a new addition, a tough defenseman from Austria. He was a giant of a man, over six feet three, a physical player fans called a hulk and "eisenhart," hard as iron. Dr. Aribert Heim might have been new to the Red Devils, but he had played against Riessersee before, back when he represented Eissport Klub Engelmann, playing both with and against many of his East Prussian teammates. Now he was skating in the American-built stadium in Bad Nauheim, where the ice was emblazoned with the U.S. coat of arms and the insignia of the XV Corps of the Seventh Army.

The life of a professional athlete was neither glamorous nor well compensated in those days, and hockey was nowhere near as popular a sport as soccer. The hockey players' first uniforms were red jerseys swiped from a U.S. Army football team. Herbert Schibukat, one of the team's stars, was put up in a dank little hotel room when he came to Bad Nauheim. Players sometimes had to trade sticks and even gloves as they made their line changes. But the games were major events.

The big defenseman, Heim, had a day job, working shifts at the Sanatorium Hahn, in an elegant four-story building with intricate iron balconies at Karlstrasse 27, an easy stroll from the city center. Heim assisted the head physician there, Dr. Luft, while also helping him out with his general practice. Ice hockey fans remembered Heim by the nickname Kleiderschrank, after the tall, wide wardrobes where Germans keep their clothes.

On the hockey team, Heim developed a reputation not only as a fierce defender but also for some rather odd habits. He always kept himself out of photographs, even team pictures. He frequently inquired about whether anyone was hanging around outside, loitering in front of the door to the dressing room. People didn't ask many questions in those postwar days. Plenty had pasts they did not want to talk about. "He's afraid," teammates whispered to one another, "that he's going to get nabbed." And he had every reason to be concerned.

Karl Kaufmann had continued to pursue his campaign for Heim's arrest and prosecution. He was angered by the fact that the Austrian police could not simply drive into German territory and arrest the suspect based on his allegations. Matters were complicated by the fact that neither Austria nor Germany was a sovereign nation in 1948. The occupation authorities would have to approve any extradition request. Investigators began to build a case with Kaufmann's statements. He told them that he "could write a novel about this mass murderer."

Kaufmann alleged that Heim took part in regular corporal punishments of inmates with twenty-five to a hundred blows with a cane, but instead of beating them across the buttocks as was normal, Heim aimed "always for the kidneys, so that many died as a result of internal bleeding." Kaufmann explained that he had spent six years in Mauthausen, three years as an orderly.

He described Heim as "very tall, he was somewhat smaller than two meters, he must have been 1.98 m and was very sturdy. He had blond, combed-back hair, beautiful teeth, a long face. What was distinctive about him was his unnatural size." In Europe, where they use the metric system, two meters, or a little under six feet seven, is the benchmark between the merely tall and the gigantic. According to Kaufmann, Heim was six feet six, and "by my estimate, he would be 36 to 38 years old presently. During the war he was a prominent ice hockey player and was constantly going to Vienna from Mauthausen. His name appeared often in the newspapers."

Kaufmann also told the judge a little bit about Heim's background, saying that he came from Styria, northwest of Graz near the town of Leoben, "where his parents had a large farm." It was unclear where he had gotten that information, which was inaccurate. Heim's hometown of Radkersburg lay to the south of Graz, and his widowed mother had no such farm.

Still, in May 1948 the Eissport Klub Engelmann responded to a request from the court in Vienna, confirming that "Dr. Heim was employed by our ice hockey team and enlisted in the year 1939. From this time we have no connection with Herr Dr. Heim." The letter from the secretariat of the club included one more piece of information that would put investigators onto the doctor's trail: "We are told that Dr. Heim was seen in Bad Nauheim (American Zone in Germany)."

CHAPTER 10

Eleonore Ackermann, daughter of the Oberschopfheim tailor who remade Alfred Aedtner's uniform, was skeptical of the young veteran at first. On her way home from work she would notice the young man from Silesia in the front yard, kicking the soccer ball with the Haag boy who had been blinded in the war. Alfred, on the other hand, was smitten with the young woman they called Lore.

She worked in the kitchen at an orphanage in the nearby city of Offenburg. Most of the boys and girls were the illegitimate offspring of German women and French soldiers. Her mother said the job would be a way not only to earn money but also to learn to be a better cook.

After a time Alfred won her affections and they agreed to marry, but her parents refused to consent. Not without a job, her parents said, a career, a profession. Painting the occasional house did not count. Aedtner had wanted to be a soldier, but occupied Germany had no army. He had no high school diploma and no money. His family was scattered in the Soviet zone and the territory ceded to Poland. He would need a new plan if he wanted to win his bride.

It was Lore who found the help-wanted advertisement in the local newspaper. The police were hiring. He answered the ad and on January 2, 1948, started work as a gendarme. It was not a glamorous job by any means. Instead of a squad car, he had a bicycle. Instead of hunting murderers, he was writing tickets and quieting down drunks.

He was posted to Gaggenau, about an hour north of Oberschopf-heim on the northern edge of the Black Forest. They married on July 20, 1948, she in a beautiful white gown and veil, Alfred in his green officer's uniform. They had their own apartment, and Lore was soon pregnant. The young police officer had no inkling of the role that Dr. Aribert Heim and other former Nazis would play in his life.

By June 15, 1948, Heim had given up his position at the sanatorium in Bad Nauheim. The next winter he began working in nearby Friedberg at the Bürgerhospital there. Starting in November 1948, Heim worked for six months in internal medicine and six months on the surgical ward. "He ran the ward entrusted to him diligently and assisted with all of the large and small surgeries of the abdomen and trauma surgeries," wrote Dr. Wilhelm Kramer, a surgeon and the hospital's chief doctor, in a letter of recommendation. As for his person, Dr. Kramer found that through his "upstanding and reserved manner he was a pleasant and reliable colleague."

The conditions in Friedberg as compared with those in Bad Nauheim showed once again how even a few miles could be the difference between bad luck and good fortune. During the war Friedberg had an important railway juncture between Giessen-Kassel and Frankfurt, making it a prime target for Allied planes. Black-and-white photographs from the time show railroad tracks twisted up from the ground like chewed cocktail straws. Houses along the city's Bismarckstrasse were blown up, buildings shorn of their roofs, retaining walls destroyed. Piles of bricks rose half a story high, and beams were scattered like toothpicks by the aerial assault. Even the sugar factory was hit.

But things had improved in the western occupation zones after the currency reform of 1948, which introduced the deutsche mark. The Americans printed and shipped five hundred tons of bills, worth 5.7 billion deutsche marks, to Germany, where on June 28, 1948, they began to circulate, with a ten-to-one exchange rate to the reichsmark. It was too soon for Germans in the western zones to realize, but the postwar period of agonizing deprivation had largely come to a close. The new currency was an instant success, quickly shutting down the black market. Goods returned to the store shelves practically overnight.

———

In May 1949, Karl Kaufmann finally appeared at the courthouse in Linz with a thorough report, in which he described what he remembered about Heim's time at the concentration camp. He recalled that the young doctor had begun working at Mauthausen in 1941, at a time when several transports filled with Dutch Jews were arriving at the camp. Three or four times a week after evening roll call Heim would take twenty-six to thirty inmates and dispatch them with injections of gasoline "in the vein or in the heart." On several Sundays when he was on duty he killed "30 to 35 Jews, all of whom were healthy."

Kaufmann said that Dr. Heim had once cut a young Jew from Prague's stomach open, "while he was completely conscious, from top to bottom." Heim proceeded to examine the young man's organs, cutting a section of his liver and removing his spleen. According to Kaufmann, "He made no exceptions, whether the prisoners were Austrian or German or belonged to any other nation." Jews were killed, young or old, whereas those from other nations were only killed if they "were weak and unable to work."

In his report, Kaufmann recommended two other witnesses to Heim's murders, a man named Sommer living in Upper Austria and a master locksmith named Karl Lotter. Rupert Sommer appeared before the court in Münichholz bei Steyr on June 24, 1949. His statement was very short, but he declared that Kaufmann's report was correct down to the last detail, *haargenau* in German. "I and Kaufmann were in the same room, therefore we have the same experiences.

"I myself was treated well by the accused," he explained. "But he was vicious to the Jews. With a smiling expression he said with his arms crossed to a Jew: 'You too must die. Is your wife beautiful?'" He described how, on the other hand, Heim treated Aryan prisoners better, including punishing an Aryan capo with a slap for mistreating a fellow Aryan inmate. Like Kaufmann, Sommer referred investigators to other witnesses.

Karl Lotter was interviewed at the court in Mürzzuschlag about the man he described as "an absolute mass murderer, who with a cold-blooded look on his face killed dozens of people. How many people he killed I can't say because he also went to the barracks. He had a special hatred for the Jews. He killed the Jews in masses." It was mostly, according to Lotter, Czech and Dutch Jews who were killed with injections after anesthesia. Heim worked with "a Viennese pharmacist" to try out different solutions and test their effects, even "standing beside them with a stopwatch, and determined which solutions were the best and worked the fastest and were the cheapest to use."

The emphasis remained not just on cataloging his crimes but on finding Heim. "To my knowledge," Lotter recalled, "Heim is Viennese and a famous ice hockey player. In the winter of 1941/42 he played for the Vienna all-star team." Lotter described the athlete as having a "conspicuous appearance," due to his height and his large feet. Lotter was of the opinion that Heim had also committed murders at the concentration camp Sachsenhausen, sometimes called Oranienburg. He overheard him threatening an inmate he had known there that he would "handle things like in Oranienburg, and you know what I mean."

Lotter said he personally witnessed Heim commit seven murders but had seen "entire mountains of corpses" from the injection procedures. "Above all, it was terrible because he had cordial conversations with the people, and then killed them through injections to the heart," Lotter said. As for how he knew that Heim was a hockey player, Lotter said he was certain because he had seen the articles about his games with the Viennese hockey team.

Lotter pointed out another witness, Josef Kohl, who more than two years after his first testimony once again told the authorities his story about Heim. All of the doctors had to give the lethal injections, Kohl said, but Heim did so "in a particularly sadistic manner." Like Lotter, Kohl described how Heim began conversations with the victims, in a seemingly humane approach, asking about their family situations, how individual family members were doing. Then the discussion would turn to whether the family was taken care of, if something should happen to them. "This appeared to be . . . the moment when his sadistic lust was stilled . . . [and] he gave the inmate the injection that brought his death."

There were inconsistencies. Lotter told investigators that Heim was at Mauthausen for around six months. Kohl put the SS doctor there for a much longer stay, from September 1940 to June 1942. Sommer thought that he was there in 1942, maybe even 1943. The focus in the questioning revolved less around the precise timing than the gruesome details. Kohl said he personally saw how Heim operated on two healthy young Dutch Jews, one of whom died when the doctor cut out his heart, the other of whom he dispatched with an injection. Their skulls, he said, ended up on Heim's desk.

The Austrian Interior Ministry now had a clearer idea of Dr. Heim's location. The public safety division of the state ministry in Hesse informed the Austrians in a letter dated February 23, 1949, that Heim was living in Bad Nauheim, working as an assistant doctor at the hospital in Friedberg. They even had a correct date of birth: June 28, 1914.

It is unclear how Heim might have learned that the police were closing in, though his elder sister, Hilda, worked for the court in Graz and might have had access to inquiries into his case and been able to warn him. The one thing that is certain is that he was gone before the authorities could catch up with him.

The suddenness of Dr. Heim's departure was recorded in the official history of the Red Devils hockey team. "By night and fog the doctor gave up his position at the Friedberg hospital and vanished as well from the spa town. The prosecutors were at his heels."

Up to the point when she met Aribert Heim, Friedl Bechtold had led a charmed life. She grew up across the Neckar River from the stone remains of Heidelberg's great castle, a hulking ruin that inspired the writers of the German Romantic school that flowered there in the nineteenth century. She was raised in a stately three-story house, a confection of imitation German Renaissance motifs, with gables and an oriel window and even a little dome with a pointed tower on top. Her mother ran a boarding school for girls, an international mix of daughters of the wealthy and the well-heeled.

The Bechtolds sent their daughter to a college preparatory school— known as a *Gymnasium* in Germany. Friedl was precocious, finishing high school a year early. When she entered Heidelberg University, she took a required first-aid course that convinced her that she wanted to become a doctor. She finished her dissertation at twenty-three, on fractures of the upper femur, the same year the war ended. The Bechtolds had been spared the worst of it. Friedl was an only child; there were no sons to die at the front. Her father, a World War I veteran, was appointed mayor and supply commander for a French town. He was later relieved of duty, suspected of insufficient loyalty to the Nazis, and thus avoided internment in a POW camp.

After the war Mr. Bechtold had to ride a bicycle or catch a ride to the country to trade with the farmers, whose foodstuffs were far more important than all the little luxuries, the cuckoo clocks and jewelry, filling grand homes like theirs in the foodless cities. He managed to trade a camera with an American officer for coffee and cigarettes. When Friedl rode home on her bicycle from the Ludolf Krehl Clinic in the Bergheim neighborhood of Heidelberg where she worked, her Red Cross band on her arm, the American GIs driving by in their jeeps would shout, "Hello, Blondie!"

She found them quite "reputable" on the whole, but she was not looking to marry a young American. Still, it was a very difficult time for a woman of her age who wanted to marry and have a family. Half the men of her generation had been killed. In parts of Germany there were three times as many women between the ages of twenty and thirty as there were men. Prospects for even an educated young lady from a good family were bleak.

One day in 1948, on her way home from the clinic in Heidelberg, Friedl caught the eye of a tall, striking man. They realized they were looking at each other, and both laughed, then struck up a conversation. She found him congenial as well as handsome. What was most important to her about the young man, who turned out to be a doctor as well, was that he had what she saw as "a natural charm, no patter."

Germans sometimes find Austrians to be *charmeurs,* smooth but a little too slick. But the seriousness that Heim had inherited from his father, the gendarme, was anything but frivolous. They were only together for a few minutes, but the man made an impression. Although she did not tell him who she was or where she lived, he told her, "I'll be in touch again at the clinic."

She was just leaving town on vacation and assumed that by the time she returned, he would have lost interest. But Heim was waiting to see her on her return. "The funny thing was," she said, that they were "medical doctor and medical doctor, you know? At some point it just feels like fate." He called at the clinic, and they agreed to meet again.

Although the young doctor was not perfect—he couldn't dance very well—it was soon clear that their relationship was serious. Heim became the first young man that Friedl brought home and formally introduced to her parents. He made a good impression on them too.

There were a few whispers. Her family's property holdings had been damaged in the war but were still significant. Some questioned whether the handsome young Austrian had "hooked a goldfish," as one family member put it. "The way she got to know him, she fell for him immediately," the relative recounted. "Then again, the way he was, with his manner, you probably would have fallen for him too."

He lived in an apartment building on Dürerstrasse in Mannheim but would often take the train down to see her in Heidelberg. As they got to know each other, one subject they didn't talk about much was Heim's military service. She knew that he was in the Waffen-SS but thought little of it. Several boys in her class had been too. Besides, he was a physician. It didn't matter much what uniform you wore when you were saving lives, did it?

Unaware of Aribert's Nazi past, Friedl focused on her wedding. Ever practical, she eschewed the traditional white gown and instead wore a simple suit. There had been no engagement party either. No members of his family made it to the wedding from Austria. Times were difficult, he explained, and none of them had a car. Still, while the event might not have been fancy, the look in her eyes on their wedding day, July 30, 1949, was one of joy, anticipation, and excitement.

The day ended, however, on an unfortunate note, with the new Mrs. Heim in bed, suffering from what she thought was food poisoning but what was actually the onset of hepatitis B. Friedl gave blood in the clinic where she worked as regularly as possible. They could always use a little more. In those days they only boiled the needles to sterilize them, which was not enough to kill some of the more pernicious viruses, and she contracted hepatitis. The pains in her liver began on her wedding night. Dr. Heim moved in with her parents and commuted to work so he could help take care of her.

On March 28, 1950, with Friedl Heim newly pregnant, the Austrian government put out a warrant for the arrest of "Dr. Heribert Heim," accusing him of murder, torture, abuse, and "crimes against dignity and humanity" at Mauthausen. The warrant concluded: "If the crime caused the death of the person concerned, it is punishable by death." Investigators had the correct date of birth, June 28, 1914, but not only were they searching for Heribert rather than Aribert; they had an incorrect birthplace as well. They were searching for a man from a place called Ingstfeld rather than Radkersburg.

In May the American military approved the extradition of Heim to Austria. American investigators traveled to Friedberg and Bad Nauheim to make inquiries but with no success. A year after he skated in front of sellout crowds, no one seemed to have heard of him. There was no trace of him at the local residents' registration office. The investigators inquired at Dr. Luft's sanatorium in Bad Nauheim but got nowhere. There was no record that he had worked there, they were told. The Bürgerhospital in neighboring Friedberg said the same.

In fact, there were references to Dr. Heim in the hospital files. At least one secretary in personnel was aware that he had moved to Mannheim. Heim had been hired and paid directly by the chief physician, Dr. Kramer. Other members of the staff were shocked by his unexpected disappearance. None of this came out a year later when the Americans made their inquiries. Whether it was an oversight or a favor for a colleague, it is impossible to say, but the locals in Friedberg and Bad Nauheim provided no assistance.

The Americans could only tell the Austrians that they had failed to find him. In a letter dated December 21, 1950, the office of the general counsel of the high commissioner for Germany wrote to his Austrian counterpart, "You are advised that Heim cannot be located in the United States Zone of Germany. We are therefore returning the file and closing this matter administratively, pending the receipt of information [regarding] Heim's whereabouts."

After years of documenting Nazi war crimes and recording testimonials from survivors, Simon Wiesenthal had begun to wonder if it wasn't time for him to close his office in Linz. He had caught around two hundred former Nazis by 1952, but the task had gotten more and more difficult. The displaced persons who provided the ranks of his witnesses and the bulk of his leads had slowly moved on. The United States, under pressure from the Soviets, had begun cooperating with some of the more unsavory remnants of the Nazi regime.

Klaus Barbie, the Gestapo chief of intelligence in Lyon, for instance, went to work in April 1947 as an informant for the CIC, the army intelligence group tasked with tracking down war criminals. The United States wanted Barbie to help penetrate Soviet networks and allowed him to live with his wife and their two children, safe from prosecution, even though he was wanted for murder in France and named on the CROWCASS list of war criminals. Barbie had been cruelly effective during the war, capturing key figures in the French Resistance and using brutal methods to make them talk.

"It is felt that his value as an informant infinitely outweighs any use he may have in prison," wrote the CIC agent Robert S. Taylor in May 1947. When the French learned that Barbie was in the American zone, they began clamoring for his extradition. Since this might have proved embarrassing, especially because the Americans had been spying on their

French counterparts, instead the CIC decided to make the person, and therefore the problem, disappear.

The 430th CIC Detachment in Austria had its own system for helping informants leave Europe, something known as a rat line. A Croatian priest in Italy, Krunoslav Draganović, could provide Red Cross passports and visas to countries in South America for between $1,000 and $1,400. An American headed the eligibility office of the International Refugee Organization in Rome, easing the way when it came to official documents and permits. Barbie was given a new identity under the name Klaus Altmann, including a Red Cross passport and a visa to Bolivia. He set sail on March 23, 1951.

But Father Draganović was not working exclusively with the United States. He had sympathized with the Croatian fascists, the Ustaše, during the war and helped his compatriots to escape. Some of the worst Nazi criminals managed to flee through the rat lines. Wiesenthal's obsession, Adolf Eichmann, had escaped to Austria and over the Alps into Italy, where he received a Red Cross passport under the name Ricardo Klement. As Klement, he left Genoa bound for Buenos Aires in July 1950. On the far side of the Atlantic he felt safe enough to bring his wife and children to join him. Auschwitz's notorious Angel of Death, Dr. Josef Mengele, followed a similar path. Mengele had kept his head down, working at a farm in a Bavarian village from the time he left a POW camp in 1945 until 1949, when he too left for Argentina.

It was a fateful year for Germany. Talks had broken down completely between the Western Allies and the Soviets. Finally, Germany was broken into two states, the German Democratic Republic in the east and the Federal Republic of Germany in the west. In his first government address in September 1949, the newly elected chancellor of West Germany, Konrad Adenauer, spoke for much of the nation when he declared, "Through the denazification much misfortune and much misery has been wreaked." He promised to pursue the worst war criminals but implicitly forgave the rest. "Those truly guilty of the crimes committed during the National Socialist period and in war should be punished with all severity," Adenauer said.

The term "truly guilty" implicitly limited the circle of perpetrators worthy of prosecution. The pressure to discontinue the hunt for Nazi perpetrators continued to mount. That same year a group of lawyers founded the Heidelberger Juristenkreis, a lobbying and legal aid group for detainees and convicted war criminals. Among the prominent members was Hans Laternser, a Nuremberg defense attorney who specialized in such trials in the postwar era. Even in the Soviet sector realpolitik calculations and desire to win over the Germans under their control brought the Russian search for Nazi war criminals to a halt. After convicting some seventy thousand prisoners of war, the Soviets declared an end to their own Nazi trials on September 14, 1950.

For a silent majority in Germany there was not so much support for Nazi sentiments as a desire to move on. Although many Germans were in favor of holding the most senior Nazi leadership accountable, they also believed the thousands of Wehrmacht soldiers still held captive in Siberia needed to come home. Leading politicians argued that the remaining detainees in the hands of the Americans, British, and French should also be released. In the recently founded Federal Republic of Germany, the rank-and-file soldiers needed to be given a second chance.

Even those already found guilty had their defenders. Adenauer promised that his government would pursue amnesty for those convicted by the Allies. In the face of intense lobbying from the church and politicians, the U.S. Army Modification Board lightened sentences. For concentration camp survivors like Wiesenthal, the tens of thousands of war criminals who lived without fear of prosecution were even harder to swallow than those who at least had been forced to flee.

Dr. Hans Eisele, for instance, had conducted painful, sometimes deadly experiments on concentration camp inmates and killed many of the survivors. According to an American colonel who worked on his case, Dr. Eisele had grown into a sadist, the transformation reflected in the nicknames the prisoners gave him, initially "the Angel," later "the Butcher." Twice Eisele was sentenced to death for his crimes, once in December 1945 and again in April 1947. In both instances his sentence had been commuted. On February 26, 1952, he was released from Landsberg Prison. The son of a church painter who had joined the Nazi Party in 1933 and worked at Buchenwald and Dachau, he was allowed to practice medicine in Munich and live there openly with his wife and three children.

Tuviah Friedman, Wiesenthal's fellow Nazi hunter in Austria, had decided by 1950 that he had had enough. Vienna was still inhospitable to Jews, and the authorities in postwar Europe were not interested in pursuing his leads. In 1953, Israel opened its Holocaust memorial, Yad Vashem, which was also a documentation and research center. Friedman moved to Israel to work there and later built his own Haifa Institute for the Documentation of Nazi War Crimes. Like Wiesenthal, he was obsessed with catching Adolf Eichmann and offered a $10,000 reward for the SS officer, even though he did not have the money to pay for a successful tip. Friedman helped broker an agreement to sell Wiesenthal's records to the Yad Vashem center in 1954.

By that time, Wiesenthal had some 3,289 completed questionnaires. He had collected not just testimony about suspects but more general information on the operation of the camps and on the implementation of the plan to annihilate Europe's Jews. In addition, he had a list of some Einsatzgruppen personnel, testimony about forced labor in IG Farben and Krupp facilities, reports on racial research, and Nazi propaganda, including examples from *The Eternal Jew*, an anti-Semitic exhibition in Munich in 1937 and 1938.

In Wiesenthal's telling he held on to one file and one file only, and that was Eichmann's. In 1954 he saw a letter mentioning that Eichmann was in Argentina. "He lives near Buenos Aires and works for a water company," the letter said. Wiesenthal passed the information along to the Israelis. The chances that Eichmann would ever be captured were slim, but Wiesenthal could not give up hope.

After a few years on the police force in Gaggenau, Alfred Aedtner had graduated from pedaling a bicycle to riding a motorcycle with a sidecar and then to driving a Volkswagen Beetle. Now he aspired to a Mercedes of his own. He wanted a suit instead of a uniform and a detective's badge to go with it. He did not particularly enjoy the work of a small-town policeman—the car accidents and disturbances of the peace—and longed for a promotion and more challenging employment.

But he had a wife and young son to care for, and the job he had would have to suffice. They lived comfortably but modestly in a small apartment in Gaggenau, a few miles of winding roads away from the glamour of Baden-Baden, with its casino and its fancy patisseries, which his wife liked to visit for a slice of cake if she had an excuse. Still, Aedtner was on the lookout for something better. He needed a chance to prove that he was more than a guy without a high school diploma directing traffic. He believed he was made for bigger things, if he could only get the opportunity. Aedtner could not have guessed that the war, nearly a decade past and a period he would just as soon have forgotten, would provide his break.

CHAPTER 13

When Aribert and Friedl Heim first moved into the stately villa in Baden-Baden in 1953, the house still needed repairs, not to mention a decent coat of paint. The heat did not work, and several war refugees were still living there. Friedl's parents, Jakob and Käthe Bechtold, had bought the villa for the young couple after they had been married a few years and were still living in the parents' house in Heidelberg. When the repairs were finished, movers brought furniture, furnishings, and artwork that the Bechtolds had bought at auctions.

The house, on Maria-Viktoria-Strasse, was an undeniably beautiful property. There was a large garden in the back and a well-landscaped circular drive in the front. The household staff handled the daily chores, the female servants still wearing traditional black skirts and white aprons. There were a housemaid and a nanny, both of whom lived with the family, and a gardener and a cleaning lady who came in to help.

The marriage was by all reports an agreeable one. Aribert had a gynecology practice in downtown Baden-Baden, above the old Hofapotheke, a pharmacy. Friedl had a small practice of her own but also was preoccupied with raising their young firstborn son, Aribert Christian. In 1955, just before Christmas, a second son was born, Rolf Rüdiger. He had an Rh-negative reaction, meaning that antibodies in his system were attacking his own blood. The doctors treated him with a transfusion, replacing the entire volume of the baby's blood. He recovered well and was doted on by his mother and especially his grandmother Käthe Bechtold, who was a regular presence in the house.

The Heims were well matched. Neither cared much for high fashion, frequent parties, or entertaining at home. Friedl could not drink because of liver complications from her bout with hepatitis, and Aribert only had a glass of wine or a beer when they went out. Although Friedl played tennis and went horseback riding, her husband, the former world-class athlete, had little time for sports. When he played games, it was with his little boys, teaching them to play soccer and table tennis. Acquaintances and former patients often described him with the same word: *korrekt*. Though it can be easily translated into the English "correct," in German it means something more intangible, implying propriety and decency.

The Heim family vacationed in Italy and Switzerland, where Friedl's parents owned a place in Lugano. If they did entertain at home, they had cakes from Baden-Baden's elegant Café König, a favorite of Heim's. They would go to local restaurants during asparagus season, a tradition in Germany, or to the town where Friedl was born, Bad Dürkheim, for its annual wine festival. Such outings were relatively infrequent, but they enjoyed driving across the French border to nearby Strasbourg, where they would dine at the restaurant Maison Kammerzell on the Place de la Cathédrale. As many times as they went, Heim always ordered the roast chicken. He had simple tastes, like many of the generation raised through the Depression and the war.

The Heims contributed to and enjoyed West Germany's unprecedented economic growth and newfound stability in the 1950s, known as the economic miracle. The Bechtolds were grateful to Heim for all the work he put into rebuilding their war-damaged properties as well as managing them, a role that grew after Jakob Bechtold's death. It took a great deal of work, but Heim's name was never added to the deeds. He began to invest in property on the side with his sister and brother-in-law.

For a doctor he had a very sharp business sense, as well as a way with people. When Friedl's young cousin Fritz had finished his schooling and needed a job, Heim simply drove to the nearby Daimler-Benz facility in Gaggenau and struck up a conversation with the boss. By the end of their talk, Heim had persuaded the man to give Fritz a temporary position.

CHAPTER 14

West Germany still lacked its own military but had no shortage of soldiers. Most found other work, but a few stuck to their profession, which meant seeking their fortunes abroad. Germans were welcomed not only in Latin America, where they emigrated in droves, but also in Egypt, where their military expertise was prized and their pasts or political leanings were of little concern. The first handful of German military advisers arrived in Cairo around 1950.

The Egyptian government assumed the moving costs of military advisers and their families, giving them salaries of 150 Egyptian pounds and insurance policies worth 10,000 deutsche marks. Advisers were hired on two-year contracts. News of these opportunities spread, and by the end of 1951 the group consisted of ten—the artillery general Wilhelm Fahrmbacher and nine other officers. There was precedent for this sort of flight to Egypt. The nineteenth-century reformer Muhammad Ali had employed many French officers after Napoleon's army was defeated.

The Germans found a warm reception in Egypt. A sizable number of Egyptian elites had studied in Germany in the 1920s and 1930s. Many of the same Egyptian officers behind the Free Officers Movement, which launched the coup in 1952 that ended the monarchy and led to the Nasser era, had quietly, and occasionally actively, supported Germany in World War II. They hoped that a Nazi victory would put an end to British colonial influence in Egypt. The Free Officers did not change the arrangement. In fact, the new regime encouraged the relocation of yet more German soldiers and technical experts.

The Wehrmacht veterans remained German citizens and in their capacity as advisers did not have the right to give orders or command troops. They worked with the Ministry of War and the Egyptian general staff on training and evaluating military equipment. General Fahrmbacher and a number of other high-ranking officers formed a group that called itself the Central Planning Board. Dr. Wilhelm Voss, a former SS *Standartenführer* and onetime head of the Reichswerke industrial conglomerate, founded ammunition and small-arms factories to help the Egyptians upgrade their arsenal. Another German, named Kurt Hermann Füllner, worked with a private company called PAG Near East, which West German embassy officials speculated was a conduit for Germans working for Egyptian intelligence. There were numerous media reports that former Gestapo and SS members augmented the secret police and even helped build concentration camps for opponents of the Nasser regime.

The Egyptians played the West Germans and the East Germans against each other to extract the maximum possible assistance. "Contact with the German military advisers won over a fundamentally positive attitude toward the federal republic," wrote a West German embassy staffer named Schirmer, "which has repeatedly made itself felt agreeably in negotiations." When a military adviser, Ernst-Günther Gerhartz, was criminally charged as a result of his divorce proceeding in Germany, the embassy argued for letting him stay in Cairo.

"Right now Mr. Gerhartz is the only tank expert in the German military advisory group and as such chief adviser at the Egyptian army's tank school," Schirmer wrote. More important, his presence "renders unnecessary" experts from East Germany. An attempt to extradite the highly prized Gerhartz would "cause serious damage to the position of the local military advisers and through that, indirectly, the reputation of the federal republic." As a result, the embassy advised the government in Bonn against bringing extradition proceedings against Gerhartz. Another embassy official pointed out, as did his Egyptian attorney Ragai Youssef Rifaat, that there was no extradition treaty between the two countries. If pressed, Gerhartz might even defect to East Germany. Gerhartz offered his resignation, but his Egyptian superior refused to accept it. Personal matters were of no interest to him, he said.

The number of Nazi prosecutions had tailed off almost completely by the mid-1950s. Konrad Adenauer had recently made his historic visit to Moscow, securing the return of the surviving German POWs from their detention and work camps in Siberia. On December 31, 1955, West Germany put an end to denazification in almost every corner of the country.

Most legislators and investigators in West Germany might have been happy to see the *Spruchkammer* law creating the denazification panels lapse, but West Berlin's interior minister, Joachim Lipschitz, was not. Just because a Nazi had evaded detection for a decade did not mean he should get away scot-free. Only thirty-seven years old at the time, Lipschitz had already endured his share of hardship. As the son of a Jewish doctor, he was harassed and persecuted in Nazi Germany but still considered fit for active duty on the front. He lost his left arm fighting for a Nazi regime that despised him and after the war had to flee East Berlin for West Germany under pressure from Communist authorities. He was elected to the city parliament in West Berlin and eventually took over law-enforcement matters.

He was known for making life difficult for the remaining Nazi supporters and for finding ways to honor their forgotten opponents. A *Spruchkammer* was a good way to seize ill-gotten gains or otherwise sanction major Nazi figures. Lipschitz got the city parliament to pass the Second Law for the Conclusion of Denazification. Under the law, the *Spruchkammer* could levy "unlimited fines" against Nazi perpetrators in West Berlin and could do so in perpetuity. The exceptional nature of Berlin's law was not widely known, even among those who should have been paying attention.

Heim spent the 1950s building his gynecology practice in Baden-Baden and traveling around West Germany as a pharmaceutical representative. In Germany's divided capital he saw the opportunity to buy an investment property of his own. A man was selling a fifty-year-old prewar building in the West Berlin neighborhood of Moabit, and Heim went to have a look. Centrally located, Tile-Wardenberg-Strasse 28 was close to public transportation as well as shopping centers. Many of the spacious prewar apartments had been divided as a result of the postwar housing shortage, and there were thirty-four units in all. The entryway had double wooden doors, and behind them there were marble flourishes on the floor and walls of the lobby. The staircase was made of oak. Heim purchased the building on February 8, 1958, for just under 160,000 deutsche marks with the help of a loan from his mother-in-law.

It was a peaceful corner of the city one block from the Spree River. The neighborhood was a mix of old buildings, new apartment blocks, and a few empty spaces left by Allied bombs. One gaping hole was next to the Heinrich von Kleist School on Levetzowstrasse, just around the corner from Heim's new investment. A large synagogue, which could seat more than two thousand, had once stood at Levetzowstrasse 7–8. The house of worship was completed in 1914, the year World War I began, a conflict that claimed the lives of many patriotic German Jews serving in the Wehrmacht and the navy. Less than a quarter century later the building was set ablaze by their fellow Germans on Kristallnacht.

The Nazis used the burned-out building as an assembly point for the deportation of Jews to the camps. The synagogue was damaged further during the war, but local residents said that the structure seemed sturdy enough. Nevertheless, with its worshippers gone, the Levetzowstrasse synagogue was torn down in 1955. A modest plaque noting its existence was all that remained.

Germans and Austrians like Heim could have reasonably assumed that their nations had put the war behind them. There would be a few plaques and a few commemoration ceremonies, it seemed, but even the worst of the Nazi war criminals focused on their futures rather than worrying about the past. It was a logical assumption to make, but it was wrong. In fact the reckoning with the past was only just beginning, and with it the pursuit and prosecution of Nazi fugitives like Aribert Heim gathered momentum.

On January 18, 1954, Bernd Fischer was hired as the director of a refugee camp in Ulm-Wilhelmsburg in North Württemberg. He worked at a lot of jobs after the war, from agriculture to a chemical factory, even as a vacuum salesman. He had a good reputation as a manager, but authorities were suspicious when he wrote down different dates for his birthday on various forms. A background check by the Americans revealed that Bernd Fischer was actually Bernhard Fischer-Schweder, a man with more to conceal than his name.

Though in his official questionnaire he denied any connection to the Nazi Party, this was not true. Even before joining the Nazis, Fischer-Schweder was a member of two right-wing paramilitary groups, the Freikorps "Fürstner" starting in 1921 and the "Schwarze Reichswehr" in 1923. Two years later, in August 1925, Fischer-Schweder joined the Nazi Party with the membership number 17,141, joining the brown-shirted storm troopers known as the SA. When the Nazis took power in 1933, he was one of the long-standing Nazis, known as the "old fighters," enrolled at the police academy in Berlin. His path within the party was not entirely smooth. He was briefly held in a concentration camp after the Röhm Putsch, when Hitler purged his rivals in the SA. But he must have proved his loyalty to the Führer because he continued his career in the SS. In October 1940 he became police director of the East Prussian town of Memel. When questioned more than a decade later, he justified his omissions in terms of self-preservation. "Only the very biggest calves look for their own butcher," he said.

Still the authorities did not respond to these revelations about his past by arresting him or charging him with any crimes. He was not called to account for lying on his *Fragebogen* or to the *Spruchkammer*. That was not how things worked in West Germany in the 1950s. Instead, his supervisors in Ulm quietly asked him to resign from his position. It was not worth a public scandal, but neither was it considered appropriate for a senior member of the Gestapo to command a refugee camp. Fischer-Schweder resigned, albeit grudgingly, and took a job working for the American firm Remington Rand. A middle-class existence in a booming country was his for the taking, but a future in government or law enforcement was denied to him.

It must have been particularly difficult for him to swallow with so many of his former comrades working as policemen and prosecutors, with all the former Nazis in positions of power all the way up to Adenauer's chancellery; Hans Globke, Adenauer's national security adviser, had even written anti-Jewish laws for the Nazi regime. Fischer-Schweder did apply for another law-enforcement job, this time in South Baden, and was turned down. Rather than accept that his past now disqualified him from public employment, he retracted his resignation and sued to be reinstated to his former job at the refugee camp.

The newspapers picked up the story of an SS *Obersturmführer* insisting on his right to a job working with displaced persons. As a result, his wartime activities received greater scrutiny. He was recognized not just as a Nazi but also as an executioner. After his appointment as police director in Memel, Fischer-Schweder had been sent to the eastern front. There his job was to slaughter Jews as a member of Einsatzkommando Tilsit, one of the roving units that massacred Jews, Communists, and other opponents of Nazi rule.

Although the authorities tried to handle it discreetly, the small controversy in Ulm grew into a major scandal that could no longer be downplayed. On May 2, 1956, the police arrested him. The case expanded beyond just the one SS officer who refused to keep mum about his past. The prosecutor's investigative files grew to thirty-five hundred pages, and ultimately ten former Gestapo and SS officers were charged for their roles in massacring thousands. Their trial opened on April 28, 1958, and over the course of the proceedings 173 witnesses took the stand. The atrocities of the eastern front, including the execution of frightened, naked women with children clutched in their arms, were revealed in harrowing detail.

The trial in Ulm was led not by the Americans or the Soviets but by West German prosecutors. Chilling dispatches appeared in all the country's major newspapers. The Ulm trials marked a breakthrough for postwar Germany's relationship with its past. While some tried to ignore what had emerged in the courtroom and the press, the Germans had begun, however fitfully, to investigate and prosecute the former Nazis.

On May 30 of the same year, Wilhelm Jellinek, a businessman from Aschaffenburg, gave the Munich police a sworn statement that Dr. Hans Eisele, a physician living comfortably in the suburb of Pasing, had killed at least two hundred concentration camp inmates as an SS doctor. Jellinek said that he personally witnessed Dr. Eisele commit the murders with injections of an Evipan-Natrium solution.

The Munich police took Jellinek's statement but did not immediately arrest the doctor, who continued to practice medicine, including treating state-insured patients. It was not until three weeks later, on June 20, that the police forwarded the case to the appropriate prosecutor. By that time the story had already made it into the newspapers.

At first Eisele defended himself vigorously, even writing a letter to the editor of one of the newspapers that published the accusations against him. Then a sympathetic individual in the government warned Eisele that his arrest was imminent. The man who had beaten two death sentences vanished from West Germany and quickly resurfaced in Egypt. The West Germans tried to have him extradited, but according to Egyptian law the murders and attempted murders he was accused of committing had already passed their statute of limitations. Like the tank officer Gerhartz before him, Dr. Eisele was allowed to build a new life in the Middle East.

On August 29, 1958, the court in Ulm found ten defendants, including Bernhard Fischer-Schweder, guilty in connection with the Einsatzkommando case. Though the men were convicted, they were only determined by the court to be culpable as accessories, and they were given between three and fifteen years in prison. Their defense that they were just following orders spared them more serious sentences. The verdicts disappointed many hoping to see real justice done, however belatedly.

But the case had a ripple effect. Under pressure from the media and with an eye on diplomatic reaction, West German state ministers created a special body to investigate war crimes with the prosecutor in charge of the Ulm Trial, Erwin Schüle, at its helm. The Central Office of the State Justice Administrations for the Investigation of National Socialist Crimes began its work on December 1, 1958, in Ludwigsburg, near Stuttgart, making Baden-Württemberg the center of Nazi investigations in Germany. By the end of the first month the office had opened sixty-four cases. On July 23, 1959, Schüle could lay claim to the group's first big victory when police arrested the head of the criminal police in the Rhineland-Palatinate, Georg Heuser, for taking part in mass shootings in Minsk. After a year, the number of active cases had reached four hundred.

Among the first employees to report for work at the new Nazi-hunting unit was the ambitious thirty-four-year-old police officer Alfred Aedtner. He had already secured a transfer from his post as beat cop to one watching trains arriving from East Germany for suspicious activity, perhaps not the most exciting job, but of greater significance than writing up fender benders in Gaggenau. Aedtner would now turn his attention to war crimes. He thought it would probably take "at the most a year" to clear up the remaining cases and then move on.

But as the small band of prosecutors began to read through the multitude of witness statements, the magnitude of the crimes came into focus. Their problem was finding the funds and manpower to handle the investigations. Aedtner was immediately given some of the toughest cases.

The Frankfurt prosecutor Fritz Bauer had begun pursuing criminal prosecutions for the murders committed at Auschwitz. By April, Aedtner was delving into the investigation. He heard how new arrivals at Auschwitz were lined up and executed before the notorious Black Wall, which had stood between the crematorium and the barracks where medical experiments were performed. A man who had shaken pellets of Zyklon B into the gas chamber with his own hands explained to Aedtner how he stood before the vents on the roof and emptied the deadly canister of pellets onto the victims packed below him.

Aedtner quickly realized that the case before him went far beyond routine violations of the rules of war. These cases had to be solved, they had to be prosecuted and the perpetrators punished, of that he was certain.

CHAPTER 16

When the Nazis came to power in 1933, the Stuttgart district judge Fritz Bauer knew the new government had two strikes against him: he was a Social Democrat, and he came from a German-Jewish family. The thirty-year-old was forced to resign and spent several months in the Heuberg concentration camp. Once freed in 1935, he first moved to Denmark and then, after nearly being recaptured, escaped to Sweden, where he worked on an opposition newspaper with his fellow Social Democrat Willy Brandt.

Bauer returned to Germany after the war intent on meting out justice through the legal system. There were former Nazis at every level of German government, and Bauer was determined to prosecute them. Threats, sabotage, and suspiciously missing files did not intimidate him. With his ample jowls, under his shock of white hair, Bauer made a lasting impression. He had begun building what he hoped would be a successful case against the perpetrators of Auschwitz, and in December 1956 he issued an arrest warrant for Eichmann.

The following year Lothar Hermann, a Holocaust survivor and immigrant to Argentina, wrote to Bauer stating that he knew where Eichmann was. Hermann's teenage daughter, Sylvia, had been dating Eichmann's son Nick, who was living in Buenos Aires under his own name and talking a little too openly about the past. Bauer was not the first person Hermann had told about his discovery of Eichmann's whereabouts. He had informed the local Jewish organization as well as Tuviah Friedman in Israel. But nothing had happened.

Bauer did not like his chances if he pursued the case himself. There were so many former Nazis in the ranks of the police, prosecutors, and government officials that he believed Eichmann would be warned before he could be found, much less arrested and extradited. The German ambassador to Argentina had once been an aide to the Nazi foreign minister Joachim von Ribbentrop. Instead, Bauer chose to meet secretly with Israel's representative in Germany, Felix Shinar. They met at a nondescript highway motel. Bauer pointed out that by handing over the information to an agent of a foreign government, he was committing treason. Shinar promised that Israel would act.

But the Israelis equivocated, saying they needed more evidence. Instead of sending experienced agents, they had directed Hermann, blind from beatings he had received at Dachau, and his young daughter to look for proof that the man living as Ricardo Klement was actually Adolf Eichmann. Sylvia found the modest house where Eichmann said he was living and went all alone to seek him out. The amateur detectives were surprisingly effective, but Bauer was furious. The Mossad was just sitting on the information. In December 1959, Bauer decided to fly to Israel and demand action.

He set up a meeting at the Ministry of Justice in Jerusalem. "Any second-class policeman would be able to follow such a lead!" Bauer shouted at the Israeli officials. "Just go and ask the nearest butcher or greengrocer and you will learn all there is to know about him!" Bauer had brought further proof with him, details about how Eichmann had used the rat lines to flee Germany. Bauer threatened to extradite Eichmann himself unless the Israelis acted. They tried to mollify him, promising that with the new information they would move against Eichmann as quickly as possible. Bauer returned to Germany and waited to see if they kept their word.

On May 11, 1960, Ricardo Klement was walking home from the bus stop after his shift at the Mercedes-Benz factory. He passed a car that had broken down on Garibaldi Street. Two men were working on it. "Un momentito, señor," one of them said to him, and before he knew it, Eichmann was pinned to the ground by the men, who wrestled him into the car and drove to a safe house. The Nazi was questioned, drugged, dressed in an El Al airlines uniform, and carried onto a jet. The agents charged with getting him onto the plane said he was a pilot who had partied a little too hard. They were there to take him home.

Simon Wiesenthal learned of Adolf Eichmann's capture when Prime Minister David Ben-Gurion addressed the Israeli Parliament on May 23, 1960. "I must inform the Knesset that some time ago, Israeli security forces tracked down one of the greater Nazi criminals, Adolf Eichmann, who was in charge, together with the Nazi leadership, of what they referred to as 'The Final Solution to the Jewish problem,'" he told the chamber. "Adolf Eichmann is already held in custody in Israel and will soon be brought to trial."

The prime minister received a standing ovation. The architect of the Holocaust, one of the most wanted Nazi war criminals, was in Israel, where he would be tried for murder. None of the details of his spectacular capture by the Mossad and the Shin Bet were made public. While it was a moment of great pride for the young nation, the Argentine government was protesting that its sovereignty had been violated. Nationalists in Buenos Aires began attacking Jews and Jewish sites. Argentina went to the United Nations demanding action.

It was not the time to trumpet the details of their operation. Nor could Fritz Bauer take credit for his part in the capture for fear of prosecution. His role remained a closely kept secret. Chancellor Adenauer had already protested the Israeli action and said that Eichmann should be sent to Germany. To deflect criticism, Ben-Gurion's government claimed that it was not the Mossad who captured the Nazi but an independent group of Jews who had taken it upon themselves to seize the *Obersturmbannführer*. Beyond that the details were sketchy.

Meanwhile, Wiesenthal had already received a cable from Yad Vashem, congratulating him. He had once passed on information that Eichmann was in Argentina. His files, along with Tuviah Friedman's, were now being used to help with the criminal's interrogation. Wiesenthal began to give interviews. After six years, the Nazi hunter was back, with a new global profile.

No trial since Nuremberg had received such attention when the Eichmann trial opened on April 11, 1961. Israeli officials wanted to tell the world what the Nazis had done during the war. Famous writers like Hannah Arendt descended on the courtroom, making controversial declarations about the "banality of evil." Unlike the Nuremberg trials, Eichmann's was televised. For the first time the world was forced to recognize the severity of the crimes during the Holocaust. Eichmann's trial would keep the Jewish demand for justice from becoming a historical footnote.

CHAPTER 17

The dance floor at the Casino Gala Evening in Baden-Baden was full of men and women in black tie. On the edge of the crowd, a blonde with carefully curled, shoulder-length hair danced with a tall man with a receding hairline. The moment was captured in a black-and-white photograph that took up an entire page in *Baden-Baden* magazine. Friedl and Aribert Heim saved the magazine as a keepsake. A dozen years into their marriage, they were enjoying life in a beautiful spa town.

After working in numerous hospitals, performing clinical drug trials, and publishing an article in a medical journal, Heim was thriving at his gynecological practice on Lange Strasse. Word traveled quickly that Dr. Heim was an attractive physician with a pleasing bedside manner. At home he tried to spend what little free time he had with his two young boys. He built a goal in the backyard for the kids to practice playing soccer. There was no net, just two posts and a crossbar. When it rained, they played table tennis. Heim put great emphasis on sport and physical activity.

In the summers Heim's mother, Anna, and his older sister, Hilda, would come from Austria and stay with his younger sister, Herta, in an affluent bedroom community a twenty-minute drive from Frankfurt. When Dr. Heim and his children visited, the two boys would follow their cousin Birgit around. Birgit adored her uncle, though she was angry when he banished her beloved dachshund from sleeping in her bed on the grounds that she might catch toxoplasmosis. Otherwise her world was a happy one, roughhousing with the local boys or playing at the tennis club. The wall that had divided Berlin in 1961 was a frightening but distant thought. She was more concerned with getting her hands on the latest record by Peter Kraus, the teenage heartthrob.

Noticing that she spent a good deal of time playing with boys, her mother felt it was time to teach her the facts of life. Instead of sitting her daughter down herself, she turned to Uncle Ferdi. He took Birgit into the study with a pencil and a notebook. But the tomboy could not understand why his diagrams meant she should stop playing cops and robbers with the neighborhood boys. Still, Herta was satisfied that her brother had taken care of the issue. "What do you have such a brother for," his sister asked, "if not to handle such a job?"

It was during this otherwise peaceful time that Heim began to fear his past might catch up with him. He had received an inquiry about his wartime service from investigators, specifically his service at the Mauthausen concentration camp. He decided to visit Frankfurt's leading defense attorneys for Nazi cases, the former Nuremberg lawyer Hans Laternser and his young protégé Fritz Steinacker.

Steinacker had stumbled into his unusual legal specialty almost by accident. The young man from Hesse always thought he would grow up to be a doctor. Born in 1921, he did not even get to finish high school. He went straight from the Hitler Youth to the Luftwaffe. Steinacker was trained as a bomber pilot. He flew Heinkel 111s and Ju 88s for the Luftwaffe, and he flew them well. He received one of the highest decorations, the German Cross in Gold, for extraordinary acts of valor.

On one mission he took heavy antiaircraft fire and had to crash-land near the town of Taufkirchen. His injuries weren't life threatening, and when he was taken to the hospital, he lay on the stretcher waiting for treatment as doctors tended to the more serious cases. The smells in the infirmary, the mixtures of human odors and disinfectants, made him sick to the point of passing out. Steinacker survived his wounds and survived the war, but the smell stuck with him. He realized he could not train on cadavers, could not work among those medical odors. They made him nauseated and light-headed. It did not take long before he realized that he would never be a physician.

He went to law school instead. It was, he thought, "an honorable job as well." The young lawyer studied civil law, but a friend asked him if he could substitute for another attorney on a criminal case. He protested that he was not trained for it, but his friend said he just needed to sit there next to the accused, a place holder with a law degree. He was diligent and effective, surpassing the expectations of Hans Laternser, the experienced attorney on the case, who had worked as a defender at the Nuremberg trials and later been part of the Heidelberger Juristenkreis, the lobbying and legal aid group for Nazi detainees.

The two men hit it off, and Laternser asked if they could continue working together. The older lawyer's specialty was defending Nazis. Many German attorneys avoided such cases for moral reasons or out of fear that it would hurt their other business. But Laternser had built his practice on exactly such cases. Steinacker had no such qualms and quickly accepted. By 1962 they had a full client list of former Nazis and a growing reputation.

The day Heim went to their office, Laternser was away, so Steinacker received the visitor by himself. Heim explained that for a short period of one or two months he was stationed as an SS doctor at the Mauthausen concentration camp. He said that he had not been concerned about possible legal repercussions until the previous year, when two men had contacted him to question him about it.

The meeting had taken place at the Heidelberg train station. It was not a confrontational conversation, but they had brought a file with them and wanted to know whether he was the man mentioned in the paperwork. Heim said yes, but as he examined the documents, he had the feeling that he could have walked away with the file, the proceeding was so informal. Heim said that he had gone to the police station in Baden-Baden to inquire whether there was any sort of criminal case against him. The police told him that there was none that they were aware of, but shortly thereafter he was warned—he did not say how—that proceedings were brewing against him. As early as 1961 he had been advised that it would be impossible to get a fair trial in such a case. He believed that even a single witness giving incriminating testimony would be enough to win a conviction.

"I know that there's a case against me, and I'm giving you power of attorney to represent me," Heim told Steinacker. He wrote out a statement naming Steinacker and Laternser as his legal representatives, then gave the young lawyer his address. They could always reach his wife there. He explained that his sister would handle any financial issues that arose, including Steinacker's fee. The two men stood up and shook hands. "You'll be hearing from me," Heim said.

Meanwhile, his appeals exhausted, Adolf Eichmann awaited his death sentence in the Ramleh prison in Israel. Shortly before midnight on May 31, 1962, he was taken to a wooden platform with a trapdoor. A noose hung from an iron frame above his head. The guards tied his legs together to prevent him from kicking. He declined a hood to cover his face.

"Long live Germany, long live Argentina, long live Austria," Eichmann said. "I shall not forget them."

He was the first and only prisoner ever executed by the state of Israel. He was cremated and his ashes placed in a small nickel canister. Later the ashes were sprinkled at sea. There would be no grave, no shrine. Eichmann's sentence was complete.

CHAPTER 18

There were many possible explanations for the growing amount of time that Dr. Heim spent away from home in the spring and summer of 1962. His medical practice absorbed a great deal of his attention, and managing the Bechtold family properties since the death of Friedl's father took up more and more of his energy. He also was a frequent visitor at Herta's house in Buchschlag. There were many plausible explanations for his absences until the bracelet appeared. After that it was difficult for Friedl Heim to dispel her fear that Aribert was having an affair.

His distraction, short temper, and sudden trips all seemed to fit a man with a mistress. The couple slept in separate bedrooms, and the family cleaning lady, Helene Possekel, had been tidying up in Heim's when she found a gold bracelet. She gave it to Friedl, who handed it to her husband, saying, "This was found in your bedroom, no doubt a memento of beautiful hours." Heim insisted that he was not having an affair. The bracelet was a present for his niece, Birgit, for her confirmation. This did not put an end to Friedl's concerns nor ease the growing tension in the Heim household. Her husband doted a little too much on his sister Herta and constantly praised her in his wife's presence. The amount of time that he spent with the Barth family, and away from home, was troubling.

Friedl had already forgiven him for the distasteful matter of his illegitimate daughter, whom he had confessed to having. Or more like half confessed. Heim claimed to have signed the birth certificate of a fatherless child, knowing that the promiscuous mother had dallied with his SS colleagues. By signing the certificate, he made her eligible for the Lebensborn program to promote the Aryan race, guaranteeing the girl a minimum of support from the state. It was an unpleasant subject, and Friedl preferred to forget it.

Until the spring of that year the couple's live-in maid, Ursula Kammerer, thought of their relationship as "balanced and harmonious." Then the household staff sensed a changing mood. The growing pressure on Heim was palpable. The couple's increasingly frequent fights "did not remain concealed from me," Ms. Kammerer said, in spite of the fact that "as it grew strained between the Heim couple I would receive days off at the most improbable moments, whereas before my free time was granted according to a definite plan."

When he was home, Aribert remained a devoted father. His younger son, Rüdiger, had a deviated septum that made him prone to ear infections and other nagging ailments. One night his father came into his room to check up on him and found the boy still awake. The two went downstairs to the kitchen, and Aribert fried a couple of eggs for the boy. They sat together in the kitchen until little Rü felt better. When his father brought him back upstairs, he was finally able to fall asleep.

It was a tender moment, but Heim was also a strict parent, especially as the pressure of discovery grew. As the school year was ending in the summer of 1962, Heim inquired how his son was doing in his classes. The teacher answered that if his work continued so poorly, he might not advance to the next grade. When Rüdiger came home from school, he saw that his desk had been moved to the middle of the living room.

"So what's this you've been telling me all along that you're doing well?" his father asked. His fuse was shorter in those days, his temper quicker. "You might be held back. Why did you lie to me?"

Rüdiger had to sit there at the little desk under his father's stern gaze and do math problems and practice spelling. After two hours he began to whimper, asking if he could go outside. His mother said, "Let the poor child go," but Heim was unmoved, and when Rüdiger began to cry, his father spanked him with the carpet beater. It was the first time Rü had been corporally punished. Like the maid and the cleaning lady, the little boy could sense the tension rising in the house.

Busy and distracted as he was, Heim did not cancel the family summer vacation at Lake Lugano. It was a happy few weeks, and everything felt normal again. In September they returned for the start of the school year.

I n 1962 the frenzy of attention around the year-old Berlin Wall continued. The threat of nuclear war between the Soviet Union and the United States was a constant concern as their stockpiles grew, but there was little the Germans on either side of the border could do. West German politicians chose to focus on economic growth and the country's burgeoning strength as an industrial exporter. German businessmen were preoccupied with the "offensive" of Japanese cars on the world market and whether they might cut too deeply into the business of Mercedes-Benz, BMW, and Volkswagen.

At Baden-Baden's Metropol movie theater, the cultural shifts of the 1960s were already in evidence. The scandalous film *Lulu* was playing, starring the Austrian actress Nadja Tiller, whose character was described as "a broad like Satan," along with Billy Wilder's cross-dressing comedy with Marilyn Monroe, *Some Like It Hot.*

Late one night that September the Heims' housekeeper, Ms. Kammerer, could hear the doctor and his wife fighting, even though her room was in the attic and they were down on the ground floor. "They carried on a loud and in part heated discussion, the content of which, since I was in my room, I had no chance to discover," she later recalled. She said she could not tell if the mother-in-law, Mrs. Bechtold, had taken part in the argument in order to, as she put it, "take her daughter's side."

The next day, Heim came to Ms. Kammerer's bedroom extremely early, around 4:15 a.m., and woke her up. She said she knew right away that something was wrong. "Compared with his otherwise normally calm and even-tempered manner, he appeared to be agitated and nervous, so I asked him if something had happened. He answered that he had to go and that he was in a hurry; probably I would never see him again."

The maid said he asked her to support his wife, "especially on account of the children, to the best of my strength, and to overlook anything that his mother-in-law might do that bothered me." She made him breakfast and watched as he loaded his suitcase and briefcase into the Mercedes with the Frankfurt license plates. His wife, Friedl, was still in bed when he left.

Friedl described the arrival of the police that afternoon "like an ambush." Half a dozen men in plain clothes came into the house and went through the rooms looking for Heim. She stopped them in front of the room where their elder son, Aribert, was doing his homework.

"Please leave the boy," she told the police. "Look around. Do what you must, but please don't speak to him. Don't tell him that you're looking for his father." Before departing, one of the officers told her, "You should be glad it's no longer the Third Reich. Then we would have gone about all of this very differently."

When Mrs. Possekel, the cleaning lady, returned to the villa a few days later, she noticed Heim's absence. She assumed that he had left because of the quarrel with his wife over the bracelet. But as the weeks went by without his return, she realized something more serious had happened. The entire family's mood was gloomy, and "Frau Dr. Heim wandered around with tearstained eyes."

It was not unusual for Birgit Barth to have her uncle stay with them in Buchschlag. It was almost like Aribert's second home. The five-bedroom house sat back from the street and was decorated in a tasteful mix of antique and modern. A metal fence ran around the property. The yard was filled with evergreens, birch trees, and an old apple tree. One day the family gathered outside in front of the garden fence to bid Aribert farewell.

This time he appeared to be going on a trip longer than the two-hour drive back to Baden-Baden. Birgit thought he was going on a vacation since he was taking the sports car. She noticed that her mother had packed his things into Birgit's little blue suitcase. With his usual advice to do well in school, Heim left her home for what she did not realize was the last time. The teenager sulked as her beloved suitcase as well as her tweezers and nail file disappeared into the trunk of the Mercedes convertible. "You better get in," her father said to Aribert. "They're over there."

Birgit thought he meant the chatty neighbors down the street, but he actually meant the state police who had begun canvassing the neighborhood with a photograph, asking neighbors if they recognized Dr. Heim. The neighbors knew him, of course, but told the police they had no idea.

A police investigator rang Herta Barth's doorbell again in February. The officer found Mrs. Barth "indignant" when she discovered that the police were searching for her brother. "She answered questions only grudgingly," one of the policemen wrote in his report.

Asked when her brother had last been there, she told him mid-January. She did not ask why her brother was being sought, which seemed like the natural question if she did not know that he was a wanted fugitive. The officer explained that they had leads suggesting that Heim had been staying with her.

German law does not permit the prosecution of direct blood relatives for aiding and abetting fugitive family members. Close relations—fathers and mothers, sons and daughters, brothers and sisters—are not expected to cooperate. The ties of blood are stronger, the law presumes, than the individual's loyalty to the state. That was certainly the case in the Heim family.

Around the same time, Friedl received a card from Heim bearing the postmark of his sister's suburb. When the police returned to interview her again, Herta was like another person. "Now Mrs. Barth was friendliness itself," the policeman wrote. Her brother had not visited for some time, she explained, because the two of them had had a difference of opinion. She did not elaborate on the subject of the dispute, but she was now curious enough to ask why the police were looking for her Aribert. The officer did not answer. Instead, he gave her what amounted to a warning: if Heim did not turn himself in, the police would have to ask the public for assistance in apprehending him. Posters with his photograph would be plastered all over the place.

"Apparently, Dr. Heim has very good friends in the federal republic," the officer wrote, "with whom he can stay for weeks at a time without being noticed." He had not registered his whereabouts, as German law required, nor was there evidence that he was staying in a hotel. "The search continues," the investigator wrote in February 1963, five months after the doctor's disappearance from Baden-Baden and shortly after his sister said he had left Buchschlag.

The Hessian police returned to Bad Nauheim, where Heim had played hockey, to look for clues. Unlike their American counterparts, who had turned up no evidence that Heim had lived there, the Hessian police found that he was still remembered a dozen years later. A doctor told them that Heim had lived at the Sanatorium Hahn in downtown Bad Nauheim.

In the neighboring town of Friedberg, Fräulein Welsch in the personnel department of the hospital found a reference to Heim in her files. She recalled how the doctor had "disappeared unexpectedly from Friedberg." They were even aware of his next stop. Fräulein Welsch told the investigators that she "surmised that he had then moved to Mannheim," which was in fact the case. Heim was registered there and could have been easily located by anyone who checked with the local municipal office, under his correct name and place of birth, at Dürerstrasse 7. The chief doctor had not been at all forthcoming a decade earlier when questioned by the Americans. "The possibility has to be considered that Dr. Kramer gave the American authorities false information about Dr. Heim at that time," the German investigator wrote in his report.

In April 1963, less than a year after he fled Baden-Baden, Heim visited West Berlin to check on his property. He stayed at the Hotel Frühling, not far from the Zoologischer Garten train station and a short walk to the real-estate firm Wilhelm Droste. Heim had come to the office to inform the staff that his sister Herta would now handle the property and that the proceeds from the apartment building should be sent to her. That was the last confirmed sighting of Dr. Aribert Heim in Germany.

CHAPTER 20

Alfred Aedtner relished his job at the Central Office of the State Justice Administrations for the Investigation of National Socialist Crimes. It provided the challenging assignments he was looking for but also meant that he spent less and less time at home with his wife and young son. Rather than drive an hour each way from Gaggenau, Aedtner rented a small apartment near Ludwigsburg, where he worked. Investigations took him all over Germany as well as abroad. He came home on the weekends exhausted.

Even then he had work. While his son splashed at the public swimming pool, Alfred read case files or studied. He needed an *Abitur*, the highest level of high school degree, to achieve his goal of becoming a *Kriminalkommissar*, or detective superintendent. He finally received his diploma at the age of thirty-six. Once he had his *Abitur*, he was able to study at the police academy in Freiburg, and by 1964 he was promoted.

The detective was still a bit of a dandy. He only wore hand-tailored suits and only drove Mercedes cars. A handsome man with a full head of hair, Aedtner marched to work each day in a trench coat, briefcase under his arm and cigarette dangling from his lip. His wife stretched his public-employee salary to shop at the clothier Z. Müller in Gaggenau. His handmade hats came from her sister, who was in the business. He only wore Seidensticker shirts, with the black rose emblem stitched into the side. He was equally loyal to his Peer Export cigarettes, smoking his way through three of the red packs every day. He used American Ronson cigarette lighters, even though the company once made tanks for the United States, which the German soldiers nicknamed Ronsons for their propensity to catch fire.

But just because state justice officials founded an office for the investigation of Nazi war crimes did not mean that they supported it. Aedtner was disappointed by the quality of the policemen assigned to the unit, green recruits, traffic cops, officers with no experience working complex investigations. "You can't fix a complicated machine with unskilled labor," was Aedtner's way of putting it. It quickly became clear that the decision to start the central office was intended more to serve as political cover than to create an actual task force.

Under the leadership of Erwin Schüle, the Ulm prosecutor who became the head of the central office, the group combed through archives from London to Jerusalem, from Washington to Amsterdam, searching for evidence of war crimes. The enormity of the task—often compared to Hercules cleansing the Augean Stables—became clearer the deeper they delved, discovering, for instance, that the Gestapo had issued false identity papers to its officers in the spring of 1945. But the group pursued its cases so diligently and effectively that even the president of the World Jewish Congress, Dr. Nahum Goldmann, praised its work and Schüle personally.

There was no small amount of schadenfreude among the opponents of Nazi prosecution when it emerged that Schüle had been a member of the Nazi Party and the stormtroopers known as the SA. As Schüle arrived in Warsaw in February 1965 to examine archival material about Nazi war crimes the East German news agency ADN reported his membership in the party. His superiors had already known about his past and he was able to cling to his job, even as he was excoriated in the press, received death threats at home, and was mocked on television comedy shows. But after the Soviets alleged that Schüle had been personally involved in executions on the eastern front during the war as a member of the 215th Infantry Division, he resigned the following year.

"Isn't it time twenty years after the war to end the denazification?" asked Franz Xaver Unertl, a conservative member of the Bundestag at a political gathering. *Der Spiegel* described the applause as "thunderous."

The Schüle scandal only compounded the already difficult task of trying to build cases in an uncooperative and at times obstructive justice system. Officials were as likely to warn former comrades of an imminent arrest as to help Aedtner apprehend the accused. Police officers regularly asked Aedtner how he could stand to betray his own. The investigators were called "*Nestbeschmutzer*," literally ones who soiled their own nests, but in spirit more like those who denigrate their country. They were cursed to their faces. Taxi drivers often refused fares to their headquarters, so they had to give nearby addresses in order to be picked up. "As a result of these hostilities," Aedtner said, "more than a few asked to be relieved from the special commission. They were replaced with others for whom it did not go any differently."

Aedtner described how he once appeared at the Stuttgart apartment of a police commander who had overseen the murder of more than ten thousand Jews, Communists, and partisans in the region around Minsk when he was a member of Police Battalion 322 during the war. The man's wife loudly cursed Aedtner and his colleagues, saying the impending arrest was "worse than Gestapo methods." She told him that it was beneath her husband to be arrested by such "little people."

Many former members of Police Battalion 322 were working for the police department again after the war. The defendants were up to date on the finest details of the investigators' schedules, always prepared in advance when they appeared to question them. "Wherever we showed up, everyone knew the score already," Aedtner wrote. Witnesses who at first had described the mass shootings in detail, seemingly relieved to confess, stopped cooperating, fearing for their jobs. "For us," Aedtner said, "this development was more than depressing."

For a man dedicated to justice, the enormity of the crimes and the fact that so many in the government resisted solving them began to chafe. One case in particular nagged at him. It involved a man who was convicted as an accessory in the murder of 16,500 people who was sentenced to just two and a half years' imprisonment, little more than an hour for each victim's life. Still Aedtner remained single-minded in tracking down such perpetrators, tenacious as well as patient.

He kept up his spirits by going out with his colleagues, playing the popular card game skat for beers. The war-crimes unit was tight-knit, "a sworn fellowship," as his son described the group. On the road, in the office, on weekends, Aedtner could be found with his stout counterpart Ernst Faller, who was his best friend on the force. Aedtner drank pilsner in great quantities and developed a bit of a paunch over the years from his love of hearty German fare, dumplings and spätzle, roasts and schnitzels. On the weekends he never missed his *Stammtisch* at the local bar back home, the regular gathering of locals at a designated table, something like a drinking club.

He was just thirty-nine when he testified on January 8, 1965, in the Auschwitz trials, as much a sensation inside Germany as the Eichmann trial had been abroad. Aedtner told the court that it was his style to let the perpetrators talk without interruption, as in the case of an SS man named Stark who worked at Auschwitz. "The accused was very willing to make a statement. He described things himself without having to be asked much," Aedtner told the judges. "It was even the case that he talked about things that we at that point knew nothing about, internal matters about his conduct or to be precise his concrete actions in the camp."

The accused often seemed relieved, "liberated," Aedtner said, following their testimony. "At that point we had a few Jewish statements in hand, from Jewish witnesses who more or less said from the photograph, that's Stark and he was involved like the others, but nothing specific. Then [Stark] described all the individual things, such as how he participated in the gassings."

After seven years at the central office in Ludwigsburg, Aedtner was sent to Stuttgart to work at state police headquarters. While the central office identified active cases, it was the job of the individual state authorities to arrest and prosecute the suspects. Even in a normal week there was a great deal of travel in his job, including going to Tel Aviv to take depositions from Holocaust survivors. The constant tales of death and suffering inflicted by his fellow Germans, not only by the Nazis, but also by regular soldiers like him, began to take its toll.

CHAPTER 21

There were plenty of foreigners in the Moroccan city of Tangier, holdovers from the time the Mediterranean port was administered by international powers. Dr. Aribert Heim, who had arrived via Spain, did not stand out. Tangier was still a popular tourist destination, where after a day at the beach a vacationer could sip a mint julep at the El Minzah hotel bar, said to be one of the inspirations for Rick's Café in *Casablanca*.

Heim's sister and his mother-in-law, Käthe Bechtold, traveled there together from Germany in 1963 using indirect flights in case they were followed and spending a night in a Madrid hotel before arriving in Morocco. Heim was living in a private room in extremely spartan conditions. Herta believed that if it were entirely up to her brother, he would have stayed and faced the charges against him, but his mother-in-law argued that Heim had a duty to spare his wife and their two young sons the trauma of his trial and possible imprisonment. The Baden-Baden jail was not far from his sons' school. If he chose to flee, she agreed to help him. Herta was surprised to see the wealthy older lady bent over a basin washing her son-in-law's laundry by hand. The two women helped Heim take the necessary financial steps to turn an impromptu flight into a longer arrangement until the mood in Germany had changed or the statute of limitations on the crimes Heim was accused of had expired.

In the meantime, Tangier was proving unsuitable as a semipermanent home. He found the city welcoming enough but worried about the potential danger posed by its sizable Jewish population. It turned out that Heim had unwittingly moved to the old Jewish quarter. Once his affairs were in order, he would have to move again.

As far as the police were concerned, there was no telling where Heim might be. All sorts of rumors circulated about groups that were said to have helped Nazis on the run. In the popular imagination they had solidified under the name Odessa—the Organization of Former SS Members. The group's escape arm, known as Die Spinne, or the Spider, was rumored to have been run from Spain by Hitler's top commando, Otto Skorzeny. A hulking, scar-faced SS man, Skorzeny was known for a daring raid to rescue Hitler's ally Benito Mussolini from captivity as well as for a plot to assassinate Dwight D. Eisenhower.

Word that Aribert Heim was hiding in Egypt persisted. Both the maid and the cleaning lady at the Heim villa told the police that the doctor had moved to Egypt. Ms. Kammerer recalled that Ms. Rieben, who rented a wing of the villa for many years, confirmed the story. Mrs. Possekel heard the same thing at the local grocery store. But when questioned by police, Ms. Rieben admitted she had never seen letters postmarked from Egypt. "The widespread rumors in Baden-Baden that Dr. Heim is located in Egypt were given attention, however they were not followed up," a local detective named Heitz said, "Such talk has long circulated and does not represent something new."

The activities of the German military experts in Egypt did not go unnoticed. The cover of *Der Spiegel* in May 1963 showed a rocket launching skyward in the desert northwest of Cairo. The article was titled "German Rockets for Nasser." Inside, a map showed how the shorter-range el-Safir, which means "ambassador" in Arabic, could reach Israel, and the el-Kahir, or "conqueror," was almost powerful enough to reach Beirut.

"Where thousands of years ago a nameless army of slaves built pyramids to the glory of the first pharaoh, roughly 500 highly paid German armorers manufacture the weapons of the new pharaoh of the colored world: jet aircrafts and rockets for Gamal Abd el-Nasser," the magazine wrote, describing a world of "professors who carry pistols, engineers whose telephone numbers are listed in no phone books, and skilled technicians who each morning must show their gray-green photo identity cards from the Egyptian Ministry of War to the khaki patrols with machine guns checking them, to enter the secret armament center of the United Arab Republic.

"If the German weapons makers successfully complete their work," the magazine concluded, Nasser would "have at his command every means necessary for a war of annihilation against Israel." Golda Meir, then Israel's foreign minister, warned in the Knesset, "The German government cannot sit idly by as 18 years after the fall of Hitler's regime, which exterminated millions of Jews, members of this people are responsible for actions that serve the destruction of the state of Israel."

In Cairo, the Germans were concentrated in the upscale districts of Helwan and Maadi. They could enjoy German fare at the Löwenbräu restaurant or see American, French, and Italian films at the Rivoli Cinema. "It was a golden era," recalled one German woman who lived in Cairo at the time and said there was "little or no difference" from home in the lifestyle or the treatment of women. In cosmopolitan Cairo, women dressed in skirts and few wore head scarves. In the capital there were trattorias and bars where Greek waiters served alcohol to young military officers.

The Suez Crisis of 1956 significantly altered Egypt's security calculations. Following Nasser's decision to nationalize the Suez Canal, Egypt found itself under attack by Britain, France, and Israel. They were forced to end hostilities in response to condemnation from around the world, and in particular the opposition of both the United States and the Soviet Union. That did not put an end to the enmity provoked by the fighting.

In the wake of the crisis the British canceled delivery of fighter jets to Egypt, and the Soviets failed to deliver spare parts for the out-of-date MiG-15 fighters the Egyptians already had. Nasser deemed it necessary to build his own domestic weapons industry and relied heavily on German expertise. "Aircraft plant in North Africa seeks skilled workers of all kinds," read the advertisements in German newspapers. The work was done for two Switzerland-based front companies, Meco, short for Mechanical Corporation, and MTP-AG, for machines, turbines, and pumps. The two had been set up by Hassan Sayed Kamil, a jeweler, engineer, and arms dealer married to Helene, Duchess of Mecklenburg.

The Israelis decided that diplomatic pressure was insufficient. The Mossad began a series of covert actions to undermine the rocket program. On July 7, 1962, Hassan Sayed Kamil's charter flight crashed for unknown reasons, killing his wife, the duchess. In September, a German businessman supplying materials for Nasser's rocket program disappeared, and an anonymous note was found saying that he was dead. Two Israeli agents were arrested in Switzerland after they were caught on tape threatening the children of a former scientist from Peenemünde, the rocket facility that developed the German V-2 rocket, who was working in Egypt.

The Israelis struck inside Egypt as well. At the end of November, the weapons factory in Helwan received several packages from Hamburg containing explosives. Five Egyptian workers were killed, and a German secretary, Hannelore Wende, was permanently disfigured by a letter bomb. Another explosive was sent to a doctor in the neighborhood of Maadi, a Cairo suburb filled with old villas. Dr. Carl Debouche's only connection to the rocket program seemed to be treating the wives of the scientists and attending their social functions, but he was better known in Europe and Israel as "the Butcher" Hans Eisele. The bomb failed to reach its target, exploding instead in the hand of the postman who was trying to deliver it, costing the man an eye in the process.

Though there was no evidence that Heim and Eisele knew each other, the two SS doctors had both served briefly at Buchenwald during the same period in June 1941. Heim likely would have been familiar with Eisele's case, which made headlines in the newspapers in southern Germany. It was a telling fact that Egyptian authorities had refused to extradite him.

The following year Heim moved from Morocco to Egypt, landing at the brand-new Cairo International Airport. A World War II airfield turned over to the civil-aviation authority, the airport had opened in 1963. It was a crowning moment for the dynamic revolutionary leader Nasser, who had become an icon throughout the Arab world a decade earlier and was watching his plans for the nation come to fruition. It was an exciting, optimistic moment to be in Egypt for Heim as well.

CHAPTER 22

Heim's sister Herta and her daughter Birgit's visits to the nearby town of Walldorf now followed a regular routine. Mrs. Barth would chat with her friend Mrs. Weil, and Birgit would visit with the four Weil children. Mr. Weil had inherited a bicycle shop, and the six of them lived in a small stone bungalow. The two families owned a piece of property together, so there was always business to discuss and Herta tended to depart carrying an unmarked manila envelope. It was not something that anyone noticed. There was nothing out of the ordinary about a housewife and her teenage daughter visiting family friends.

One afternoon in 1964, just two years after her brother's disappearance, Herta was in a greater rush than usual to see the Weils. Birgit now insisted on sitting up front in the Mercedes "like in the American films." Her father always said that it bothered him that the older car did not have seat belts, but that might just have been his latest excuse to try to upgrade to a new model. Mother and daughter pulled up to the T intersection at the B44 highway. Herta was about to make a turn across traffic when she spotted a truck coming toward her from the left. What she could not see was that another car was passing the truck, going the wrong way in her lane. By the time Herta became aware of it, she had already started to cross the intersection.

Birgit could see the collision as it was happening and remembered thinking it was "as if the motor of our car was leaping into the front of the other car." There was a loud bang, and she was thrown into the windshield, leaving a spiderweb of cracks where her head struck the glass. When the vehicles came to rest and everyone stumbled out, they could see that the front of Herta's car was smashed in. Birgit was bleeding, not profusely, but enough to cause some concern.

Herta rushed to the gas station at the corner and called their physician, Dr. Niemöller, who was also a family friend. The doctor hurried over and removed several shards of glass from Birgit's head and then drove them home, leaving the scene of the accident without waiting for the police. Mr. Barth answered the door, finding his daughter with a bandage on her forehead and his wife still shaking.

"Your wife had a small accident," the doctor told him.

"Ach, and my car's fucked up?" he asked. This was not the reaction his wife was expecting.

"I will never drive a car of yours again," Herta said coldly.

"Mom, Papa can see that we're okay," Birgit said. "We walked in. We weren't carried in. We weren't on stretchers. We weren't in intensive care." She knew just how angry her mother was. Birgit was told to go upstairs to the maid's room. It struck the teenager even at the time as odd that she was not sent to her own room.

Birgit could still hear her parents talking and heard her mother say that the police should not be allowed to talk to her. "She stays upstairs." The police came and went without questioning Birgit. Mrs. Barth did not speak to her husband for a good month thereafter. She also stopped driving. Once Birgit had her license, it was her job to chauffeur her mother on errands, whether to the Weils' or the office of the lawyer in Frankfurt representing her uncle Ferdi.

It was as though the family had become spies. They took whispering walks in the garden to talk in case there were listening devices in the house. They picked up letters from the Weils the same day that they arrived. After reading them, Herta made a few cryptic notes and burned them. The trips to Switzerland to wire Aribert Heim money were nerve-racking, even after years of practice. Many well-to-do Germans spirited money into the legendary secrecy of Swiss bank accounts. But crossing the border with thousands of deutsche marks hidden in the lining of her purse made Herta nervous. Even a routine check might reveal who her brother was, and with it the purpose of her trip.

Her visits to Aribert were infrequent, requiring as they did the kind of zigzag pattern that she had used when she met him in Tangier. Now Herta boarded a flight to Paris, then flew to Beirut. From the Lebanese capital she journeyed to the new Cairo International Airport. Just as her fugitive brother appeared to greet her, Herta bumped into a man who lived no more than four streets away from her in Buchschlag. She saw that he recognized her.

After all their efforts to fool the police, they would be undone by an improbable coincidence. But the man never said a word to her nor, as far as she could tell, to anyone else. Herta considered the man's own reputation as a notorious philanderer and concluded he was extending her the same courtesy he wanted for himself.

Still, all was not right. At one point her husband's security clearance was not renewed for his next building project, jeopardizing the family's income, which they spent about as fast as he brought it in. The Barths feared it was because her brother Aribert was a wanted man. Underneath the family's stylish, affluent veneer ran a steady undercurrent of anxiety.

The family could often tell when the phone was tapped. The sound was different, and if the conversation wandered from any investigative interest, a click was audible. Once, when they were out of town, their maid, a kind but mentally challenged girl from Austria, was questioned. Every knock at the door was the source of apprehension. Salesmen, repairmen, all visitors, were suspected of snooping and spying for the police. But Herta remained convinced that her brother was innocent of any war crimes. She told her daughter that if she had not believed in him, she would not have helped him. Yet she was beginning to feel the strain of supporting his life underground.

Not long after the car accident, Herta received another visit from the police. The two officers, Chief Inspector Beihl and Inspector Schäffner, appeared unannounced at 9:30 one morning. The maid had told them that madam was unavailable. They came back about an hour later, and her son from her first marriage, Joachim, answered the door. He left them in the parlor to wait for his mother. Chief Inspector Beihl could barely make it through the end of his opening statement when she interrupted.

"What does that have to do with me? Do we have guilt by association here?" The police started to ask where her brother was hiding but were again sharply interrupted. "No questions, no more answers, please go!" At that point the two state officers left the house. "At least you've comported yourselves decently, but there have already been others here," she said, adding, "I'd like once and for all to no longer be confronted with these things. We have no guilt by association. I'd like to finally have my peace."

CHAPTER 23

One weekend around the time that Alfred Aedtner's son, Harald, had finished his mandatory military service in the late 1960s, the detective brought him to the office. The young man was more interested in working at the gas station and earning money to buy his own car than in history lessons, but since he did not get to see that much of his father, Harald was happy to spend the day with him. He knew that his father pursued former Nazis for war crimes, but his teachers had barely taught the subject in school. As a result, Harald did not understand what the Nazis had done.

His father took him to Ludwigsburg, a garrison town where the Duke of Württemberg began construction on a magnificent baroque palace in 1704. The central office on Schorndorfer Strasse was just a short drive away from the palace. The Nazi hunters had moved into a century-old former women's prison, where in 1938 Ludwigsburg's Jewish residents were held. It was before the era of computers, and the prosecutors and police officers had to keep an enormous catalog of index cards, naming perpetrators, witnesses, military units, and locations of atrocities. They also had evidence, which Aedtner decided to use for educational purposes.

He set up a projector and loaded the first reel of film. Father and son sat together in the dark as scenes from before Harald's birth played out in front of them. Frightened civilians were forced to strip down in front of a mass grave. They stood at the edge and soldiers fired at their backs, sending their bodies plummeting into the pit. As these inhuman events were projected, Aedtner explained everything. It was not something they would discuss again. It was understood that Germans of Aedtner's generation did not talk about their feelings. But afterward, when Harald would go to the bar with his father, he noticed that the policeman never discussed his work there either.

Aedtner was traveling so much his wife started asking where he hadn't been instead of where he had. Often he didn't come home even on the weekend. But both his son and his wife knew just how much his job took out of him. "He worked like a madman," his wife said. "It wore him down," she added, using the German word *mitgenommen*, literally "took him with it," which in a sense it had. The barbs hurt, the taunts of "traitor."

"These people have to be brought to account. I hate them like the plague," his son recalled Aedtner spontaneously declaring one day, after reading an article about the Nazis in the newspaper. He only said it once, but it stuck with Harald. His father never talked about where this antipathy had come from, what had happened that made him dedicate his life to catching a group of criminals that most of his countrymen would have rather pretended didn't exist.

But his son could speculate. His father maintained a friendship with a Jewish goldsmith in Pforzheim. The man had made the watch Harald received for his eighteenth birthday, as well as the rings with the blue lapis lazuli stones that he and his father wore. Perhaps Aedtner was moved by Jewish friendships from his youth? Also, the war had ended with Aedtner's hometown being annexed by another country, most of his family trapped behind the Iron Curtain. But Harald thought it was more visceral than that. The end of the war was a terrible time, and scared young recruits who ran from the fighting were executed as deserters. When Aedtner had been wounded in action, the man beside him died. There were so many possible explanations.

Even Aedtner might not have understood his own commitment. It might have been something fundamental about him as a person. His wife recalled how deeply affected he had been when, while still a beat cop, he worked at the site of an automobile accident that had killed a young man. Maybe his dedication to his calling grew out of nothing more than an ingrained opposition to suffering, and he could never get over the extreme, almost limitless suffering that the Nazis had caused. One thing was for sure, his son said, it was not a coincidence that Aedtner worked in the Nazi-hunting unit, despite the abuse and frustrations that came with it. "He wanted that job," said his son. "He wanted to get them."

Harald himself could never shake the images from the films his father showed him. He left the former women's prison with its archive of war-crimes evidence almost numb with shock. But the scenes on the movie screen answered any remaining questions he might have had about why his father pursued his job and at such personal cost.

CHAPTER 24

On the morning of June 7, 1967, in the middle of the Six-Day War, Simon Wiesenthal called a press conference in Vienna. "In contrast to Nazi criminals who live freely in other countries, the Nazi criminals who live in the Middle East are engaging themselves deeply in politics and their role was built into the plan for the fight against Israel," he said.

Amid the roll call of forty-three names was "SS-Hauptsturmführer Dr. Heribert Heim, camp doctor from Mauthausen, who performed countless experiments on inmates in this camp that led to deadly outcomes. Wanted in Austria, he has been a police doctor in Egypt since 1954. To conceal himself, he has changed his name many times." The press conference was intended to link the Arab attack on Israel to the Holocaust. Wiesenthal duly sent his list of war criminals to the central office in Ludwigsburg for them to pursue. Adalbert Rückerl, who the year before had replaced his colleague Erwin Schüle as the head of the central office, explained in a letter to the famous Nazi hunter that they could find only nineteen of the forty-three individuals in their records, and of the nineteen they knew about, five were not connected to Nazi crimes, two were dead, and two were definitely not in Egypt, because they were already in German custody.

There were other mistakes in the hastily arranged conference. One of the names on his own list struck Wiesenthal as a little odd, that of Leopold Gleim. Wiesenthal checked his SS catalog and decided it must have been "a phonetic mistake" and that it was the quite common name of Klein rather than Gleim. And the aforementioned Heribert Heim had been working as a police doctor in Egypt since 1954, eight years before Aribert Heim left Baden-Baden. Yet the Nazi hunter was correct in that Heim had relocated to Egypt, just as he had been correct when he said that Eichmann was in Argentina. The central office used the same misspelling of Heim's first name and gave an incorrect place of birth as Ingstfeld. "The person concerned is the former SS doctor in the concentration camps of Mauthausen and Oranienburg," Rückerl from the central office reported. "His exact location is unknown."

In 1969, Wiesenthal wrote a letter to the State Institute for War Documentation in Holland trying to find a photograph of Heim. By that time he had the correct spelling of Heim's first name and as a precaution put "Heribert" in parentheses. He also appealed to the central office in Ludwigsburg for information, which repeated back to him Wiesenthal's own suspicion that the former Nazi was in Egypt, working as a police doctor. In the meantime, Wiesenthal received an anonymous tip that Heim was living with a woman in Riezlern in Kleinwalsertal, an isolated Austrian mountain valley near the German border. The man's name was Leopold Heim, and the woman's Anni. It proved a false lead. The trail had gone cold.

Meanwhile, with the ample time at his disposal, Heim became interested in tourism, studying statistics on the travel patterns of Western European vacationers to beachfront properties in Majorca and Crete. He believed Egypt's coast could be turned into a destination to rival Spain or Italy. He even wrote a report titled "Beach-Bathing Tourism," which he sent to the Egyptian minister of tourism and to the German ambassador. English and German travelers would be especially interested because of their "joint history interests from World War II" at El Alamein. He was referring to the tens of thousands of casualties suffered in the North Africa campaign.

His sister Herta was still managing their properties in Germany, the source of the income that allowed him to invest in a seaside lot outside Alexandria. In his absence his wife had begun looking after her family properties herself, no longer able to lean on her husband for assistance. She and her mother had been called in again to answer questions about his disappearance.

The two women were told that Dr. Heim was wanted for suspicion of murdering inmates at Mauthausen between 1941 and 1942. Both told the police inspector that they believed in his innocence. Both said they did not know his whereabouts. The police countered that it was then hard to understand why Heim had not turned himself in, to which they replied that he would very likely have been held for years in pretrial detention. The inspector did not find it credible that Friedl knew nothing about her husband's whereabouts.

A few months later, in February 1967, Friedl decided to file for divorce, listing their home in Baden-Baden as Heim's last known address and "now unknown residence." According to the filing, her husband told her he was wanted in connection with the Nazi euthanasia cases but that he was innocent, before he "packed with the greatest speed and drove off to an unknown destination." Promises that they would be reunited had not been fulfilled. "The respondent [had] told the plaintiff it would only be a short separation. Today, after four years, the respondent is still away . . . Naturally, the burden of the maintenance of the family since 1962 has fallen on the shoulders of the plaintiff and her mother . . . After the above-presented developments, the plaintiff no longer has any marital feelings toward the respondent. The dissolution of the marriage is also in the interest of the children." The reality of Heim's long stay in Egypt began to sink in.

Life as a fugitive presented constant problems, and their resolution usually fell to Herta. Often it was trouble with money transfers from Switzerland to Egypt, or in one instance help acquiring a car in Europe and getting it through Egyptian customs. Even after her brother's departure, Herta traveled frequently to Baden-Baden to visit with her sister-in-law and to share the absent father's letters to his sons. She burned their business correspondence but ferried the innocent missives to the children.

Once, as she was leaving the mansion, tears began to roll down her cheeks. "What's wrong?" Birgit asked. "I thought you wanted to come."

"But when I think about how he has to live . . ." She could not continue. The thought of her brother living all alone, thousands of miles from his family, was sometimes more than she could bear. That his children were growing up without a father was even harder. A letter here and there, a spoken message on spooled magnetic tape, this was not the same as having a father. She knew. She had lost her own father at about the same age as Rüdiger, the younger of the two Heim boys, had lost his.

Heim's German passport expired, and he could not risk renewing it. He had once planned a possible move to Spain, but with his property investment in Alexandria that plan was now "passé." He intended to stay in Egypt for ten more years. He asked his lawyer, Steinacker, to compose a letter to Heim's mother-in-law, in which he tried to convince both his ex-wife, Friedl, and her mother to send the boys to him in Egypt.

"Herr Dr. H. informed me that his sons could begin their studies in the country where he is living at any time," the lawyer wrote. Their father could handle the applications and only needed copies of their passports and birth certificates. "The climate and the sports facilities are world famous." He mentioned the nineteenth-century German doctors Robert Koch and Theodor Bilharz and noted that their successful research had been pursued in this unnamed country, even though both had famously worked in Egypt. Heim knew several of the teaching professors at the university and assured his wife and mother-in-law that they had trained in England and the United States. "The children could pursue their studies with complete independence as if they were alone in a major city," Steinacker wrote on behalf of his client. "Naturally, Dr. H. would stand ready with help and advice."

Nothing came of the proposal. There was little evidence that Friedl wanted anything other than for the two Heim boys to remain close to home and as far as possible out of harm's way.

Over the next few years the political and social climate changed dramatically while Heim was in hiding. The relative calm of Germany's postwar years came decisively to a close after student demonstrations broke out in 1968. The extreme elements of the left-wing protest movement transformed into a potent terrorist group, calling itself the Red Army Faction and dubbed the Baader-Meinhof Gang by the press. They considered the West German state little more than a successor to the Nazi regime with its own fascist agenda.

The Red Army Faction seized the West German embassy in Stockholm, killing two hostages and blowing up part of the building. The terrorist group was in the middle of a spree of kidnappings and shootings, even though their leaders were held in the maximum-security prison in Stammheim, just a fifteen-minute drive from Alfred Aedtner's office.

In the midst of this severe turmoil, investigators had quietly redoubled their efforts on a war-crimes case that was thirty years old and begun searching intensively for a suspect who had fled more than a dozen years earlier. The police believed they now had information that Aribert Heim was alive and still in contact with his family in Germany. The investigation took on a new urgency.

Aedtner, who had been put in charge of his department in 1973, became obsessed with the concentration camp doctor who had lived undiscovered a short drive away in Baden-Baden. "His goal was to hunt down this Aribert Heim," said Karl-Heinz Weisshaupt, a colleague who socialized with Aedtner after work. "One could almost say it was his dream."

German police officers were working with their counterparts in Switzerland to expand their search in and around Lugano, where Heim's wife's family had property. They had few fresh clues to work with, only contradictory theories. Heim might have been in Germany, living under an assumed name, or across the border in his native Austria in an isolated mountain village. He could have gone to Argentina like Adolf Eichmann or to Bolivia like Klaus Barbie. Barbie had been discovered in 1972, but the South American country refused to extradite him. It was yet another hurdle Aedtner might have to face.

He decided to start over, beginning with the witnesses. On a July afternoon in 1975 he traveled from Stuttgart to the police station in the Bavarian town of Schongau to speak with Gustav Rieger, sixty-seven, a doctor of law and a camp survivor. Aedtner had questions about the young Austrian physician Rieger had known at the concentration camp more than thirty years earlier.

"I had seen Dr. Heim already in the sick bay, but it was through his and my tasks in the camp bordello," said Rieger, "that I came to know him somewhat better." He looked at a photo lineup of four pictures and correctly identified the SS doctor as number 3. "I remember Dr. Heim well," the former inmate said. "He was very tall," Rieger recalled, over six feet three, and "he boasted that he was a good hockey player."

The subject Rieger dwelled on during his interview with the investigator was the bordello where he and Dr. Heim worked. The former inmate described his duties with the women euphemistically, as "cleaning up the inmates before and after the exercise." It was Heim's responsibility to examine the women for sexually transmitted diseases several times a week. According to Rieger, the Austrian liked to visit the women for more than professional purposes and encouraged Rieger to do so as well. Rieger described in some detail the infection and multiple operations that prevented him from taking part. He recalled how he had tricked Heim once, going off with the oldest woman, the one they called "the procuress," and letting the SS doctor think they had had sex.

But Aedtner had not driven the two and a half hours from Stuttgart to this small town to talk about the bordello. Only capital crimes were still prosecutable under the German statute of limitations, and he was there to investigate multiple homicides. The warrant issued for Heim's arrest declared that the doctor was strongly suspected of killing "a large but as of yet undetermined number of inmates." The warrant described his "bloodlust" as he injected gasoline directly into the hearts of his victims. Then there were the operations in which the surgeon was accused of opening his patients' abdominal cavities and removing internal organs while the victims were still alive. The ultimate badges of inhumanity were the trophies he made out of victims. "He sent all the inmates out of the operating room, cut off the heads of the two corpses, and let them cook until the flesh separated from the bone. Several days later the two skulls stood on his desk," the arrest warrant said.

"What do you know about Dr. Heim's tasks in the sick bay generally, and especially the deaths of inmates effected by him?" Aedtner asked him.

"I am aware that Dr. Heim performed operations," Rieger answered. "I believe that there was no actual reason for many of these, but instead they were performed by him out of his own interests. When an inmate . . . died after the operation, it was registered in the operation book merely as *exitus letalis*," fatal outcome. Rieger had not himself witnessed cases where Dr. Heim dispatched patients through lethal injections to the heart but said that he was "of the opinion that he acted the same way, if perhaps not to the same extent, as the other SS doctors." It was a fairly standard procedure to euthanize sickly inmates given the Nazi obsession with breeding a superrace.

Rieger had worked in the laboratory as well as the bordello, testing blood, urine, and phlegm with Nikolaus Howorka, a fellow inmate. Several doctors were known among the inmates for their decency, Rieger said, but he did not list Heim among them. He suggested to Aedtner that two other former inmates named Lotter and Sommer, both of whom were in Austria, would be better able to help him with his investigation. Rieger was a little fuzzy on the dates. He had been released from the camp around Christmas in 1942 and was under the impression that Heim was still there at that time. Rieger added that Heim was friends with the SS dentist but could not remember his name. At the end of Rieger's testimony, he and Aedtner both signed the transcript of his statement.

It was difficult to actually prove what had happened all those years ago. At one point after the war Rieger had been investigated himself over possible involvement in killings, though he had been exonerated. Still, as damning as Rieger's statement sounded, it was not going to help convict the Nazi physician. "I am aware that Dr. Heim" was a caveat that flagged every statement. Rieger could not—or would not—name a single instance in which Heim had killed a specific patient. Aedtner needed more.

Two days later he was in Munich, interviewing another survivor, Ramón Verge Armengol from Barcelona, but the Spaniard did not remember the tall, hockey-playing doctor in the slightest. It was just another dead end. Another witness who lived in Munich, Gebhard Westner, was on vacation. Missed chance; Aedtner would have to return to depose Westner later. More frustrating still were those camp survivors he would never reach. Gustav Claussen had died in 1968, and Howorka, Rieger's partner in the lab, had passed away in 1966. Franz Powolny, who reportedly worked in the infirmary, had died in 1962, and Vladimir Kostujak, another sick-bay worker, in 1960.

More than twelve years after his disappearance the police had not gotten any closer to finding Heim than they were in the years immediately following his disappearance. In March the police began tapping the Barths' phones, but without much success. "The analysis of the audiotapes from the telephone surveillance of the sister of the accused yielded no concrete clues as to the whereabouts of the accused Dr. Heim," Aedtner wrote in his report. The best he could hope for was that his watch on the sister and brother-in-law would provide a break.

I n 1975, Rüdiger Heim, approaching his twentieth birthday, decided that he had to see his father again. He remembered little from his childhood. He recalled the soccer goal his father had built and how he would try to keep up with his older brother as the three of them kicked the ball around. Rüdiger also remembered spending time at his father's medical practice.

His mother and grandmother told the boys that their father was living in Berlin. As a small child Rüdiger received letters from him and wrote notes in return, in one describing how good he was in school, "above all in arithmetic." On the back of the letter, Rüdiger drew a house with two chimneys under a large sun. He often asked his father when he was coming home. He listened over and over to the tape recordings in which Heim talked to his sons in a calm and reassuring voice.

Through his aunt, Rüdiger received books from his father, such as primers on how to learn English. Heim stressed the importance of studying foreign languages from a very early age and recommended that his older son visit Greece to learn about antiquity. In the letters Heim sent to Herta, there were many recommendations—directions really—for the children's schooling, their participation in sports, and even when and how to talk to the boys about girls and contraception. He was a gynecologist, after all, but no longer there to give the talk himself.

As Rüdiger grew older, he eventually came to understand that his father was not in Berlin. But he was never told where Heim had really gone. The boys' home in Baden-Baden was loving but stifling for a teen-ager. Rüdiger had more restrictions than any of his friends, always having to tell his mother and grandmother where he was going. It was difficult for him to leave the house alone after 7:00 p.m. in the sleepy spa town without causing them alarm. The two women seemed to have overblown fears that he might be kidnapped or that someone would want to hurt him. As the 1960s generation came of age, the silence around the war began to break down. As his teachers discussed Germany's Nazi past, Rüdiger wondered if this explained why his father had left.

The restrictions on his autonomy had become oppressive. At a time when personal freedom and self-expression swept the country, Rüdiger pressed for more independence. He did not join any of the left-wing groups springing up in Germany, but he wanted to be sent to boarding school. At seventeen he left Baden-Baden to go to St. Gallen, Switzerland.

In the international atmosphere he found himself shying away from the other Germans and making friends among the Italians. After gradu-ation he spent a few months in Lausanne studying French, then moved to Florence to study Italian. He had applied to medical school in Pisa, expecting to follow in the footsteps of his father, his mother, and by now his older brother, who was studying in Heidelberg. As he thought about his future, he became determined to see his father again.

He knew that Aunt Herta had close contact with her brother, and she seemed pleased that he wanted to see him. His aunt told him it was more complicated and dangerous than a trip to Berlin. But she helped him arrange a visit. Although his mother expressed reservations about the trip, she gave him the money to pay for it.

As Heim looked forward to seeing his younger son, he was increasingly careful about the locations he visited. Not only had the Israelis captured Adolf Eichmann, but in Uruguay the Mossad had also executed the SS captain Herbert Cukurs, known as "the Hangman of Riga." Cukurs was accused of killing thirty-two thousand Latvian Jews in 1941. His body was found in a large trunk in the bedroom of a beach house, with a note saying he had been executed by "Those Who Shall Never Forget."

Even Cairo's German community had been infiltrated by Israeli intelligence. In 1965, Egyptian authorities arrested a wealthy horse breeder and former Wehrmacht officer named Wolfgang Lotz on espionage charges. Lotz threw lavish booze-soaked parties for Egyptian generals, cabinet members, and German scientists, rising quickly to the top of Egyptian society while making no effort to dispel rumors that he had been in the SS.

Lotz even attended parties hosted by a Ministry of Information official named Omar Amin, where inebriated guests sang the Nazi anthem known as the "Horst-Wessel-Lied." Omar Amin was not an Egyptian but rather a convert to Islam once known as Johann von Leers. He had been a leading anti-Semitic propagandist under Joseph Goebbels. Heim had met von Leers a few times, but it was not an acquaintance he had any interest in deepening.

Heim's distance from his fellow Germans might have protected him. Lotz was not who he claimed to be. Rather than serving with Field Marshal Erwin Rommel, he had fought against him with the British army. He had been born in Germany, and his fluent German led the Mossad to recruit him and send him to Egypt as an agent. The lavish parties were part of his cover, and after his arrest by the Egyptians he earned the nickname "the Champagne Spy."

Others besides the Israelis and Wiesenthal made it their business to chase Nazi war criminals. Serge and Beate Klarsfeld, part of the 1968 protest generation, joined the hunt when Kurt Georg Kiesinger became chancellor of West Germany. Beate wrote an article for the Parisian daily *Combat* saying that Kiesinger's work on Nazi propaganda should have disqualified him from holding office. For her outspokenness she was fired by the Franco-German Alliance for Youth, which only increased her zeal.

In 1968 she publicly slapped Chancellor Kiesinger in the face at a party congress for his conservative Christian Democratic Union. Shaming former Nazis was not enough for the couple. Their tactics became even more extreme. In 1971 they unsuccessfully attempted to kidnap the former Gestapo chief for Jewish affairs in France, Kurt Lischka, from Cologne and bring him back to France by force. The following year, Beate identified a man named Klaus Altmann, who had recently been living in Peru, as the German Gestapo chief of Lyon, Klaus Barbie. New identities were not always enough to prevent discovery was the lesson for those still in hiding.

Reading all the headlines, Heim distrusted anyone who displayed interest in him. At one point he ended up chatting briefly with a motorcyclist in Alexandria. The man might have been just a curious traveler, but he also could have been working for a Western intelligence service. Heim excused himself from the conversation, only to receive a written message from the man at the hotel where Heim was staying.

"I think that you don't give the chance to anyone to talk to you," it read. "Traveling and meeting people or friends is something fun, especially fellow motorcyclists." He left his name and his phone number "if you need any help." Heim filed the message with his documents, noting that he had refused to engage because the man "definitely worked for some group."

Later Heim had a great scare, finding himself face-to-face with a woman who had worked at the very pharmacy downstairs from his medical practice in Baden-Baden. She greeted him saying, "Herr Dr. Heim, what are you doing here?" apparently as surprised as he was. Dr. Heim, or the man who looked strikingly like him, kept walking, pretending he did not recognize her.

Not only the fear of discovery but significant shifts in Middle East politics offered a fresh source of worry as his months of exile stretched to years. When Gamal Abdel Nasser died in September 1970, Heim feared a change in Egypt's relationship with Israel could jeopardize his safety. In 1974, Israel and Egypt signed an agreement, and in June 1975 the Suez Canal reopened. The days of safety for Germans in Egypt were coming to a close.

CHAPTER 27

n 1975 officials in Stuttgart believed that "the odds are that in the near future [Heim's] location will be tracked down," or so Aedtner's office informed the Austrians in asking for their assistance. Aedtner's own assessment was more restrained, but he prepared himself for the trip to Heim's former home. The German detective arrived in Vienna on September 8, 1975. His schedule called for him to question witnesses all over Austria in the course of twelve days. In accordance with the legal requirement for foreign detectives, the Austrians assigned an inspector of their own, Bendl, to the investigation. Technically, Aedtner was just observing while Bendl did the police work. It soon became apparent that gathering new evidence in Austria was going to be difficult.

Two of the four key witnesses, Karl Kaufmann and Josef Kohl, were dead. When Aedtner sat down with a third, Rupert Sommer, he found the man "obviously making an effort to remember concrete events" but barely able to recall any specific incidents. Sommer was seventy-one years old by the time Aedtner spoke with him. His host of ailments required treatments with numerous medications, some through injections. Aedtner observed that the man was suffering a "general physical breakdown." Sommer identified Heim correctly in the photo lineup but then said he was not certain. In Aedtner's judgment, he was no longer useful.

Nor was Sommer the only disappointment. Ernst Martin, one of the main witnesses at the U.S. military trial of Mauthausen perpetrators in

1946 and someone Bendl considered reliable, "no longer had his powers of recollection at his disposal," Aedtner wrote in his report. "Somehow the name is familiar" was all the survivor could say. Another former prisoner, who had served seven and a half years in jail for cooperating with the SS at Mauthausen, told the police officers that the name Heim "awakens no memory." Another inmate, whose job had been removing corpses, neither remembered the name nor recognized the doctor.

Even the leading expert on Mauthausen could offer little in the way of assistance. Hans Maršálek was part cop, part historian, and himself a survivor of the concentration camp. He had been active first in Austria's Social Democratic Party and then in the Communist Party. He was sent to Mauthausen in 1942. During his time at the camp he joined the underground resistance. After he was released, he became a police officer tasked with bringing war criminals to trial. By the time Aedtner came to see him, he was serving as the head of the Mauthausen Memorial. Maršálek said he arrived at the camp in 1942 after Heim's departure.

Stories about Heim had coursed through the camp, but Maršálek only knew them secondhand. Heim was known to have shown great interest in the heads of skeletons. It was quite possible that he had also worked at the Gusen satellite camp, where the skeletons of "scientifically interesting prisoners" were preserved in the pathology department, some two hundred in all. He referred Aedtner to a young inmate who had grown up to become the head of the Polish Red Cross and another who had worked under the camp pharmacist who prepared the lethal injections. Both suggestions were time-consuming dead ends.

Nearly a week into their journey Aedtner and Bendl arrived in Mürzzuschlag, a town of roughly eleven thousand inhabitants. There they at last found a witness who not only remembered Heim but recalled the doctor's actions in detail. At seventy-three Karl Lotter could still remember the five years he spent working as an orderly at the infirmary in Mauthausen. Dr. Heim stood out, Lotter told Aedtner, because the staff in the operating room wore wooden clogs. Heim's feet were so big, Lotter said, that he had to ask the camp carpenter to make a custom pair for the SS officer.

Dr. Heim was a "strikingly athletic figure," the former orderly recalled, and a competitive ice hockey player. At the time the *Völkischer*

Beobachter, which called itself the "fighting paper of the National Social-ist movement of Greater Germany," described how Dr. Heim played on an Austrian all-star team against the Germans. The young doctor had a scar on his cheek, Lotter believed, from a fencing duel. He treated the staff at the sick bay relatively well, Lotter said.

Every evening, ill and injured inmates came to the infirmary for examination and were told to return in the morning for treatment. The next day the simpler cases were put at the front of the line, the more seri-ous ones at the back. Dr. Heim tended to the blisters, bruises, and coughs of the patients who were in basically good health. Then Heim explained to the seriously ill and debilitated patients, "The German state could not afford to feed sick people, and the simplest solution was to give them lethal injections." He then pushed needles into their chests and injected deadly chemical solutions directly into their hearts.

The former orderly had a clear memory of specific instances of cruelty, as when a Jewish boy of about twelve lay on the operating table with his hands folded and said, "Good-bye, Mommy." Dr. Heim said that he had to die because the Jews were responsible for the war. In another instance a Jewish inmate who had been partially anesthetized called Dr. Heim a murderer. The physician stopped the anesthesia and when the man was fully conscious told the patient that the Jews had caused the war, before dispatching him with an injection to the heart. On another occasion Heim anesthetized a relatively healthy young man, then "lightning-quick made a powerful cut through his stomach, from bottom to top," Lotter said. "I saw too how the intestines bulged out and immediately found a pretext to leave the room."

In spite of his age, Aedtner judged Lotter's memory to be excellent. He stood by his earlier statements in depositions and corroborated the testimony of the late Kaufmann and Kohl. "He has to be considered the most valuable witness," Aedtner wrote. He was particularly intrigued by what Lotter told him about Gustav Rieger. According to an off-the-record remark Aedtner jotted down, Rieger spent only a short time each day working in the camp bordello and the rest of the time as Heim's anesthetist. Lotter believed that Rieger must have been a witness to the killing of at least one of the victims. Aedtner now believed Rieger had held back in his testimony. According to Lotter's official statement, the reason for this was Rieger's good relationship with Heim. Aedtner began to believe that there might have been an even more compelling reason, his own fear of prosecution.

Although he remained in Austria several more days, Aedtner would not find a better witness. Another former corpse bearer, though he did not remember Heim, did remember a decapitated head prepared in the crematorium, cooked until all that remained was the bare skull. Aedtner left behind copies of the lineup photographs of Heim with Inspector Bendl so that he could show them when speaking with additional witnesses.

The German detective returned home with copies of two pages from the operation book at Mauthausen bearing Heim's looping signature. He also had leads for several other camp survivors, living everywhere from Communist Poland to Jackson Heights, Queens. What he did not find was any information as to the doctor's present whereabouts. For all of his boss's optimism, Aedtner's assessment stood: there was no concrete information about the location of the fugitive.

CHAPTER 28

Rüdiger Heim arrived in Egypt in December 1975 to meet his father for the first time since he was six years old. He had traveled from Florence, where he had recently moved to study Italian, first heading to Rome to catch his flight and then transferring through Athens. On the airplane Rüdiger felt nervous and excited wondering whether he was being followed.

He did not have his father's exact address or telephone number. He sent a letter general delivery to the central post office addressed to Camvaro Company, a firm that did not exist. In the letter, he told his father that he would look for him each day between eleven o'clock in the morning and three o'clock in the afternoon at the outdoor café at the Nile Hilton. Nasser had inaugurated the modern glass-front hotel in 1959. He met with the Palestinian leader Yasir Arafat at the hotel in 1970 and it was rumored, probably apocryphally, that Nasser's successor, Anwar el-Sadat, gave him a fatal dose of poison in his coffee.

Rüdiger wandered back and forth among the vacationing families and businessmen. With his shaggy hair, T-shirt, and blue jeans, he stood out at the luxury hotel, all the more because he was six feet four, with the same broad shoulders and athletic build as his father. At least that was what Heim looked like in family photographs. Rüdiger did not know how much the doctor had changed, but when he finally spotted him, wearing a striped shirt and carrying a briefcase, Rüdiger had no doubt the man was his father. They did not call out or embrace for fear of being recognized.

At the age of sixty-one, Aribert Heim was still a vital presence. Rüdiger was taken aback by his father's barrage of questions. Heim wanted to know about not just his ex-wife and elder son but his sister and niece, his friends and business associates from home. He also wanted to hear all about Rüdiger's future medical studies. Across from him, his son was having difficulty absorbing everything. Although the nineteen-year-old had no doubt the man was his father, his first impression was of "foreignness." Rüdiger had the feeling, too, that he, a long-haired young man who idolized Bob Dylan, was not quite the son his father, who had left a much more conservative, traditional Germany in the early 1960s, had been expecting.

Another issue loomed over their reunion, the reason Aribert Heim was in Egypt. Was his father a Nazi? It was not a question Rüdiger knew how to ask, so he did not. Instead, he buried his reservations in rote answers and let his father show him his adopted country, fascinated but never quite able to quell the fear that they would be discovered.

Early in his visit, Rüdiger awoke in the middle of the night to loud pounding on his door. His heart was beating fast as he got out of bed. "Who is it?" he asked.

"Let me in," said a voice in accented English. "This is my room."

"No," Rüdiger answered. "It's my room." His father had brought him to the Mena House, a luxurious hotel in Giza, insisting that his son see the Great Pyramid and the Sphinx before leaving. At the time, the Mena House was filled not only with travelers but also with United Nations peacekeepers.

The pounding continued. "This is my room. Let me in."

"You must be wrong. This is my room. Go to the concierge." It might have been an innocent misunderstanding, a confused tourist, or a drunken soldier on the wrong floor. It might have been an attempt to rob him. But he could not banish the thought that it might be someone who wanted information about his father. Rüdiger waited by the door, but he did not open it. At last the man gave up. In the morning Heim made his son move to a less expensive, and less conspicuous, hotel.

Rüdiger checked in to the Scarabee Hotel on 26 July Street. The grand boulevard, formerly Fouad Street after King Fouad I, had been renamed in honor of the date of his successor's abdication in 1952. The Scarabee looked as if it were built in the same era. It was clean and orderly, but unlike at the Hilton or the Mena House, European visitors were rare. It was frequented for the most part by fellow Egyptians and Sudanese who wanted to stay downtown for business.

His father showed him the European quarter of the city where French architects had laid out the grid of streets in the nineteenth century. Heim would buy slightly outdated copies of the *Frankfurter Allgemeine Zeitung* and the weekly news magazine *Der Spiegel*. If the local vendors did not have what he was looking for, he could try the nearby German-language bookshop, Lehnert & Landrock. He took his son to the expensive but increasingly shabby Western spots for coffee and pastries, including the café Al Americaine and the famous Groppi café. With foreigners Aribert spoke English; in the local quarters he used his fluent Arabic.

Father and son walked together to Midan Ataba, the square where the twisting lanes of Islamic Cairo met the orderly grid of the European quarter. The square itself mixed elements of the two. It was bustling and chaotic, full of Fiat taxicabs and horse-drawn carts. Booksellers and market stalls lined the narrow alleyways. But there were also grand buildings, like the former Tiring department store topped with three stone figures holding a globe like a trio of Atlases, the old fire station with its turreted tower, and the domed central post office. This was where his father fetched the mail for the fictional Camvaro Company from one of the service windows in a courtyard ringed with mosaics depicting the ancient Egyptian gods Horus with the head of a falcon and Anubis with the head of a jackal.

Aribert Heim lived across the way at the Karnak Hotel, of which he was a partial owner. He had a small room with a view of the square. It was one of several property investments he had made in Egypt. The purchases were complicated by ownership rules that forbade foreigners to buy property, but with the help of local partners he owned a share of the postwar building in Cairo, an apartment in Alexandria, and a plot of land he was trying to develop in the coastal resort of Agamy Beach. He intended to show them all to his son. He had many plans—and even more opinions.

He gave Rüdiger advice about his health and about relationships, his medical studies, and his career. Aribert showed great interest in his son's efforts to break into professional tennis by playing in satellite tournaments and qualifier events around Europe. Heim, once an athletic trainer before the war during his time in Rostock, wanted to watch his son play and set him up against a coach he knew at a local club. Rüdiger gamely donned an ill-fitting pair of borrowed pants and played against the instructor, only to find himself constantly critiqued by his father. "Go to the net. You're tall. Serve and get to the net!"

Rüdiger's worry about his hippie appearance proved well-founded as his father repeatedly complained about the length of his hair. No matter what the fashion might have been in Europe, Heim explained, in Egypt men simply did not wear their hair long. Finally, he took his son to a barbershop where Rüdiger let the man cut his hair as his father wished. He also went to a local ear, nose, and throat specialist, who examined his deviated septum and recommended surgery. His father concurred, but Rüdiger wanted to wait until he returned to Europe.

Together with his father, Rüdiger traveled by train from Cairo's Ramses Station northwest through the Nile delta to the ancient capital of Alexandria. The journey made a deep impression on the young German. From the dense and dirty Egyptian capital he found himself soothed by the rhythmic motion of the train moving through the country's agricultural heartland and the passing bucolic scenes of fellahin working the fields in their long jellabiyas. It seemed to Rüdiger as if little had changed in the rhythm of their lives in hundreds of years, maybe thousands, even as political turmoil swept the country's largest cities.

In Alexandria, Rüdiger met the tall, debonair Egyptian Nagy Khafagy, who helped his father with his investment in the Karnak Hotel. Khafagy worked at the Montazah Gardens and El Salamlek Palace on the western edge of the city, the king's summer palace before the revolution. He was always ready with a joke or a kind word. A Cleopatra-brand cigarette dangled perpetually from his lip, yet somehow his pressed white shirts remained pristine.

They visited the beachfront property in Agamy, between the water and the first coastal road. Heim had purchased the plot of land in 1966 for 60,000 Swiss francs, 30,000 francs down plus installments of 7,500 francs each of the next four years. The plan was to construct a building on the empty lot with multiple apartments, some for Heim and his family and some for his other business partner, a man named Rifat. At sixty-one, Heim was already thinking about what he could leave behind for his children.

One evening during their stay in Alexandria, Rüdiger and his father turned onto a small side street and stopped in a local restaurant, the kind of place where only the Egyptians go to eat for 2 or 3 pounds. The furniture was nothing fancy, just cheap tables and chairs. There they had simple, filling Egyptian fare like the fava bean stew known as *ful* and roast chicken. His father chatted amiably with the people there in Arabic. They knew his father, and Heim introduced him, saying, "This is my son."

The boy still wanted to ask about his father's sudden departure and the reasons behind it, but he never found the right moment. Questions about Heim's military service and possible war crimes were never broached. Instead, Rüdiger studied his father, asking himself, "Is this how a Nazi behaves? Was he one?" Rüdiger's notion of Nazis was based on Hollywood films, which presented those Germans as racists who felt justified in exterminating those to whom they felt superior. They were people who killed without being troubled by the act.

CHAPTER 29

Berlin had changed since the war. Musicians like Iggy Pop and David Bowie moved to West Berlin in the 1970s for the artistic ferment but also, in Bowie's words, to "shoot drugs in the heroin capital of the world." The Zoologischer Garten train station was a hangout for junkies and teenage prostitutes. West Berliners did not have to serve the compulsory year of military service, which helped draw counterculture types from all over Germany, as well as many left-wing revolutionaries. Soldiers from the American Berlin Brigade partied at Rolf Eden's racy nightclubs on the once-proper Kurfürstendamm. Looming over it all stood the bomb-damaged steeple of the Kaiser Wilhelm Memorial Church, left in jagged ruins as a reminder of the war.

The Berlin Wall did not so much separate East and West Berlin as it surrounded West Berlin, making it an island of freedom. Two East Germans had been killed at the wall in 1975 trying to escape to the West. A guard shot down a third man who was merely trying to get to his home near the heavily fortified border after a night of drinking. There were other accidents. A five-year-old Turkish boy in the West died after chasing a ball to the Spree River. He fell into the water, and rescuers on the West Berlin side could not get permission to dive in to find him as the Communists controlled the water itself. The boy's body was fished out barely fifteen feet from the western bank. Then, rather than being handed over to his family, his body was taken to East Berlin's Charité Hospital and autopsied.

When Alfred Aedtner arrived in the divided city in February 1976, there had been no recent fatalities. The Soviet sector included the city's historic downtown, the grand avenue Unter den Linden with its splendid opera house and celebrated university. The Brandenburg Gate stood at the end, sealed off from the West by the wall. Aedtner was tracking the owner of a piece of property in the British sector, an apartment block at Tile-Wardenberg-Strasse 28.

Investigators had known about Heim's apartment building almost from the beginning of the hunt but initially just considered it a possible hiding place. The Berlin police had been asked to search in the "vicinity of the apartment building." They complied but found nothing, saying, "No indications came out of it that could have delivered clues as to his whereabouts."

Aedtner, on the other hand, was interested in the building itself, specifically what happened to the tenants' rent. Tax inspectors suspected that Heim was dead and the money was going to his sister Herta. The management company, Wilhelm Droste, regularly transferred money to her at the Volksbank Dreieich "because the brother was often traveling overseas [so] the money was transferred to her account . . . Whenever her brother came to visit, she withdrew large amounts of money and handed it over to him directly." There was no proof that he had received the money, but she was not paying income taxes on it. The inspectors had checked with officials in Baden-Baden and found it odd that Dr. Heim claimed no other income. Barth's statements "raised doubts." "The suspicion arises that her brother is already dead and the receipts flow to Mrs. Herta Barth and she must pay taxes on them." Aedtner decided to visit Heim's property managers.

A native Berliner, Rolf Gallner had worked at Wilhelm Droste for sixteen years and never met the doctor. Gallner's job was to send the rent after expenses to Baden-Baden. He had heard rumors that Heim's absence had something to do with accusations of war crimes. Now, seated across from Aedtner, he felt sure this was the case.

He told the detective that Heim was one of their customers but, without looking at the files, he could not say how long the company had handled the account. It was at least as long as the sixteen years that Gallner had been working there. He quickly ruled out the possibility that the suspect had hidden in one of his own apartments. He said all correspondence went through Dr. Heim's sister. "Over the course of time I came to learn through conversations why Dr. Heim did not handle his own affairs. The way I heard it, Dr. Heim is being sought by German authorities because he committed crimes along the lines of euthanasia in the past under the Third Reich."

From time to time Heim sent handwritten letters through his sister, generally about once a year. The last time they had received any communication was just before Christmas. Heim had thanked the managers for their good work and even given instructions for bonuses and holiday tips for Droste's employees. When legal forms were needed, they arrived already signed. Gallner did not know if there was a return address as the envelopes were already opened when they landed in his in-box. Maybe they could figure out where Dr. Heim was from the paper, the real-estate manager suggested.

Aedtner acquired a search warrant for the premises. He, Gallner, and an officer from the Berlin police went to the offices, where Gallner gave them access to the files. Heim's file filled two binders. Aedtner left with nine handwritten letters. "The striking thing," Aedtner wrote, is the "foreign paper format," common in Austria, Switzerland, and the United States. After checking with experts, he learned that the style was also common to international hotels, and thus could have been purchased in Germany. The glue at the top edge indicated it had come from a pad he could have taken with him.

The records revealed Heim to be an absolute stickler for detail. Even with the police in pursuit, he was writing to Droste about the heating system for his apartment building. The old coal boiler had been replaced by a new gas system, and Dr. Heim gave detailed instructions for paying the remaining balance. One thing was certain: the apartment building allowed the doctor to finance what was probably a quite comfortable lifestyle. The building housed thirty-four tenants, paying anywhere from 118 to 475 deutsche marks a month. One firm even paid 15 deutsche marks for the privilege of hanging a cigarette vending machine by the front door. In all, Gallner estimated that the properties yielded 24,000 deutsche marks per year, sent to Heim's sister. It was not a fortune, but it was more than enough to live on, more than a lot of German police officers made at the time.

The fact that Heim did not have to work in order to survive made it easier for him to remain out of view. For the same reason Josef Mengele, who came from a wealthy family, also managed to elude capture. The considerable resources of Heim's in-laws meant that there were many places out of sight but in considerable luxury where he could hide. His wife's family owned property in Germany and Switzerland. Lake Lugano, where they owned an apartment, seemed like the sort of place a fugitive would live, right on the border between Switzerland and Italy, where one could easily cross a frontier if necessary. Or Heim could pass the time at one of the three apartments in Bad Kissingen that his brother-in-law Georg Barth owned. They were rented to spa guests, with lots of people always coming and going.

Aedtner had one other stop before he could leave Berlin. He traveled to Zehlendorf in the city's southwest, a neighborhood filled with villas and fine homes. His destination, though, was a modest cluster of buildings in the Heimatschutz style, an architectural movement in Germany from the turn of the century to revive traditional building styles. It was not the buildings, however, but the vast archive that lay in the bunker beneath them that brought Aedtner there.

Aedtner parked at the Berlin Document Center, which thirty years after the war still contained personnel files of members of the SA and SS. According to his file, Heim had served in Prague, Vienna, and Berlin. He inspected concentration camps for two months in 1941 and was a doctor at Buchenwald for a month. Nowhere in his personnel file did it mention working at Mauthausen. According to the papers, Heim spent the final years of the war with a division of mountain troops.

Again, Aedtner focused on the money trail. Here, to the investigator's surprise, he discovered that Heim's pay included an allowance for an illegitimate daughter, born on July 28, 1942, and listed under the name Waltraud Böser, which was a slight but persistent misspelling of her first name, Waltraut. The transfers were sent to the Sparkasse Graz, in the care of Heim's elder sister, with an address listed in the Austrian city of Graz. On May 1, 1945, in the bloody waning days of World War II, another name was briefly listed in the records, that of Gertrud Böser, living in the Austrian ski resort town of Kitzbühel. Shortly after, her name was crossed off and the payments sent to Heim's sister Hilda. "It has to be assumed," Aedtner wrote, "that this Gertrud Böser is the mother of the child."

Aedtner saw that Hilda was still legally registered in Graz, but efforts to find Gertrud Böser were less successful. The street address, listed as Sonnenhofgebiet 467, appeared to be incorrect. The closest investigators came was a Sonnentalhof. Aedtner noted that locating the Bösers was a priority. "There is definitely the possibility," Aedtner wrote, "that the accused remains in contact with his illegitimate daughter or potentially with the child's mother."

Aedtner continued to pursue every lead he could. One former victim said that he had known Dr. Heim at Sachsenhausen, but was aware of the lethal injections only secondhand. "For me the man in the photo is simply the murderer from Sachsenhausen." Back in Austria, Aedtner interviewed the former inmate Franz Kuczera, who claimed that he had seen Heim "removing the skin from the corpse of a tattooed inmate" in the autopsy room.

But what Aedtner needed most of all was concrete information that would lead him to the doctor's whereabouts. Finally, in 1977, his search for Heim's illegitimate daughter bore fruit. Swiss authorities informed him that Waltraut Böser was now in Switzerland, working as a pharmacist in Geneva. This was particularly intriguing, considering that Heim's wife owned property in Lugano. "There is definitely a chance," Aedtner wrote, "that Waltraud Böser is in contact with her father." He asked the Swiss prosecutors to look into the young woman's life. Don't let her guess "that she is being checked out," he wrote. "It cannot be ruled out that the accused is in her close personal circle."

The Austrians, meanwhile, had tracked down her mother, who was living in Innsbruck. Gertrud Böser had a difficult life from the start. She was born in the Austrian town of Marburg, which after World War I became part of Yugoslavia. Her entire family contracted tuberculosis when she was young. Her father died, her mother went to a sanatorium, and Gertrud and her sister were sent for some time to an orphanage. She pursued her dream of singing and acting and performed as an opera singer in Milan and Vienna, including at the Theater in der Josefstadt, where Beethoven and Wagner had both conducted. A dark-haired beauty, she also worked as an actress in Frankfurt and Berlin and raved about the latter as the greatest city of all for artists.

Gertrud had a long affair with the handsome young doctor Aribert Heim, whom she had known since his student days in Graz, when she worked in the school cafeteria. Once he completed his medical studies, Heim joined the military and was stationed all over, including in Berlin and Vienna. She became pregnant while he was at Mauthausen. Gertrud saw him exactly one more time after Waltraut was born. He appeared a few months later to sign the birth certificate. All she knew after that was that he was fighting on the eastern front. She never saw him again.

After she gave birth to her second child, Peter, she developed varicose veins and had a difficult time standing for long periods on the stage. She moved to the mountain town of Kitzbühel with her mother, a seamstress, who helped pay the bills and watched the children. Gerturd began performing with a puppet theater at schools, often towing the wooden theater and puppets behind her bicycle up and down the Alpine roads.

Her little daughter, blond like her father, took after him in many other ways. She was a talented downhill skier, already racing at the age of five. Because her father was believed killed in the war, Waltraut received while at school a small orphan's pension from the Austrian government, the same bureau responsible for the disabled.

Her children grown up, Gertrud owned her own home on Innsbruck's Kugelfangweg. Since 1973 she had received a monthly pension of 3,900 schillings. According to the police report, she claimed she received financial support from her children. She had never married and lived alone since her own mother passed away, putting on puppet-theater performances now and then, on invitation from the local schools. "Gertrud Böser enjoys a good reputation in her neighborhood," the report noted.

On April 26, 1977, six days after her sixty-third birthday, Aedtner appeared at the postwar apartment building where she lived. He found himself answering more questions than he asked. Gertrud wanted to know where Heim was. If he were alive, he would owe child support. What was his address? How could she reach him? Gertrud seemed unaware of the more or less publicly available address for Heim in Baden-Baden.

Aedtner said he was pursuing a criminal matter, but they ultimately agreed that if he located the doctor, he would pass along the address, and she in return agreed that if Heim contacted her, she would notify the Austrian authorities. Gertrud told Aedtner that she had tried to locate

Heim right after the war and how in 1966 her daughter had placed a request through the Red Cross in Munich to find her father. The Red Cross officials could say no more than that he was missing in action. By the end of the meeting, Aedtner found Gertrud to be "completely ingenuous" and was convinced that neither she nor her daughter knew where Heim lived.

Gertrud did not inform her daughter about the police officer's visit, nor the fact that her father might still be alive. The girl had made a good life for herself in Switzerland as a pharmacist, and Gertrud did not wish her disturbed.

CHAPTER 31

Oblivious to the fact that police had intensified their search for his father, Rüdiger returned to Florence in January 1976, where he worked on his application for medical school. Now that he had made contact with Heim, he kept in close touch. He wrote a letter telling his father he was glad he made the trip and that he "had reassured me of many things I was in doubt of." Rüdiger also apologized for the fact that he had not had a haircut since leaving Egypt, admitting that it was because "a girl told me not to," but promised that as soon as his hair interfered with his tennis game, he would get it trimmed. He said that if he failed to get into the Italian university, he might come and live in Cairo for a year. He signed the letter, "Your 'true one.'" But, like his Aunt Herta, he could not shake a sense of sorrow at his father's solitary life so far away.

The young man had the operation to correct the deviated septum diagnosed in Egypt, putting an end to his constant earaches. He dutifully thanked his father but found the influence of other of Heim's opinions weakening. Even as he announced his relief at getting into medical school, he wrote about his passionate interest in photography and his growing portfolio of pictures. An upcoming exhibition and meetings with photo editors at magazines clearly had greater appeal than chemistry and biology.

But he was brutally honest in a way that children rarely are with their parents. He was comfortable writing about masturbation and satisfying his sexual needs "to a certain point" with a girlfriend. His father became his sounding board, and Rüdiger had much to discuss. His writings reveal a young man of artistic temperament, out of step with the people around him, searching for authenticity and honesty. "Some days I feel terribly miserable because I could walk for miles in the streets of the city without being paid attention to," he wrote. "From time to time I want to explode, hit someone's bloody face, kick someone, or whatever because this 'indifference' around me is hard to bear. But what is the most terrifying thing is I can't even explode. I'm too fucking afraid to do so." In the very next paragraph, however, he said he often feels "free and a part of this world." He described trips to an art gallery and his rising nervousness as they discussed his pictures. "I'm trying to learn as much as possible . . . but again all kinds of walls are building up in front of me."

Aribert's side of the correspondence showed that although he missed his family, he expected more support from them than he felt he was receiving. He relied on his sister for more than money and expected her to help curb his loneliness through regular visits. His own letters often complained that he had not heard from her sooner or more often. As much as he had integrated into Cairo society, life there was not easy for him. The country's infrastructure had deteriorated significantly under Nasser. Blackouts were common. Telephone lines were overloaded at peak hours, making calls impossible. Buses were so overcrowded people would hang dangerously on the outsides. The population of the Cairo metropolitan area had roughly doubled to 9 million over the previous decade. Some 200,000 newcomers were arriving every year. It could be a hard city to call home.

Rüdiger kept up the correspondence with his father as he had promised. He told him that he was reading Lawrence Durrell's Alexandria Quartet novels, about the city on the coast that they had visited. "I feel that I should know more about this town," Rüdiger wrote. On another occasion Rüdiger assured Heim that he and his aunt had sent difficult-to-acquire equipment for his father's friend, an Egyptian dentist. "Most probably they got lost on their way as they didn't reach you," Rüdiger wrote. "Anyway, there is no reason to blame your sister."

Herta had always done all she could to help her brother with anything he asked. When Nagy Khafagy, Heim's Egyptian friend and business associate, needed assistance importing a Peugeot to be used as a taxi, she handled the European side of the transaction. In addition, she had always taken care of her brother's bills, transfers of money, and taxes. Now tax officials had begun demanding either proof that she was sending the rent from the Tile-Wardenberg apartments to her brother or a payment of 10,000 deutsche marks. Given that her brother was a fugitive in hiding, he could hardly fly back to Germany, march into a courtroom, and affirm his identity.

The family took great precautions to avoid divulging his location. Not only was mail sent to the Weil family, Herta's friends, who handed her the plain manila envelopes, but they also used their own improvised code to identify people in correspondence. Herta was Gerda; their sister, Hilda, was Lyda. Heim was Gretel, and Friedl was Dora. On the Egyptian side, Rifat became Richard, and the suave Khafagy became the dashing Don Alfonso. The money itself was called pralines.

There was one more member of the group, a man who was referred to as Rainer. His real name was Steinacker, the prominent defense attorney for Nazis accused of war crimes. Steinacker never received mail directly from Heim; it was always routed through Herta Barth. Heim's sister handled his correspondence as well as his financial matters. She asked if the lawyer would meet personally with her brother and see if he could resolve the tax problem. For 1,760 deutsche marks Steinacker booked a seat on Lufthansa flight 626 on March 30, 1977, bound for Cairo.

I t had been six years since the lawyer and his client last met. On Steinacker's first trip to Cairo they had discussed routine business, investments, money transfers, his car, and other matters. Now his sister's role in handling Heim's business had caused her significant and potentially costly difficulties.

Heim was thinner and tanner but still instantly recognizable, tall and broad shouldered, a man with a great deal of presence. The two sat together at a café on the Nile and discussed the best way to handle the tax dispute. There was little movement visible in the criminal case against him, but it still hardly seemed wise to Steinacker for Heim to travel to Germany. Instead, Steinacker asked his client to sign a statement that it was he and not his sister who ultimately received the rents collected in Germany. The lawyer could then affirm before the court that his client had written the letter in his presence, but there remained the very real possibility that the court would not find Steinacker's word sufficient. So Steinacker prepared a fallback plan. Using a reel-to-reel recorder, they made a tape of Dr. Heim saying that he was alive and the lawful recipient of the funds in question.

Attorney and client said their farewells and parted ways. Steinacker returned to Germany after spending only a single night in Egypt. There were complications given Dr. Heim's fugitive status, but otherwise the case seemed straightforward. All parties assumed the criminal case had fallen into hibernation. The lawyer prepared letters to tax offices both in Hesse, where Herta lived, and in Baden-Württemberg, where Heim had

his last known address, including along with them copies of Heim's letter and Steinacker's sworn statement that he had personally laid eyes on
the fugitive doctor.

Heim meanwhile was preoccupied with questions of guilt. He could
visit with friends, work out, and manage investments, but without his
wife and children, without his practice, he was left with a great deal of
time to reflect on his circumstances. He read widely, clipping articles
about Christ and Hitler, the partition of Poland, and the Soviet Polit-
buro. At one point he analyzed the promise of Israel to the Jews, examin-
ing the Old Testament and the New Testament, before noting that it was
"already well cultivated by the Philistines and the Canaanites who pos-
sessed a highly developed copper and steel industry." In the next paragraph he mused on the Second Vatican Council's examination of Jewish
guilt for the crucifixion of Jesus Christ.

But Heim kept coming back to two particular historical events. The
first was the April 9, 1948, attack by Zionist paramilitary groups on the
village of Deir Yassin, not far from Jerusalem, in what was then the British Mandate of Palestine. The Irgun and the Lehi killed more than two
hundred Arabs, including women and children, in the village. Captives
were paraded through the streets of West Jerusalem. The incident was
infamous throughout the Arab world. News reports of the massacre at
Deir Yassin caused Arabs to flee in panic and helped provoke the Arab
invasion. Heim noted bitterly that Menachem Begin, the leader of the
Irgun at the time of the attack, was not in jail or in hiding but poised to
become prime minister of Israel.

The second incident was the American massacre of Vietnamese civilians at the village of My Lai in 1968. Heim clipped and saved numerous
articles about William L. Calley Jr. Out of twenty-five enlisted men and
officers, only Calley was convicted of the premeditated murder of Vietnamese civilians. After Calley was found guilty in 1971, he received a
surge of support from the American public, including a hit song with the
lyrics "My name is William Calley / I'm a soldier of this land / I've tried
to do my duty / And to gain the upper hand / But they've made me out a
villain / They have stamped me with a brand / As we go marching on."
Within three days of his conviction the record had already sold 202,000
copies.

Unlike West German politicians, Heim wrote, American politicians defended their soldier. They even used the same argument German defenders had employed—and American prosecutors had rejected—at the Nuremberg trials: he was only following orders. Sentenced to life imprisonment, Calley spent only three months confined at Fort Leavenworth before President Richard Nixon ordered him released pending appeal. He then spent three years under house arrest in a "comfortable two-bedroom apartment," according to the *New York Times*.

For Heim, the difference between the treatment of former Nazis like himself and that of Israelis and Americans was a double standard. Soviet leaders responsible for purges had also gone unpunished. Heim had spent nearly three years as a POW and postwar detainee. He had lived in exile for more than fourteen years. As time passed, the doctor would focus more and more on Israel and the Jewish lobby in the United States, which he believed had pressured postwar West Germany into abandoning its own soldiers.

An article published in English in the *Egyptian Gazette* in the autumn of 1976 had captured Heim's attention. Titled "Counterfeit Semites," the article reviewed a new book by the novelist Arthur Koestler, *The Thirteenth Tribe*. Koestler was a literary lion, a Zionist turned Communist who finally became a staunch anti-Communist. His best-known novel, *Darkness at Noon*, was inspired by Stalin's show trials. His views could be idiosyncratic. Although members of his family perished in the Holocaust, Koestler opposed the death penalty and wrote an impassioned plea for Eichmann's life. His reputation declined rather sharply later in life with his growing interest in the occult and the supernatural.

Koestler blended history, genetics, and a fair amount of conjecture in *The Thirteenth Tribe*, arguing that the majority of the world's Jews were descended not from the people of Israel but from a Turkic tribe known as the Khazars who had converted to Judaism. The book was widely rejected by Western scholars, the facts as well as the author's motives questioned. "The lingering influence of Judaism's racial and historical message, though based on illusion, acts as a powerful emotional brake by appealing to tribal loyalty," Koestler wrote.

Koestler foresaw the implications his book would have in the debate over Israel's legitimacy. He wrote, "While this book deals with past history, it unavoidably carries certain implications for the present and future . . . I am aware of the danger that it may be maliciously misinterpreted as a denial of the state of Israel's right to exist." He insisted that the partition of Palestine and a century of peaceful Jewish immigration provided the ethical justification for the state's legal existence.

Despite his protestations, the book found a rapt audience in the Arab world, which saw Koestler's work as undermining the Jewish claim to Israel. The reviewer in the *Egyptian Gazette* suggested that the Balfour Declaration should have promised a national home for the Jewish people between the Black Sea and the Caspian Sea, where the Khazar Empire had once reigned. He wrote, "Mr. Koestler, a distinguished Jewish author, should be congratulated on the courage of his convictions and on a scholarly exposition of a little known episode in history which may have a great influence on events in future."

Heim's copy of the article was heavily underlined in red ink. "Indeed if Mr. Koestler's point is accepted by the world at large then the term anti-Semitism will have no meaning and the world will have come to realise that for many centuries it had been the victim of a colossal hoax." The words "anti-Semitism will have no meaning" became Heim's preoccupation.

Aedtner rented an empty apartment in Frankfurt's West End. At 6 deutsche marks a day the rent for his ten days there in the spring of 1977 came to 60 deutsche marks, which was billed to the Baden-Württemberg state police. It was neither the price nor the size of the apartment that impressed Aedtner but the view. Not only could he see anyone entering and leaving the building on Savignystrasse where Steinacker had his office, but he could peer in through the office window. A decade before, Steinacker had watched Aedtner testify at the Auschwitz trials. Now the detective returned the favor, the difference being that the lawyer was unaware that he was under observation.

Aedtner was working with accountants and tax collectors to quietly raise pressure on Herta Barth. He had explained to the finance officials that their tax-evasion case was his murder case. He included them in the investigation and remained in close contact with the responsible department head at the state tax office in Hesse. They all waited for Herta's response. It was probably too much to hope that the Nazi doctor would walk through the door himself, but there was always the chance. An important hearing was coming up in the tax case, and Steinacker had written in two separate letters the month before that he had personally met with Dr. Heim about the matter. The lawyer said he watched his client sign letters swearing that the rent money from the Tile-Wardenberg-Strasse apartments came to him.

As the tax case gathered speed, Aedtner did not take his eyes off Stein-acker's office. On May 24 at 3:35 p.m., he saw Herta Barth arrive at the attorney's office. From his vantage point in the building across the street, Aedtner could see into the meeting room where Steinacker received cli-ents, and witnessed what he described in his report as a "very lively dis-cussion" between Steinacker and Herta Barth. The two spoke for over two hours. Ms. Barth did not leave until 5:45 p.m. Shortly thereafter, Steinacker asked to postpone the hearing. They were far from appre-hending Heim, but it felt as if they were drawing slightly closer.

If there was ever a time when Aedtner could have been pulled off the case, this was probably it. Shortly before his latest trip to Austria, on April 7, 1977, the attorney general of Germany, Siegfried Buback, was shot to death in Baden-Württemberg by Red Army Faction terrorists. He was on his way to work just an hour's drive from the state police headquarters in Stuttgart. The Mercedes he was riding in was idling at a red light just after nine o'clock in the morning when bullets from a Heck-ler & Koch machine pistol shattered the windows. Buback, his driver, and another justice official were killed, and the assassins sped away on a Suzuki GS750 motorcycle.

At the time German society was divided between, on the one hand, angry leftists warning of a reinvented police state and, on the other, a conservative society concerned about the counterculture and terrified of terrorism. Buback had been a member of the Nazi Party for five years and had come down hard on the Baader-Meinhof Gang and its sympathizers.

While his colleagues were hunting Buback's killers, Aedtner remained on the trail of the Nazi doctor. He interviewed other doctors who had served in the SS at Mauthausen, and even their widows, but there was no evidence that Heim had stayed in any form of contact with those particu-lar colleagues. Aedtner questioned inmates whom Heim had operated upon and sought former Mauthausen prisoners from Spain through the consulate. The state police asked colleagues in Tel Aviv for help tracking down victims in Israel.

Aedtner also targeted Herta's friends, such as her confidante Katha-rina Kallmann. The police spoke with the Barth family's longtime Aus-trian housekeeper who started working there in 1961, the year before Heim disappeared. They spoke with the former fiancée of Joachim

Gäde, Herta Barth's son from her previous marriage. She insisted that she knew nothing about Heim's whereabouts. They explored whether Heim's accountant Michael Barth, no relation to Herta's husband, had any grounds on which to refuse to testify as to the suspect's whereabouts. Aedtner was convinced that the accountant was in direct contact with Heim.

As for the doctor's family, they were quietly going about their business. Heim's elder son, Aribert, was studying in Heidelberg. Rüdiger was taking courses in Italy and playing tennis tournaments around the Continent, usually for no more than room and board. Heim's ex-wife, Friedl, was living in the same Baden-Baden villa as she had with her ex-husband. The family appeared unaware that anything more than a routine tax case was going on.

Most West Germans were focused on the violence that became known as the German Autumn that followed Buback's murder. The impression among German citizens of lawlessness was growing. Hundreds of suspected anarchists were brought in for questioning and to have their alibis checked. Police in Holland, France, and Sweden joined the search.

A botched kidnapping attempt ended with the murder of the head of Dresdner Bank. A leading industrialist and former SS officer, Hanns Martin Schleyer, was also kidnapped and killed. Four members of the Popular Front for the Liberation of Palestine hijacked a Lufthansa aircraft, demanding the release of leading members of the group from Stammheim Prison near Stuttgart. The hijackers killed the captain, Jürgen Schumann, before German commandos successfully stormed the airplane in Somalia, freeing the hostages. Three of the top terrorists, Gudrun Ensslin, Jan-Carl Raspe, and Andreas Baader himself, committed suicide in the wake of the failed attempt.

"The news just came on the radio that the hostage drama in Somalia is over," Rüdiger wrote to his father. He was conflicted about the situation, a young man with an artistic bent who hung out with Italian Communists on the fringe of the Red Brigade but who was not committed to the point of condoning violence. "I'm not happy about it, but I also don't want to forget that three terrorists who brought so much suffering to people have taken their lives."

Baader was dead and the hostage crisis foiled, but the group continued, as did other groups like the June 2 Movement and the Revolutionary Cells. Putting a halt to the violence shaking West Germany remained the priority for law enforcement. Yet through his methodical work with the tax authorities, Aedtner was drawing closer to his target. In his efforts to prove that rent money from the Berlin apartment building was going to Dr. Heim in hiding and not remaining in his sister's hands, Steinacker had been forced to release an audio recording of his client's voice as a proof of life.

The tape might have helped the family save a few thousand deutsche marks, but it was a risky maneuver, announcing to the world that a wanted Nazi was alive and receiving material support. If the news traveled no farther than the courtroom, it was a canny step. If Heim's voice carried farther, it might lead to his capture. There were people outside Germany who cared about Nazi fugitives, people who cared very much.

An audiotape proving that a Nazi murderer was alive and well, living comfortably abroad or even disguised closer to home off the proceeds of his apartment building in Germany, would have been galling to any survivor of the Holocaust, but particularly to one like Simon Wiesenthal who had devoted his life to catching Nazi fugitives. There was a personal edge to the Aribert Heim case because Wiesenthal had been imprisoned at Mauthausen, nearly died there at the end of the war, and said that while an inmate there, he had heard the stories about the gruesome Dr. Death who decapitated inmates and kept their skulls as trophies.

Aedtner and Wiesenthal spoke by phone about the case and exchanged letters. They might have seemed a mismatched pair, the Holocaust survivor and the Wehrmacht veteran turned police detective, but they shared a dedication that included a willingness to bend the rules to catch their quarry. Wiesenthal scrawled handwritten notes about Heim on a flyer for the Seconda Sessione delle Udienze Internazionali Sacharov, an event dedicated to Andrei Sakharov, the Soviet physicist, human rights activist, and Nobel Peace Prize winner. There was Herta Barth's address, information about the building at Tile-Wardenberg-Strasse 28, and details concerning the tax accountant Michael Barth.

Aedtner sent Wiesenthal two photographs, as well as a physical description of Heim: six feet three and speaking an Austrian dialect. It was in 1977, just weeks after Steinacker played the recording of Heim's voice, that Wiesenthal's search began in earnest. The Nazi hunter wrote to an acquaintance in Graz in the hopes that he knew someone in Hilda Heim's circle of friends. He called Heim "one of the most sadistic and anti-Semitic camp doctors in Mauthausen," and added, "He is one of our most emotional cases."

Wiesenthal's office was at Salztorgasse 6, on the site of the former Hotel Metropol, which the Nazis used as the Gestapo's Vienna headquarters. The apartment building that replaced it was unassuming, an ugly postwar building. Wiesenthal's shelves bent under the weight of his many boxes so full of paper they looked about to spill onto the black-and-white tile floor.

Approaching his seventieth birthday, Simon Wiesenthal had hardly slowed down. His work helped raise awareness in the United States of the Holocaust perpetrators who had moved to America like Hermine Braunsteiner Ryan, the brutal "Mare of Majdanek." She was stripped of her citizenship and by 1975 was on trial with other Majdanek officers in Düsseldorf. The U.S. government, in the meantime, was in the process of founding a special unit in the Justice Department to root out further Nazi fugitives. And in 1977 the Nazi hunter struck a deal to have his name grace the new Simon Wiesenthal Center in Los Angeles.

Wiesenthal made a lasting impression in part because of his gentle public persona. Justice, not vengeance, was his stated goal (and later the title of one of his books). He chose to stay in Austria, where he spoke simply as a citizen, rather than move to Israel, where he would be perceived as representing the Jewish state. Wiesenthal's rising profile had its uses as well. People with tips—Good Samaritans and fellow Nazis with grudges against former comrades—knew they could take them to the celebrity Nazi hunter.

In his own country, Wiesenthal was still a controversial figure. Austria preferred to depict itself as the first victim of Nazi Germany, conquered in the Anschluss, rather than a willing partner in war and extermination. Abroad, especially in America, Wiesenthal was embraced as a hero. He gave lectures and published books, including the memoir *The Murderers Among Us* and a parable of guilt, *The Sunflower,* which had passages by Desmond Tutu and the Dalai Lama.

In his novel *The Odessa File*, Frederick Forsyth sends his hero, the fictional reporter Peter Miller, to meet with Simon Wiesenthal as he searches for a real-life perpetrator known as "the Butcher of Riga." Much of the book is set in Cairo, and the plot turns on the German scientists working on Egypt's rocket program. Published in 1972, *The Odessa File* went on to sell more than 2.5 million copies, earning Wiesenthal a measure of fame that went far beyond any he had known. In the 1974 film version the actor Shmuel Rodensky portrayed Wiesenthal.

There was also a character clearly inspired by Wiesenthal in the 1976 movie *Marathon Man,* which starred Dustin Hoffman. That same year a novel called *The Boys from Brazil,* by Ira Levin, the best-selling author of *Rosemary's Baby,* featured a Nazi hunter named Yakov Liebermann who runs a documentation center in Vienna. Liebermann is searching for Dr. Josef Mengele, the Auschwitz doctor who became Wiesenthal's greatest obsession after Eichmann's execution. A film based on Levin's novel was set to come out in 1978, with Gregory Peck portraying Mengele and Sir Laurence Olivier as the Wiesenthal character.

The more famous he became, the more pressure Wiesenthal could bring to bear on Austrian and German officials who clearly preferred to have the Nazi issues go away. In this, he was very useful to Detective Aedtner. Since the tax case had ended in Herta Barth's favor, there had been little or no movement in the criminal case. Wiesenthal did what he always did and bombarded officials with correspondence. The large blue print on the letterhead read "DOCUMENTATION CENTER," all in capital letters. In smaller letters it said, "Of the Association of Jewish Victims of the Nazi Regime."

He appealed to the president of the Jewish Community of Berlin, Heinz Galinski, saying, "The fugitive SS camp doctor owns a large house in Berlin-Tiergarten with 42 apartments, which a property management company called Wilhelm Droste manages. The proceeds go to his sister, who gives him the money." He drew particular attention to the unusual fact that the doctor, living underground, gave his lawyer an audiotape in which he confirms that it is his signature presented to the tax office in Berlin-Tiergarten.

"As far as I know the wealth of Nazi criminals can be taken for restitution. Does that only apply to the wealth of those who have already been convicted?" Wiesenthal asked. "Could it be the case that—because the man is still alive and won't turn himself in—it could also be done with the assets of a fugitive?" Wiesenthal had Galinski forward his inquiry to the proper authorities, which Galinski did shortly thereafter, directing it to a city official at Berlin's interior department.

On October 18, 1978, Wiesenthal wrote directly to Dr. Hans-Jochen Vogel, reminding the minister of justice that they had met personally at an event in Munich when he was still mayor there. Wiesenthal was canny, not just relying on sympathy, but always looking for an angle to drive it home, whatever the audience. "We don't know whether Dr. Heim is practicing somewhere under a fake name. If he is, one would have to consider that with his predisposition and lack of conscience, which we know from his activities at Mauthausen (the arrest warrant speaks expressly of bloodlust), he could pose a direct danger to his potential patients."

Wiesenthal also referred to Steinacker's role in the case. "No one wants to rob Dr. Heim of good legal counsel, but this legal counsel is not defending his client in court, but instead much more through his counsel making it possible for him to live carefree, helping him with the monthly receipts of DM 6,500, enough money after all to live illegally." Wiesenthal pointed to the pursuit of the Baader-Meinhof terrorists, whose lawyers "were accused of supporting a criminal organization and of having knowledge as to the location of those underground." The SS was also a criminal organization, one that had committed far worse crimes than the RAF. "Justice found a way in the case of the Baader-Meinhof attorneys," Wiesenthal wrote. Maybe justice could pressure Heim's attorney in a similar manner.

As he waited for a reply, Wiesenthal decided that the case could use a little more public attention, so on November 30, 1978, he picked up the phone and called Heinz Höhne at *Der Spiegel*, Germany's leading magazine. Höhne was well-known and respected in journalistic circles, in particular for his articles on Nazis. He worked for two years and went through more than seventy thousand documents from the Nazi archives for a *Spiegel* series on the history of the SS. After they talked, Wiesenthal sent the reporter files and photographs of both Heim and Steinacker. The reporter dug into the story. There was no question whether he could produce an article. The question was, would anyone care?

CHAPTER 35

In the autumn of 1977, a film crew transformed the working-class West Berlin neighborhood of Wedding into the Warsaw Ghetto. Government officials in Poland and the Soviet Union had refused to give the production company permits to shoot in either country. For the same reason, they could not film at the Auschwitz or Sobibor death camp. For those scenes the producers turned to the Mauthausen concentration camp in Austria. West Berlin did double duty as the capital of the German Reich and as occupied Poland. Although the German authorities allowed the movie studio to film there, the reception in Berlin was anything but universally positive. Swastikas were painted onto cameras, and rolls of film disappeared. One passerby was so angry about the Hollywood production that he threw bottles at the set. An old man screamed, "I killed you Jews once before. I'll kill you again."

The cast and crew persisted. After the blockbuster success of the miniseries *Roots,* about an African slave and his descendants, executives at rival NBC wanted their own miniseries, one with the emotional resonance of slavery. They chose the Holocaust. The director, Marvin J. Chomsky, had been one of the directors of *Roots* and was a television veteran, with episodes of *Star Trek, Gunsmoke, Mission: Impossible,* and *Hawaii Five-O* among his credits. The novelist Gerald Green, author of *The Last Angry Man,* was given the difficult task of squeezing the fates of millions of Jews into one identifiable and sympathetic group, the family Weiss. A single ambitious SS officer, Erik Dorf, played by the actor

Michael Moriarty, would serve as the primary carrier of German guilt. Meryl Streep and James Woods starred in the miniseries.

When it aired on U.S. television in 1978, *Holocaust* generated significant controversy. Writing in the *New York Times*, the television critic John J. O'Connor attacked what he called the "sterile collection of wooden characters and ridiculous coincidences" necessary to submit a single family to the events of Kristallnacht, the terrors of Auschwitz's selection ramp, the Warsaw Ghetto uprising, and more. The writer and prominent survivor Elie Wiesel called the miniseries "untrue, offensive, cheap," and "an insult to those who perished and to those who survived." Particularly galling for many was the juxtaposition of genocide with bright and gaudy commercials for household products, which many deemed indecent, if not downright obscene.

For all the criticisms, the miniseries was a professional production with star actors that brought the history of the Holocaust into millions of homes. Yet few would have predicted at the time that a mainstream entertainment aimed at an American audience would have a significant and lasting effect on Germany's attitude toward its war crimes. The result was an unlikely national catharsis that would lead to greater public support for the pursuit of war criminals decades after the war. Far from flagging with the passage of time, investigations into Nazis like Dr. Aribert Heim would be pursued with new vigor and growing resources.

German public television purchased the foreign rights in Germany for $600,000. The fact that it was state-owned television meant that the decision was politically charged from the start, urged by leading members of the left-leaning Social Democrats and largely opposed by the right-wing Christian Democrats. Helmut Oeller, the program director of Bavarian television, Bayerischer Rundfunk, said, "I say no because 'Holocaust' puts the horror within boundaries, presents it in the same familiar limiting format as Westerns and murder mysteries, all of which we view as entertainment and something not quite real, not quite the truth."

Public critiques of the program's commercialism, the soap-opera quality of its filming, and the historical inaccuracies led the directors of the main television network, ARD, to demote the miniseries to its regional stations. Expectations for the program were low and falling. Germans, it was widely believed, were tired of hearing about a war more than three decades in the past, tired of lectures about their culpability. The strange foreign word "Holocaust," taken from the Greek *holos* and *kaustos,* for "completely" and "burned," was almost unknown in Germany.

"The problem will be getting people to turn on their sets when it is broadcast," said Heinz Galinski, leader of the Jewish Community of Berlin, with whom Wiesenthal had corresponded on the Heim case.

But not everyone, it turned out, was feeling apathetic about the renewed attention to the murder of the European Jews. Right-wing groups opposed to the broadcast were in some instances ready to take action to prevent *Holocaust* from airing. At 8:40 p.m. on a Thursday evening in January 1979, a ten-kilogram bomb detonated near Koblenz, severing television cables belonging to the regional public television station. Barely twenty minutes later another explosion destroyed the cables running from an antenna not far from Münster. A right-wing radical group claimed responsibility, saying its goal had been to prevent the airing of a documentary called *The Final Solution* in the run-up to the broadcast of *Holocaust.* Weeks before the miniseries was scheduled to air, threatening phone calls to German television stations had begun.

The concerns of anti-Semites and unreconstructed Nazis were well-founded. When the four-part, seven-and-a-half-hour miniseries finally aired in Germany, viewers tuned in by the droves, with more than twenty million West Germans watching. One station, Westdeutscher Rundfunk, hosted "Midnight Discussions" after each episode, and roughly thirty-five thousand Germans called in. Viewing groups were started for singles because the program was considered too traumatic to watch alone. Nearly two-thirds of those surveyed by West German television and the Federal Office for Political Education described themselves as "deeply shaken." The Holocaust turned into an inescapable national debate in Germany, on the front page of every newspaper, the cover of every magazine, discussed from elementary schools to universities, which would soon register a surge of interest in studying the crimes of the Nazi era.

The question was whether this was what the Germans call a "straw fire," which flares up bright but burns out immediately, or whether it would have a practical impact in the search for Nazi war criminals. The Bundestag in Bonn was due to debate the statute of limitations for Nazi war crimes. A survey of twenty-eight hundred people before the program aired found only 15 percent of Germans wanted the statute of limitations removed. Two weeks later that figure had leaped to 39 percent. A majority of Germans, 51 percent, said before the miniseries aired that Nazi trials should end. After the program was broadcast, the number dropped to 35 percent.

"In the house of the hangman," *Der Spiegel* wrote, "the rope was spoken of as never before."

Tano Pisano never expected to have much of a relationship with Rüdiger Heim, the slightly withdrawn young man he got to know a little in Florence. Where the Sicilian painter was a radical and an artist, Rüdiger mostly liked to talk about tennis. He wore shorts, wristbands, and a headband to keep his long blond hair away from his face. The two men moved in some of the same social circles, and many of the people they knew in common were American students. Rüdiger was friends with one of Pisano's girlfriends, a Frenchwoman, and would tag along sometimes when the couple went out to dinner or to an event.

At one point Pisano asked Rüdiger where he was from, and he answered that he came from Germany and was supposed to study medicine at Pisa. To Pisano's eyes it did not appear that his acquaintance was spending very much time at the university at all. Pisano found himself asking more questions, a spark of interest forming in the quiet young man. He learned that Rüdiger was good at languages. They spoke Italian together, but the young man could also speak French and English as well as his native German. He had a serious interest in photography and, Pisano thought, some talent as well. He had a good sense of light.

Still, Pisano did not believe they would stay in touch when he moved from Italy to Denmark, part of his restless wandering between northern and southern Europe and a symptom of his own conflicted feelings about painting and the art market. He rankled when an art dealer told him one style or another was selling and that he should make more of those paintings. He stopped making art and opened a restaurant instead.

Pisano's restaurant was an idyllic, peaceful place in a tiny yellow cottage on a gentle sloping hillside facing the Øresund Strait in Klampenborg, north of Copenhagen. The unassuming little gatekeeper's house of a nineteenth-century spa was a historic landmark, built by the famous Danish architect Gottlieb Bindesbøll, better known for churches, town halls, and the Thorvaldsens Museum in the capital. The spa was gone, and the house had been used as a kiosk in the summer for selling food to beachgoers before Pisano and his wife received permission to turn it into a year-round restaurant.

Den Gule Cottage, or the Yellow Cottage, as the restaurant was called, was "a missionary place," in Pisano's words, an effort to bring Mediterranean cooking to the still relatively narrow Scandinavian culinary environment. Pisano would buy whatever fresh ingredients he could find at the market and create the sorts of meals he had grown up eating. He perplexed his diners the first time he served artichokes because most did not know what they were.

In the end it was tennis that brought Rüdiger and Pisano back together when Rüdiger showed up in Denmark to play in yet another tournament. He mostly played in Italy, in Palermo or Padua, but traveled to Belgium and Denmark for matches as well. It was a roving life for those on the margins of the tour and neither a very lucrative nor a comfortable one, tramping around with your rackets, staying at places that offered cheap rates for the competitors, eating at the tennis clubs. Rüdiger only won prize money a single time, in 1978 in Messina. Denmark was the worst place to play, in Rüdiger's experience, because they only let the Danes train before the events. That might have contributed to his decision to quit competing.

Rüdiger told Pisano that he didn't want to go on playing tennis or studying medicine and asked if perhaps he could work in the restaurant. "Why not?" Pisano said. The Yellow Cottage was a place where a conflicted young man could find a measure of peace.

Rüdiger had never washed dishes, waited tables, or worked in a kitchen before. Pisano knew enough about his new employee to know that he did not need the job. But the young man was a hard worker, and it seemed as though he had something to prove to himself. Meanwhile, he enjoyed meeting all kinds of new people, not just artists and intellectuals, but workers and activists. Pisano provided entry into an egalitarian world unlike Rüdiger's spa-town upbringing or his years in a Swiss boarding school. Rüdiger Heim wanted to be a part of that world if his past would let him.

His idea was to move to Copenhagen, work at the restaurant, and continue with his newfound love of photography. He was studying Danish and planned to stay. His mother was extremely disappointed that her younger son had chosen to abandon his studies, and Rüdiger believed the knowledge would drive his father crazy. "I also knew that he would certainly reject everything that I was doing. No sport. No studies," Heim said. He was not quite ready to tell his father that he had given up school to wash dishes and wait tables.

Instead, he wrote that in 1978 he competed in ten tournaments all over Europe, meeting "people from every corner of the world." There was a new optimism to his correspondence. "Here and there I had small romances but nothing solid. I hope that one of these stories will turn into something serious as I would like to have a girl to love and to be loved by," Rüdiger wrote to his father. "It's just that I don't quite know yet what really is love!" He told his father he was in Denmark but not why. "I'm afraid this is not a long letter since I can't write about myself and what I am doing and thinking. I prefer to talk about it. Let me say only that I know in which direction to go. It is only a matter of getting enough courage to start."

At the beginning of 1979, Rüdiger Heim's main worry was his father's prostate operation. He did not know that the police were keeping track of him and his family. He did not know that packages sent by his mother to Pisano's address were duly noted in the investigative file, including the artist's name. Rüdiger Heim did not know how his family's fortunes were about to change. He had paid no attention to the renewed public interest in Nazi war criminals, but he could not miss the article about his father in *Der Spiegel*. It fell to Rüdiger to warn Heim.

In the family's correspondence the code name for Aribert Heim was Gretel, the little girl who got lost in the woods with her brother, Hansel. When Rüdiger sat down to inform his father what was happening, he spun his own fairy tale modeled on the Brothers Grimm.

When Gretel awoke one morning, it had just turned the fifth week of the New Year, and she was not feeling particularly well. She decided to buy herself a Spiegel. The old one was already too old, and one couldn't recognize anything in it anymore. But no sooner had she bought the new Spiegel than she went home and looked inside. It shocked her terribly for what was inside did not please her at all. Her entire misery was mirrored in her face once more. She suddenly had a vision that came out of this Spiegel. If one day, all of a sudden, the poor girl could no longer receive bread and if water was no longer brought up to her room, well, then she would inevitably starve and die of thirst or else she would have to go out into the forest to provide for herself. But the forest was teeming with wolves, and they would most certainly tear her to pieces. There was still Rainer, however, and he could certainly help her. She simply had to make contact with him, and he would give her counsel. Oh, that would all be terrible, thought Gretel, and sat down to try to recover from the scare.

In plain language, Rüdiger wanted his father to acquire a copy of *Der Spiegel*. He had to talk to Fritz Steinacker, Rainer in code. His livelihood, and possibly his life, depended on it.

The February 5, 1979, issue of *Der Spiegel* featured a black-and-white photograph of train tracks dusted with snow leading into Auschwitz, an image of hopelessness and desolation. Inmate number 290, a survivor who had become a film director, shared his experiences at the death camp with the magazine. Another article speculated whether the Bundestag would overturn the statute of limitations for Nazi murders. Under the title "NS Crimes: Out the Back" was the story of a Nazi doctor who had escaped and was still living in hiding. One week after the national catharsis of the *Holocaust* miniseries, Aribert Heim had been designated as the new face of Nazi impunity.

The three-page article took what had been essentially a quiet police investigation and laid it out for the world to see. The circulation of *Der Spiegel* at the time was 1.1 million in a country of roughly 60 million people. Even that number understated the publication's importance to the nation. In 1962, when the magazine reported that the West German army was unprepared for war, the government declared treason and arrested the publisher and the deputy editor in chief. The public protests that followed, combined with court rulings in the magazine's favor, helped secure freedom of the press in the young democracy and establish civil society. *Der Spiegel* was the secular bible of the educated middle class. Its national reach and moral authority exceeded any other mainstream publication at the time.

The black-and-white photograph accompanying the article showed Heim unsmiling with his hair slicked back. It listed his SS membership number as 367,744 and his Nazi Party membership number as 6,116,098. "For 17 years the former KZ physician Dr. Aribert Heim has lived underground," read the bold text, "provided for financially by a Berlin apartment house, legally advised by a Frankfurt attorney." With so much support, the magazine concluded, "the investigators are powerless." The terrible crimes were described in detail, starting with the deadly injection of chemicals directly into the hearts of the victims. The suspect had killed "because he was bored at his job," taking skulls for "personal uses," including that of a young inmate with a perfect bite. He forced patients to undergo unnecessary operations, removing their organs and killing them in the process.

But Mauthausen was not the main focus of the article, which scrutinized how it was possible for someone like Heim to live undetected and unpunished for so long. The title came from a quotation from a state police officer, saying that he had the impression Heim had gone "out the back as we came in the front." The message throughout the article was that eluding justice was only possible with a lot of help, whether in the forms of warnings, tips, professional assistance, or financial help.

"Roughly 120,000 inmates were killed in the Mauthausen camp, yet by all appearances one of the murderers involved can spend his rental proceeds undisturbed because property managers, tax accountants, and lawyers stand ready to help in exchange for their honorariums." Walter Rebbe, the Frankfurt notary who helped Heim with various contracts when he went on the run, was quoted as saying, "Do I have to ask every time someone shows me their identification card?"

The residents of his apartment block, the article continued, also helped the fugitive, albeit unwittingly. "Like most renters in large buildings in big cities, the parties at Berlin's Tile-Wardenberg-Strasse 28 do not know whose building they really live in," the article began. That was because the name in the entryway was not Heim but Wilhelm Droste & Co. Heim's contact there was Rolf Gallner, whom Aedtner had already interviewed. "We have a management contract," Gallner told the magazine, and the company was "not a moral institution."

Heim's tax accountant in Heidelberg, Michael Barth, told *Der Spie-*

gel that he was "completely unaware of what Mr. Heim might have done at some point in time." He added that this was the first time he had been told there was an arrest warrant against his client. The only inkling he had had was certain "hints from Steinacker." The lawyer was featured in the article, too, with a photograph showing him wearing tinted glasses and an unbecoming smirk. When the reader looked over at the facing page, he saw a field of white crosses, grave markers for many who had died at Mauthausen.

Der Spiegel described Steinacker's work in the Arajs trial in Hamburg, the Majdanek trial in Düsseldorf, and the Fasold case in Frankfurt. When asked where his client Dr. Heim was residing, he answered that he had "a certain idea" but added he "would not like to be more concrete than that." The magazine found it "noteworthy" that Steinacker assessed the West German justice system and found it lacking. "At this point one could not advise one's client to turn himself in," the attorney said, because he couldn't get "a fair trial." The magazine described Steinacker's conduct in shielding his client as "just on the border of permissible." The head of the state police in Baden-Württemberg agreed, complaining that the investigation was much more difficult because "members of certain professions are excessively employing their rights, or, better put, their supposed rights." But the minister of justice conceded that the lawyer could not be charged for failing to reveal confidential information like the location of his client.

Alfred Aedtner's name appears nowhere in *Der Spiegel*'s article, but the fruits of his investigation and the insights from his files and official reports are seeded throughout. In the course of the investigation police had questioned more than two hundred people, the article said. There had been a tip from an intelligence service in 1967 that Heim was in Egypt, but by the end of 1969 or the beginning of 1970, Heim was believed to be back in "the German-speaking area."

The magazine also included Herta Barth's involvement in forwarding the rent money to her brother. Her husband, Georg, was named in the article, along with the fact that he had his own engineering firm. The article even gave his and Herta's home address in Buchschlag. Friedl's exact address on Maria-Viktoria-Strasse in Baden-Baden was also included. Mrs. Heim protested that her ex-husband had fooled her too. His flight from justice had "surprised her completely," and only after his departure did she learn about his past. "I wasn't even in the BDM," Friedl told the magazine, referring to the Bund Deutscher Mädel, or League of German Girls, the female version of the Hitler Youth. Käthe Bechtold, identified only as "the aged mother," said that the family had a long anti-Nazi tradition. "Three of my husband's siblings were arrested by Hitler," she told the magazine. "We fought so hard for the Jews."

Though twelve years had passed since the divorce, Aribert Heim still haunted the family. After the *Spiegel* article appeared, a man phoned the home on Maria-Viktoria-Strasse saying he was a reporter for the tabloid *Bild*. Mrs. Bechtold answered the phone and couldn't quite understand the name he gave, if he had said Berger, Börger, or Burger. When she said that her daughter was away, the man, who was not the reporter he claimed, became increasingly incensed and threatening, saying that the negative publicity was only the beginning. "Soon bombs are going to be planted at your home. That's already been decided." When Mrs. Bechtold called the newsroom at *Bild,* she was told that no one by that name worked at the paper.

"It is self-evident for our client the case has increasingly become a personal burden and beyond that a danger," the family attorney, Dr. Klaus Froebel, said. Froebel wanted to know why his client's full name and address had appeared in a national magazine, even though in the same article "it is remarked that she never knew anything." Froebel continued, "Our client has noticed that the press has at its disposal facts out of the investigation and also from the divorce proceedings."

Steinacker personally visited the family to update them on the defense. Rüdiger drove down from Denmark to be with the family. Unlike his mother and grandmother, who had kept many of the details from him, he was learning the specifics of his father's alleged crimes for the first time. His grandmother told him, "Your father swore on his children that he had not done anything."

A trip to visit his father in Egypt at that point was out of the question, since the family assumed that they were under constant surveillance. What Rüdiger learned about the government's charges against his father clearly shook him. He resolved never to tell his friends in Denmark about the charges, to keep his two worlds separate and spare himself their judgment.

ndignant, shocked, and shaken." Those were some of the words that residents of Tile-Wardenberg-Strasse 28 used to describe their reaction when they learned how their rent money was being used. "I can't believe that I am financing the flight of a Nazi criminal," one woman told the local *Tagesspiegel* newspaper. The *Holocaust* series and the related media coverage had successfully refocused German public opinion on Nazi war criminals.

Many tenants had long been dissatisfied with their absentee landlord, but they neither knew who he was nor what he had done during the war. Decades of neglect, chipped paint, cracks in the walls, burst pipes, long waits for other repairs, all took on a sudden significance. Many reacted with more than just fury. They organized protests, which in turn ensured that the case did not slip back into obscurity.

By February 1979, many of the tenants had begun questioning how they could stop assisting the fugitive. "We want to speak with an attorney about whether we can pay our rent into a frozen account," Lothar Tuchen, a thirty-four-year-old electrician, told the local *B.Z.* tabloid. "We don't want our money financing the livelihood of a Nazi criminal." Some of the older residents, however, said they couldn't care less. It was the younger renters who sent letters to their political representatives asking for help in stopping payments to the accused killer. They began collecting signatures demanding "a new owner who will make sure that our house is led correctly."

Their protest became a news story that threatened to explode into a political scandal. At one point someone burst into Droste's offices and threw stink bombs so foul the company briefly evacuated the premises. The vandal left a note declaring, "Money stinks," as a preface to angry statements about the firm's handling of Heim's business. The Berlin authorities were helpless with Dr. Heim hiding safely abroad, but the idea that he could continue to receive support was simply unacceptable from a political standpoint. Even state television was calling to find out what was going on with the Heim case. Something had to be done.

In an open letter, many of the tenants appealed to the city government not only that "the house be placed immediately under court supervision" but also that more be done to educate German youth about the past. "What will you do and what have you done up to this point to honor the opponents and victims of the National Socialist dictatorship?" the letter asked. "What position do you take on the question of the statute of limitations for the systematic eradication of people and the other murderous deeds of National Socialism?"

The younger residents discovered how the local Levetzowstrasse synagogue had been used as one of Berlin's main deportation centers to the concentration camps. After watching the *Holocaust* miniseries, several tenants told reporters they were appalled to have helped support a Nazi criminal. On March 3, 1979, the renters collected signatures at the site of the former synagogue. "Countless Jewish fellow citizens live in the immediate vicinity of Dr. Heim's rental building," scolded the neighborhood representative Gottfried Wurche in a letter to the city government. Shortly afterward the renters made good on their threat and began paying into a frozen account. "The authorities have been aware of the dark past of the building's owner, Dr. Heim, for 17 years," they wrote in a letter, "without an arrest."

Still, there was little West Berlin police could do; the criminal case was in the hands of Aedtner and the prosecutors in Baden-Württemberg. The tax authorities said that as long as Heim and his representatives paid the taxes he owed, the government was powerless. But city justice officials raised the possibility of pursuing Heim under an antiquated statute aimed at depriving the Nazi leadership of its ill-gotten gains.

The former minister of the interior, the one-armed Nazi-hating veteran Joachim Lipschitz, had died in December 1961. But he left behind the Second Law for the Conclusion of Denazification. Under it, the independent panel known as the *Spruchkammer* could levy "unlimited fines" against Nazi perpetrators. The "Berlin specialty," as the *Tagesspiegel* called it, might allow them to put Heim's crimes before a civil panel and try to take the building from him. There was the chance, as *Der Spiegel* had written, to "bring Heim's house under the hammer." Rüdiger had warned his father: "If one day, all of a sudden, the poor girl could no longer receive bread and if water was no longer brought up to her room . . ." The strategy was straightforward. Cut off Gretel's food and water, force her into the forest, and leave the rest to the wolves.

The head of Berlin's Jewish community forwarded Wiesenthal's request for help with the Heim case to the director of the Interior Ministry of West Berlin, Jürgen Brinkmeier. He, in turn, passed the request down to Rolf-Peter Magen. Magen was a short man with a pudgy face, a small, fine mouth, and a pronounced bald spot. He looked like what he was, a bespectacled, middle-aged lawyer. Magen normally handled cases involving voter rights. He was not a criminal prosecutor. He was, however, tenacious and creative, refusing to accept that there was nothing the city could do about the Aribert Heim case. The Heim case posed a legal challenge, but Magen was also interested in raising his profile politically, with an eye on higher office. The case was all over the city's newspapers and even on national television, presenting the perfect opportunity. "He immediately smelled blood," said his colleague Ernst R. Zivier, who worked on the Heim case with him.

It was not an auspicious beginning for the prosecution. The lack of firsthand testimony would hurt their case. Magen hoped to have witness statements from the early stages of the investigation in the postwar years if he could convince the Baden-Baden prosecutors to help. He also had the foremost expert in German law enforcement as it related to Aribert Heim at his side. Alfred Aedtner traveled to Berlin to walk Magen and his colleague Zivier through the depositions he had taken and the archival material he had unearthed. The detective remembered every last detail from his witness interviews, each tiny point from the files. "He had jealously driven all over the place in his search," Zivier said. "It made an impression how utterly engaged he was."

Like Aedtner, Magen went to the Berlin Document Center, where he determined that Dr. Aribert Heim had indeed been part of the Nazi army, a member of the SA and the Waffen-SS. He learned that Heim had worked as an inspector at Buchenwald. Magen's first instinct must have been to build a criminal case against the Nazi doctor. The Berlin files contained a copy of the death notice of a Berliner who died on November 3, 1941, while Heim worked at Mauthausen. But the person who provided the information did not have evidence of any specific crime. Magen wrote to the prosecutors in Baden-Baden, asking them to turn over "the results of their investigation as quickly as possible."

The officials in southwest Germany rebuffed Magen's request, writing, "I regret once again that I cannot send you the complete files to examine, but there is an ongoing need for them here." The official added that the witness statements were "extremely incriminating." Lacking the support from Baden-Baden, Magen's boss, Brinkmeier, appealed instead to Wiesenthal, who sent along a photocopy of the German arrest warrant as well as information on the Austrian investigation.

"I am under the impression that that will be sufficient for your purposes," Wiesenthal wrote. "If you should require the Austrian arrest warrant, request it please from the federal minister of justice." He commented that the case had turned into "a parody" and that he felt obliged to send a copy of the file to Justice Minister Vogel himself. Though Wiesenthal was frustrated with the progress and insulted that Vogel never answered him, he was soon pleased to learn that the West Berlin lawyers planned to use their "Berlin specialty" to go after the Nazi doctor.

The *Spruchkammer* law had been used to seize funds from the heirs of Hermann Göring and Heinrich Himmler, as well as the estate of the Buchenwald commandant Hermann Pister. It had last been used against the estate of Reinhard Heydrich, chief of the Reich Main Security Office, in 1971. The Berliners assured Wiesenthal that they could make the same case against Heim.

With every passing year the need to keep denazification panels at the ready seemed less and less pressing. When new members were nominated for the standing three-judge panel, "every time people just smiled," Magen told the *Frankfurter Rundschau* newspaper. The *Spruchkammer* was a quaint historical relic, not a tool of justice. Then the Heim case broke in 1979.

Unlike most criminal cases, where the guilt of the accused is determined before the appropriate punishment, Heim's sentence was chosen before the hearing even began. The correspondence between the authorities reveals that they would seize the building if the accused was found guilty. A letter from Berlin to the court in Linz observed that the "goal of the procedure" was to "impose a monetary penalty on Dr. Heim such that, after the verdict of the *Spruchkammer* has legal force, the rental-apartment property belonging to Dr. Heim in Berlin could be taken." In order to take that step, however, it was necessary to know what the building was worth.

The city finance ministry made a simple calculation based on similar properties. It came to the conclusion that Tile-Wardenberg-Strasse 28 was worth 690,000 deutsche marks. The building authority was more thorough. It sent inspectors to the apartment house in March 1979 for a complete assessment. They found that the elevator had not worked since the end of World War II. There were cracks in the inner and outer walls. The stucco on the facade was damaged, especially on the fourth story. The roof was leaking, and there was moisture damage as a result. Banister rungs were missing. The basement floor was sinking. The whole building needed to be rewired. The list went on and on.

"The damages determined could in large part be a result of war activities, as well as the omission of necessary repairs and upkeep," the inspector wrote. He assessed the value of the house as 590,000 deutsche marks, 100,000 marks lower than the colleague at the finance ministry.

The moment had come, but the authorities in Baden-Baden, Heim's last known address, were still not on board. The prosecutors there had handled the case since before Heim fled in September 1962. As *Der Spiegel* put it, "They fear that evidence already used in a *Spruchkammer* procedure would lose some of its strength for criminal sentencing." The magazine posited that it was dangerous to let the defense attorney see the witnesses in the civil procedure. It would make them "half as useful" if they ever brought their criminal case to trial. The Berlin authorities appealed once more to Baden-Baden, insisting that "in light of the current discussion about the hunt for Nazi criminals, the public would have little understanding" if an effort by the Berlin authority to prosecute a man accused of such serious crimes were hindered by the Baden-Württemberg officials.

Wiesenthal kept up the pressure in the media. In an interview with the *Berliner Morgenpost* paper on February 13, 1979, he repeated his assertion that he had "reason to believe that [Heim is] living not all that far from us and in all likelihood practicing his profession, but under a false name." Three days later, the director of the Interior Ministry, Brinkmeier, answered: "I hope as soon as possible to apply for the introduction of a penalty procedure before the *Spruchkammer*."

City authorities filed to request a hearing on March 29, 1979. The Berlin *Spruchkammer* granted the request on April 27, 1979, announcing that it was opening proceedings against Dr. Heim. "The personal appearance at the hearing of the person concerned is hereby ordered," said the panel.

Aedtner followed the current actions against Heim with an almost obsessive zeal. He had in the meantime learned that a Dr. Wrazlaw Busek, who had kept the list of the dead at Mauthausen along with Josef Kohl, had moved to Queens, New York. He wrote to the former inmate asking for his help, adding that Heim was "definitely still alive and we have well-founded hopes that we could soon have him in hand." The moment Fritz Steinacker submitted a letter from Heim granting him power of attorney for the case in Berlin, Aedtner got hold of it and sent it away for forensic analysis.

The forensics department at the state police headquarters in Stuttgart completed its analysis of the typeface and signatures on the letters submitted in the tax case. The typewriter was from one of five manufacturers, Adler, Triumph, Facit, Royal, or Imperial, using a particular rotating-type-ball technology first introduced in the IBM Selectric, of a model that had only existed since 1974. There was no evidence that Heim's signature had been forged. The letter appeared to be genuine, which meant that Heim was still alive and still in contact with Steinacker.

As if to prove that they were not just sitting idly by, the Baden-Baden prosecutors announced a 15,000-deutsche-mark reward for Heim on March 19. Although there had been an arrest warrant since 1962, prosecutors had never formally filed charges, a step they finally took on June 11, 1979, just two days before the trial in Berlin was scheduled to begin. Then, under severe political pressure, they finally sent the Berliners eight hundred out of the two thousand pages in their file on the accused, including witness statements but not investigative findings.

That the fugitive Heim would not attend was a foregone conclusion. It was more of a surprise that the surviving witnesses also refused to appear. The Mauthausen inmate Gustav Rieger wrote reminding them that he had already given sworn testimony before a judge. "A trip to Berlin is impossible for me for health reasons." He explained that he was in such poor physical condition he had been officially designated as handicapped, and he included his identification number with the Munich health authorities if they wanted to confirm it.

The former political inmate Johann Payerl had a very different reaction, expressing deep skepticism whether his appearance would make any difference to the outcome of the trial. Years of not-guilty verdicts and suspended sentences had taken their toll, Payerl wrote.

I would like to answer your letter of March 6 with a question. Is it so important for me to give testimony before the Berlin Spruchkammer against KZ physician Dr. Heim when he is sure to be acquitted? We KZ survivors have learned the fact that "not guilty" verdicts for former KZ murderers are reached despite the most serious incrimination by witnesses. So it was in the Sachsenhausen trial, Buchenwald, etc. and also many other NS cases.

If you can give me evidence to the contrary, then please let me know as soon as possible.

Magen replied that he could not "judge what decision the Berlin *Spruchkammer* will impose against Dr. Heim." The balking witness insisted that he might well suffer a nervous breakdown or even a stroke were he confronted in court by Heim. "Imagine for a moment," Payerl wrote back to the city attorney. "I am classified as 80% affected by a nervous disorder and this man stands in front of me?" The handwritten letter becomes illegible as Payerl writes of "a murderer before me" "who killed my buddies."

Karl Lotter, who had given Aedtner the precise descriptions of Heim, declined the invitation as well. "As a witness in the criminal matter of Dr. Heim, I inform you of the following: unfortunately, in light of my age (76 years) and in consideration of the state of my health, it is not possible for me to come to Berlin." He reminded Magen that he had been deposed twice in the case, most recently in 1976. "Both times officers came to Mürzzuschlag."

Despite the lack of flesh-and-blood witnesses in court Magen pressed ahead. He would have to work with the transcripts of past testimony. With the trial date approaching, he would have to work fast.

The hearing began at 10:30 in the morning on June 13, 1979, in the government complex on Preussen Platz in West Berlin. The large room on the eleventh floor was not a courtroom but part of the building authority's offices. It was an abnormally speedy start for a trial requested by prosecutors less than three months before. Fritz Steinacker arrived sharply dressed in suit and tie, wearing tinted glasses, his hair combed back and going white at the temples and sideburns.

The judge and chairman of the panel, Wolfgang Neesemann, opened the proceeding by asking Steinacker, "Is your client present?"

"No," the defense attorney answered.

"I specifically ordered his appearance," Neesemann said. "Do you know where he is?"

"No," Steinacker answered, "but even if I knew, I wouldn't say. I am under the attorney's obligation of secrecy." Steinacker then filed a motion to dismiss the case against his client as baseless. The motion was rejected. The hearing would proceed without Aribert Heim.

Magen presented his case. Although lawyers from his division rarely had to appear in court, he was not nervous but instead calm and collected, quite in his element that day. He described Heim as "part of the enforcement clique around Hitler," without whom "the regime would not have been capable of committing these crimes." Heim had "advanced the rule of National Socialism to a significant extent." He had overstepped orders to euthanize the ill and the infirm by killing even healthy inmates "out of lust for murder and boredom." He was, in Magen's words, "a beast in the form of a man."

The witness statements were read out loud in a flat monotone. The *Berliner Morgenpost* newspaper called it "deadly silent" as testimony from the five witnesses reaching back to 1949 was presented one after another. Karl Kaufmann, who began the process with his letter to Heim's former ice hockey team, had passed away, but his words stunned the courtroom. He knew Heim while working as the capo in the operating room in 1941. At the time there were many transports arriving at Mauthausen, including many Jews. Heim would order "26 to 30 prisoners incapable of working," without regard for nationality or religion, who would be brought to him and whom he "killed with gasoline injections in the vein or in the heart." When he had Sunday duty, he ordered "30 to 35 Jews, all of them healthy," who were killed the same way.

An old Jewish man, Kaufmann guessed around seventy years old, came to Heim and said, "Herr Obersturmführer, you like to operate. Look here, I am an old man and won't live that much longer. Operate on me. I have a bad hernia. I know that I will have to die in a few days." According to Kaufmann, Heim obliged by cutting into the Jew's abdomen and poking around at his internal organs until he died. Kaufmann then described the lethal injections. "Countless Jews were liquidated in this way without any difference made between young or old, and also those of other nations, but then only those who were weak and incapable of work," Kaufmann said.

Josef Kohl, who had been the first to give testimony about Heim to the investigator Arthur A. Becker less than a year after Mauthausen was liberated, described how Heim brought his victims to tears with "seemingly very humane" questions about their family members. Only then would he give the deadly injection. Karl Lotter called Heim "a markedly perverse mass murderer" who "with a cold-blooded look killed people by the dozens." Lotter said that he was personally present for seven murders but that Heim could have been responsible for more than a hundred. "The Jews were brought in, injected, and then thrown out."

The left-wing *Tageszeitung* newspaper described the testimony as "taking the air away, causing nausea." The correspondent noted with great disappointment that the courtroom was not full, how only "a few interested parties, above all younger people, came this Wednesday to the hearing, to recall the memory—indeed the cruelest parts—of National Socialism." The businesslike approach clashed with the depravity of the crimes in question, creating "an atmosphere like in a trial over a used car. There was no indignation, no whispering in the room."

Working against Steinacker's client was the fact that Heim presented such a memorable figure, what with his height, his athletic build, and his trips to play professional hockey. A former member of the SS who served at Mauthausen, Otto Kleingünther, did not testify to any specific crimes but confirmed the doctor's presence and his appearance. Lotter and Kaufmann both remembered that he played for the same ice hockey team in Vienna. In summing up their statements, Magen made clear that this was not a man easily confused with others.

"All testified in agreement," Magen said. "He was there, he looked like this, he did this."

Steinacker began not by defending his client but by defending himself. To assume, he told the court, that a lawyer identifies with a Nazi war criminal just because he represented the accused was false. "Whether he is supposed to be a left-wing terrorist or a right-wing criminal, every client has a right to a fair trial," Steinacker declared.

"But you live off this," shouted one of the spectators. Steinacker did not answer but continued his opening statement.

"Dr. Heim rejects all of the accusations," Steinacker said. "He spent just a few weeks at KZ Mauthausen—as troop doctor for the SS guards." The files at the Berlin Document Center in Zehlendorf clearly stated that Heim was a troop doctor and not a camp doctor. "Heim does not deny that he was there for a certain time, but he says that he came to Mauthausen in the fall of 1941 and was there for seven weeks," Steinacker said. "Based on the information available to me, Heim at no time committed the acts he stands accused of." Heim's name appeared in the operation book for the first time on October 8 and for the last time on November 29.

Josef Kohl said that Heim was at the camp from September 1940 to June 1942. Sommer said he came in 1942 or as late as 1943. Referring to a handwritten letter from his client, Steinacker returned time and again to the contradictory dates in the testimony in order, as the *Spiegel* correspondent wrote, "to devalue the witness testimony at its core."

Listening to Steinacker it was as though "a medium was speaking for the missing accused in the court chamber." The claims against his client were full of "sweeping descriptions, the Jews, the Germans." Unless the witnesses were questioned again, his client could not be found guilty. Considering that several of the most important witnesses had died since they were deposed, this was as good as saying it was too late to try his client.

"We only have paper here," Steinacker said, referring to the statements, and pointed out that after concentration camps were liberated, the inmates tended to exaggerate and conflate. The statements were too "polemical and not precise enough." Many witnesses described events as if they had seen them firsthand, then modified them by adding "I came to know" or "I learned" to their statements. Steinacker summed up the accusations against his client as "latrine rumors." The left-wing *Tageszeitung* described the lawyer as excellently prepared as he "picked apart" the statements, raised contradictions in the timelines, and imputed false memories and exaggerations. Legally, his client's fortune could not be touched.

By the time the decision was announced, Steinacker was already in a taxi on his way to West Berlin's Tegel Airport. The hearing had lasted less than a workday, and the deliberations would take only half an hour. "The crimes we heard about in court today are even more gruesome and terrible than those shown in the 'Holocaust' film," said Neesemann. The case before them was much worse "because it was no movie."

Magen did not have to worry about the fact that the witnesses did not appear or about the inconsistencies that cropped up in their testimony, despite how those incongruities had been highlighted by Steinacker. Heim's family had gathered letters of support and offered witnesses to testify to his good character, but none were heard or introduced into the record. The second *Spruchkammer* that heard his case found that Heim was a major offender, not the follower he was judged to be in 1948.

"Heim supported the violent National Socialist regime to an exceptional degree," the panel found as it convicted him in absentia. It levied a fine of 510,000 deutsche marks against him, about $255,000 at the time, as well as the costs of the court case.

The reporter from the *Tageszeitung* wrote, "The *Spruchkammer* announces the verdict, sees Heim's guilt as proven, the building is expropriated. Certainly an appeal will be filed and the case will drag on. Heim lives without his house, still unpunished. And?"

CHAPTER 41

Under the name Alfred Buediger, Heim had started out as a patient of the Egyptian dentist Abdelmoneim el Rifai. The relationship between the two men had quickly grown more personal, and Heim began calling on Rifai at home, where he met Rifai's wife and his son, Tarek. He often brought Tarek's favorite chocolate cake with him as a present. The dentist had an extensive library of Arabic literature and liked to talk to his friend about Islam. Rifai hoped that after so many years in Egypt the Christian-born Austrian might consider joining the faith. Buediger graciously accepted the gift of the books. He was a serious, well-read man.

His interests ran toward history. Indeed, he was forever toiling away on a paper about the long-gone empire of the Khazars, whose leaders had converted to Judaism in the eighth century. Most of the world's Jews were not the descendants of the people of Israel, Buediger argued, but were of ethnically Turkic origin and came from the Caucasus. Buediger had sent his report to many powerful and influential people: the United Nations secretary-general Kurt Waldheim; the American secretary of state Cyrus Vance and the national security adviser Zbigniew Brzezinski, as well as numerous senators and congressmen; *Time* and *Newsweek;* the Romanian leader Nicolae Ceauşescu and Yugoslavia's Marshal Tito; the head of Germany's conservative Christian Democratic Union, Helmut Kohl, and the foreign minister Hans-Dietrich Genscher.

The foreigner showed numerous drafts of the research to his friend. History was not Rifai's subject, but he appreciated discussions on serious topics and was impressed by the European's thoroughness. "He was someone," Rifai said, "who wanted to find the truth."

The work on the Khazars would set the historical record straight, in Buediger's view, as well as influence current public opinion. "Till now, the mass of the educated people has no knowledge of the true ethnic and religious history of Palestine," Heim wrote. Once the truth was widely understood, he believed,

> the accurate and true justice corresponding to the law would be
> the re-establishment of the single state of Palestine, eradicated in
> 1948, where should live together only the native people, the semitic
> Moslems, the semitic Hebrews and the semitic Christians, like
> they have lived throughout the millenniums before. The invaders,
> the 1 ½ million Khazars, should regain their native countries or
> join their brothers in the U.S.A.

It was a popular view among Cairo's Muslim population. Egypt had fought several wars against Israel, and Rifai found his friend very sympathetic to the Egyptian cause. He had fought in World War II with the Nazis. Rifai's family had the impression that he had some kind of difficulty with the Jews. "It was understood that there was not much of, what would I say, friendship between him and the Jews," said Tarek, who later also became a dentist. "As far as I remember . . . he came at a time when there was war between Egypt and Israel, and I think he took refuge here in Egypt for that reason, just to be far away from them and in a place that would welcome his ideas."

But Egypt's military and diplomatic relationship with Israel was changing rapidly. Menachem Begin and Anwar el-Sadat had signed the Camp David Accords in 1978 and the Egypt-Israel Peace Treaty in March 1979. "I remember that when Egypt had a peace treaty with Israel that he was afraid," said Mrs. el Rifai, the dentist's wife. "He said that he feared the peace treaty and that now Israelis were also in Egypt."

In his hotel room above the Midan Ataba in Cairo, Heim had gone over and over the testimony that Steinacker had sent him. He wrote numerous chronologies of his life both in English and in German, as if the weeks in Mauthausen would shrink when juxtaposed with the decades from his birth in 1914 to the present day in 1979. He studied the charges against him carefully and concluded that he faced a Zionist conspiracy. Simon Wiesenthal had orchestrated the campaign against him. Wiesenthal, or, as Heim code-named him in letters to the family, "Latte," the German word for the bar of a cage, was the "absolute dominator of all German agencies." The real Wiesenthal, his letters so often unanswered, could only wish that it were so.

The very point of Heim's flight from Europe had been to protect his family, "my school-age children, then 6 and 12 years old, whose schools were next to the detention center and the district court, which would have made it impossible for them to continue attending school if I had stayed." Having now failed to shield his loved ones from the criminal investigation, he viewed his years of self-imposed exile as having effectively been for nothing. Heim believed that he was being punished unjustly for the second time, the first time being his postwar detention. Hardest for him to understand was why his country continued to investigate and prosecute its own veterans.

The loss of the apartment building was a significant financial blow, removing his main means of support, though by no means his only one. He still received his share of the revenues from the hotel overlooking the square where he lived and could count on support from his sister if necessary. But the verdict clearly troubled him. There was still a sliver of hope that his appeal could be won, which spurred him to find a single piece of evidence that might clear him. In the summer between his conviction and his appeal, Heim composed a lengthy missive to the state premier of Baden-Württemberg, Lothar Späth, to try to convince him of his innocence. Heim repeatedly called the case against him "Greuelpropaganda," atrocity propaganda, which he attributed to Wiesenthal.

Heim also defended himself against the charge of anti-Semitism, highlighting what he called his history of positive interactions with Jews as a defense. At the age of ten, he recalled, he played the violin in a duet with a Jewish girl on piano. A Jewish businessman in his hometown was "the only one constantly informed about my athletic successes during my studies in Vienna." During his student days, he lived with a Jewish widow and was treated by a famous Jewish sports surgeon named Professor Mandl. One of his friends in those days was a Jewish medical student, Robert Braun. He even brought Braun back to his family home in Radkersburg one summer. Through his athletic pursuits, Heim came "into contact with athletes from other countries, thereby gaining a tolerant attitude in ethnic and religious matters." Heim also highlighted his friendship with a lawyer named Pauline Kuchelbacher, who had written a letter during his internment affirming that the doctor had helped and supported her after she was disbarred because she was not Aryan.

According to Heim, he was posted to Mauthausen unwillingly, and the brevity of his stay was due to his strenuous efforts to secure a transfer. "Only through athletic occupation could I free myself from service at KL-Mauthausen. If I'd had no athletic skills to exhibit, I could just as easily have landed in Auschwitz, and had to select on the ramp between those capable of working or not!"

If he was such a heinous criminal, Heim asked, why had none of the charges been aired during his detention? "During my internment in the year 1947, all inquiries were made, and if these atrocious allegations were based on the truth, I at that point would have certainly been made to answer for them by anonymous complaint," Heim wrote. "Maybe it bothered Wiesenthal that in 1948 I was already playing in the German ice hockey championship with Bad Nauheim, and this could not be permitted for an SS doctor who worked in a KL, because in those days it was a crime just to have been in the Waffen-SS."

Heim, who had been wounded on the eastern front and won an Iron Cross for his service there, believed that he had suffered enough. "I lost eight years to war and imprisonment in the service of the state, then worked in the hospitals all those years for nothing as an obstetrician," Heim added. "I can justifiably assert that I have spent my entire life for the betterment of my fellow men and practical Christendom."

Heim suggested that the prosecutor in the Berlin *Spruchkammer* case, Magen, who had called him "a beast in the form of a man," should "try to accomplish a dissection, step-by-step, on a living person, then he would have to concede that such a bestial act is impracticable." The worst of the accusations against him, according to Heim, was the story of the twelve-year-old Jewish boy whom the doctor was accused of killing after telling him he had to die because the Jews "were responsible for the war." According to Heim, "No one can deny that at the time I was there, October 1941, only grown-ups (men) were incarcerated at KL-Mauthausen, therefore it is an obvious, clearly proven atrocity-lie."

The fact that a prominent figure like Hans Globke, who helped write the emergency legislation that gave Hitler his extensive dictatorial powers and who served as an adviser to Eichmann's Office of Jewish Affairs, could then be the head of Konrad Adenauer's federal chancellery only underscored what Heim thought was the arbitrary manner in which former Nazis were punished. "The little man alone must atone, when in war he must heed the state and obey postings and commands to particular places, of which he could not suspect beforehand, whereas a Mr. Globke of the Nazi-race ideology could even reach the highest position in the chancellery." Heim believed, in contrast, that he was ordered to Mauthausen by the state and then singled out for punishment.

He felt betrayed by the country he served. "The citizen must be prepared to sacrifice his life for the state authority, and it would never occur to the average citizen to refuse to obey an order because the consequences would be unforeseeable," wrote Heim. In war "the citizen is the slave of the state authority."

It was an impassioned argument that must have taken no small amount of time to draft. It summed up arguments he would make again and again in his personal papers. But according to a note at the top of the letter, he never sent it.

No freedom for killers," chanted the protesters dressed in concentration camp uniforms. They barged into the Bundestag chamber and disrupted the already-charged debate over the statute of limitations for Nazi war crimes. The window for prosecutions in cases of murder had been extended for four years in 1965 and for ten years in 1969. To many conservatives it was time to say enough. But Hans-Jochen Vogel, Germany's justice minister, worried that war criminals might return from hiding the moment the statute expired.

At Wiesenthal's insistence the Jewish Documentation Center in New York had printed up thousands of postcards with a picture of a German shooting a woman with a baby in her arms. "This must never come under the statute of limitations," the postcard read in German, English, and French. The postcards were sent to Chancellor Helmut Schmidt of Germany. Wiesenthal even paid a personal visit to Franz Josef Strauss, the head of the Bavarian Christian Social Union, one of the political parties in favor of letting the prosecutions lapse. The head of the Simon Wiesenthal Center, Rabbi Marvin Hier, led a delegation to meet with Chancellor Schmidt, who was not pleased about the postcards.

The awareness that Nazi war criminals were going unpunished had grown in the United States. On March 28, 1979, the U.S. congresswoman Elizabeth Holtzman of New York announced that the Justice Department was launching the Office of Special Investigations with a budget of $2.3 million to uncover and deport Nazi fugitives in the United States.

"There should be absolutely no question that the Department of Justice and the U.S. government will act unequivocally and vigorously to deny sanctuary in the United States to persons who committed the worst crimes in the history of humanity," Holtzman said.

A mere six months after *Holocaust* aired, lawmakers in Bonn gathered to vote on the statute of limitations. A no vote would likely have served as a symbolic close to the pursuit of war criminals, even if fugitives like Josef Mengele and Aribert Heim could still have been prosecuted, because criminal charges against them had already been filed. But new prosecutions would not have been possible after December 31 if the vote failed. On July 3, the Bundestag voted to suspend the statute of limitations for capital crimes by a narrow vote of 255 to 222.

"During the debate," Heim wrote, "not one Bundestag representative dared raise the war crimes of other countries."

Rüdiger hurried back to Baden-Baden from Denmark. His grandmother had fallen in the garden and been rushed to the hospital with a broken hip. It was unclear exactly what had happened, but within the family it was believed that the elderly woman had succumbed to the stress of the ongoing scandal.

The family could feel cold stares on the street and could not help but notice silent snubs from acquaintances. One long-standing Swiss friend was indignant that no one had told her about the situation. She only learned of it when the police questioned her. The media attention made the family feel like a public spectacle. In the midst of all the excitement Mrs. Bechtold, who was living with her daughter, had either missed or ignored a letter sent to her in Heidelberg.

The follow-up notice was impossible to disregard. This time it was correctly addressed to Baden-Baden. The dispatch gave Käthe Bechtold the biggest shock of all. Rolf-Peter Magen from the Interior Ministry in Berlin demanded to know why she had not answered his letter requesting information about the status of the loan she had made to her son-in-law in 1962. "In my letter from March 12 of this year I asked you for a response," Magen wrote. Since she had not answered him, he said, "I am determining whether I can also begin a case against you under

§ 5 paragraph 2 of the Second Law for the Conclusion of Denazification of December 20, 1955."

Her attorneys responded immediately that his letter had left their client "completely taken aback." Mrs. Bechtold had first met Dr. Heim in 1949 "and knew nothing about his past," they wrote. Her own history "as an opponent of the National Socialist regime" had earned her significant trouble with the regime. She had not seen her son-in-law since 1962. Magen ultimately never brought a case against her, but the stress had taken its toll on the elderly woman.

When Rüdiger arrived, there were no longer photographers or camera crews waiting outside. The rush of attention and requests for interviews were over for now, though the household continued to receive threatening phone calls. He found his grandmother at the hospital with his exhausted mother watching over her. He relieved Friedl so she could rest but was struck by just how ill Mrs. Bechtold looked. It seemed to him there was more wrong with her than just her hip. He rushed to find the ward physician, who quickly diagnosed a potentially deadly embolism. She was hurried into intensive care.

When Rüdiger saw the letter threatening to drag his grandmother to Berlin, he was appalled. His aunt Herta and the lawyer Steinacker were clearly handling the matter, not his grandmother. The prosecution's tactics seemed to miss the mark entirely. He realized that he had approached the case with a certain naïveté, assuming that his father was innocent and that his attorney would swiftly clear everything up. The accelerated court proceedings were disorienting, in particular the question of why the defense was not allowed to call witnesses. He did not understand how the panel could determine that his father had killed hundreds of people based only on written testimony. Rüdiger thought it was against "the spirit of the republic we live in." The conclusion that he drew from the speed with which this complicated, nearly four-decade-old criminal case was handled was that people wanted to get it out of the way as soon as possible.

"Don't worry about what I think," he wrote to his father. "I accept you and am on your side."

I have the wish to visit you and talk with you, but it doesn't seem to be the right time just now. The whole thing will go on for another while and then lose its public interest. Other things will be given to the people to gossip about. Right now we live in an epoch of desperation, isolation, and continuous assassinating of all that smells of humanity. People feel and think like robots. Give them fear, they will feel afraid; give them hate, they will feel hatred toward everything, even toward their own wives or husbands.

He concluded his letter by telling his father, "I don't want to say specifically what I'm doing but be sure and confident about me! I love you."

CHAPTER 43

Heim's appeal was delayed from October to December. In his filing, Steinacker insisted that his client had performed only two emergency surgeries at Mauthausen. In one case he removed the appendix of a young inmate, who survived. He attempted to do the same for an older patient, who also suffered from cancer and died during the procedure. Steinacker questioned the constitutionality of the first ruling, saying that it violated the principle of retroactive enforcement of the law. The rules had changed, in other words, and his client was being tried after the fact.

Steinacker opened the hearing by arguing that the earlier ruling should be put on hold until the criminal case in Baden-Baden was decided. The motion was rejected. Steinacker then asked "in the interest of a fair proceeding" that the surviving witnesses be subject to cross-examination. The court deemed that unnecessary, as was the presentation of additional witnesses for the defense.

On December 17 the initial ruling was upheld. The appeals panel found that Heim had murdered several patients at Mauthausen. "At least three cases" were proven, and it was not the duty of the panel "to prove Heim's remaining countless acts or to clear up contradictions." The penalty of 510,000 deutsche marks, "the value of a Berlin apartment house that Heim owns," was also upheld. On March 7, 1980, the Berlin Interior Ministry informed Steinacker in writing that if "your client has not paid the fine of 510,000 deutsche marks as well as the trial costs within a week," the apartment building would be confiscated. In fact, taking the apartment building was not a simple legal matter.

The prosecutor's office in Baden-Baden was demanding 18,000 deutsche marks to cover its costs related to the case. The rivalry between state authorities deepened when the prosecutors in Baden-Baden seized all of Heim's assets "in the territory of the Federal Republic of Germany and West Berlin." The demands of the competing authorities would have to be reconciled and Heim's assets would have to be unfrozen before the house could be sold. The building, like its owner, had slipped into a sort of limbo.

During all this time, Aedtner continued to pursue the investigation against Heim. The detective had traveled almost the length of Germany in the hopes of finding a living witness. The *Spruchkammer* was nowhere near as rigorous as a trial in criminal court. The prosecutors had left several holes that Aedtner needed to close. With each passing year the pool of potential eyewitnesses was dwindling. But the media attention from the civil case led new witnesses to come forward. The question was, were they reliable?

Aedtner received a letter from an attorney in Lübeck on the Baltic coast, promising almost ideal testimony. A survivor, Erwin Balczuhn, had come forward. He had been in the operating room and seen Heim administer lethal injections to six inmates. Balczuhn's attorney described how his client watched the victims make "twitching and convulsing movements" as they died. Balczuhn had read an article in the *Lübecker Nachrichten* newspaper about the case against Heim, which brought back memories of what he had seen in the sick bay nearly forty years before.

At the Lübeck South police precinct, Balczuhn told Aedtner that he started working at the Mauthausen quarry in October 1940. Roughly a year later he was in the infirmary for a week having the toenail removed from his big toe. He recalled that when he was waiting in the hall outside the operating room, he heard loud screaming. About ten or fifteen minutes later, he watched Heim come out smelling powerfully of gasoline. He watched as orderlies carried out six naked corpses. Their clothes lay on the floor, where he could see the colored badges indicating that the bodies on the stretchers consisted of four Jews, one Pole, and one Russian soldier. He tried to ask a fellow inmate about what he had seen and was told, "Man, keep your mouth shut or you'll be up next."

Aedtner thought this was an affecting story but not the eyewitness account of the actual murders that Balczuhn's attorney had promised. But at least Balczuhn could place Heim at Mauthausen at precisely the time he was alleged to have committed the atrocities. Balczuhn described Heim's height and said he must have been quite young, perhaps between twenty-four and twenty-nine years old, at the time. In fact, he was twenty-seven. The former inmate even remembered the scar in the corner of Heim's mouth. He picked him out of the photo lineup.

Balczuhn had spent nearly five years at the camp, staying long enough to hear from American soldiers how they had tracked down and killed the camp commandant. But he remembered quite clearly that Heim's tenure was a short one. The doctor had probably gone by early 1942. Aedtner took the new witness seriously enough to have him deposed by a prosecutor in front of a judge, with a defense attorney standing in for Steinacker. When they did the follow-up deposition, the defense attorney quickly proved that the media attention could be a double-edged sword. He immediately objected to the photo lineup since "countless pictures of the accused had appeared in the press throughout the federal republic."

Balczuhn was not perfect, but he was a witness, a living witness. There were few enough of those. Aedtner had continued sending lists of potential witnesses to his counterparts in Vienna. His Austrian colleagues sent them back with black crosses in the margins next to many of the names, marking them as deceased.

LEFT: SS officer Dr. Aribert Heim is pictured here in a tuxedo, enjoying Germany's postwar prosperity.

BELOW: Aribert Ferdinand Heim was born in Austria on June 28, 1914, the same day that Archduke Franz Ferdinand was murdered, plunging Europe into war. His twin brother was stillborn.

LEFT: His father, Josef Ferdinand Heim, was a gendarmerie commander in the town of Radkersburg in what was then Austria-Hungary.

BELOW: Heim moved to Vienna in the fall of 1931, when he was seventeen years old, to begin studying at the university there.

ABOVE: Heim (far left, with bandage) played professional ice hockey and was so skilled he was invited to play for the Austrian national team. He suffered a gash to the corner of his mouth, which left a distinctive V-shaped scar.

RIGHT: Heim (center) at the University of Vienna, where he completed his medical degree in 1940 at the age of twenty-five, a few months after World War II broke out. He was drafted into the SS upon graduation.

LEFT: Heim's older brother, Josef Heim (right), was a staunch Nazi who took part in a failed coup attempt in Austria and then served in exile in Germany as part of Hitler's Austrian Legion until the Anschluss. He was killed during the invasion of Crete in 1941.

BELOW: Heim worked as a doctor at Mauthausen for several months in 1941. The concentration camp, located near the Danube River in Austria, was one of the harshest in the Nazi system, designed as a forced labor camp for quarrying granite.

ABOVE: Heim's signature on the Mauthausen operation book. Records show he operated 263 times while he was at the camp. All eleven of the Jewish inmates he operated on were listed as having died within a few weeks.

RIGHT: After leaving Mauthausen, Heim, pictured here in SS uniform while in Finland, was wounded on the eastern front and received the Iron Cross.

LEFT: After the war, Heim was detained by the victorious Allies for nearly three years, first at a POW camp in France and then in a series of internment facilities in the American sector of Germany. He was released in December 1947 as part of a Christmas amnesty.

BELOW: After his release, he resumed practicing medicine (right, leaning over the patient) and played in the German professional hockey championship game under his own name.

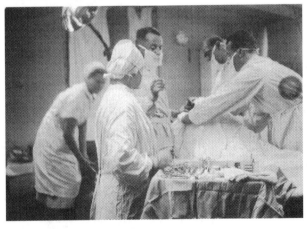

ABOVE: Heim married Friedl Bechtold in July 1949, and they moved to this villa on Maria-Viktoria-Strasse in the resort town of Baden-Baden in 1953. They lived comfortably and enjoyed vacations in Italy and Switzerland, where Friedl's parents owned a place in Lugano.

RIGHT: Heim practiced as a gynecologist and Friedl gave birth to two sons, Aribert Christian and Rolf Rüdiger (pictured with Heim).

LEFT: Realizing that the authorities were closing in on him, Heim fled his home in 1962. There were rumors that he had settled in Egypt, where a number of former Nazis and German weapons experts had found refuge. Heim, pictured here after his escape, on the Mediterranean coast.

BELOW: Fritz Steinacker (at right in a photograph taken by Heim) was widely known as a defense lawyer for Nazis, including Josef Mengele and Heim. The lawyer visited Heim in Cairo and carried back a message from Heim to his wife, asking if his sons could travel to his new home where "the climate and the sports facilities are world famous."

LEFT: Alfred Aedtner spearheaded the search for Aribert Heim as a police investigator focusing on war crimes for the West German government. He joined the war crimes unit at its inception in 1959, and by 1973, as head of the department in Stuttgart, Aedtner's primary target was the fugitive doctor.

BELOW: Aedtner developed a close working relationship with renowned Nazi hunter and Mauthausen survivor Simon Wiesenthal. From his office in Vienna, Wiesenthal used his media contacts to focus the public's attention on the SS doctor.

LEFT: Aedtner tracked down Heim's illegitimate daughter, Waltraut Böser, while she was living in Switzerland and working as a pharmacist. Although she never met her father, she inherited his love of sports and aptitude for languages.

BELOW: In 1979, German authorities seized an apartment house in Berlin that belonged to Heim, squeezing his income. He moved to the Kasr el-Madina, a hotel in a working-class Cairo neighborhood, where he rented a small room.

RIGHT: With the help of Egyptian associates, Heim was able to purchase property and remain in Egypt even after his German passport expired. At right is his Egyptian driver's license.

BELOW: Even as his exile in Egypt grew from a temporary measure to a permanent circumstance, Heim maintained his innocence, drafting numerous written arguments and letters about the case. This is the first page of a handwritten chronicle of his life.

Chronicle of my course of life!

1914	born in Radkersburg, Austria, son of Joseph Heim Gendarmerie-District-Commander
1920 - 1932	Primary school in R. and Secondary school in Graz, Mary-Institute
1933 - 1939	Study of medicine in Vienna, Victory in German-Icehockey-Championship 1939 (EKE) in Berlin
17.4.1940	Military service in Army SS Reserve Battalion Deutschland, Munich
June 1940	War against France as ordinary soldier (car driver)
18.40 - 1.2.41	Medical Battal. France, Lieutenant 1.8.40 Red-Cross Hospital Surgical Dep., Belgrade
	Resettlement of Ethnic German, Earthquake-Relief-Action Rumania
14.41 - 19.6.41	Concentration Camp Oranienburg/Berlin, Camp-Hospital, Surgical Depart., Assistant
20.6.1941	My older brother, Medical-doctor-Lieutenant of parachute-troops, killed in Action in Crete
19.6.41 - 14.7.41	Troop-doctor of the soldier-guards of Concentration Camp Buchenwald/Weimar
14.7.41 - 26.11.41	Reserve-Battalion LAH Berlin-Lichterfelde, Troop doctor, October 41 Conc.Camp Mauthausen
	Troop doctor for the soldier guards and for the camp's inmates = Camp Hospital, 7 weeks only
28.11.41 - 24.2.42	SS Hospital Vienna, Surgical Department, Assistant
24.2.42 - 21.10.42	Doctor of the examination Board for the SS Army-troops
	Brunswick dwelling at D'Ing. Egger, Büssing factories
	Munich " " Thyssen
	Nuremberg " " Bauersachs, Textile whole dealer
	Breslau " in Board-office house, First Lieutenant 1.9.42
21.10.42 - 31.2.44	SS Mountaineer fighter Division Nord, East Front, wounded, honoured with Iron
	Cross II Infantry-Attacking and Wounding Decorations, Captain 20.4.44
3.1.45 - 15.3.45	West Front, Vosges mountains, — USA War Captivity —
1945/46	in USA Prisoner of War Hospitals, surgical Department, Assistant, France
1947	American / German political Internment, Hohenasperg Ludwigsburg Jagstfeld / Saline Mine
1948/49	Icehockey-club Bad Nauheim, participation German Championship 1948 and 1948/49
	Children Hospital Jagstfeld East Hosp. Friedberg, Denazification Chamber Neckarsulm not concerned
1950 - 1962	Hospital for women, Ludwigshafen, own publications in Gynaecology-Periodicals
	and besides some years Gynaecologist-Praxis in Baden/Baden
1956	German - Austrian citizenships procedure, Mannheim
	German - Passport 14.1.1957, Police-Presidency,
1958	Apartment-House Purchase in Berlin

ABOVE: As Egypt was becoming more religiously conservative, Heim, raised a Christian, began reading the Koran and visiting mosques, including al-Azhar, the famous center of Islamic learning in Cairo.

RIGHT: In 1980, the fugitive converted to Islam. Heim, who had gone by the names Ferdinand Heim and Alfred Buediger in Cairo, adopted the Muslim name Tarek Hussein Farid, throwing investigators farther off his trail.

ALLAH ✹ ALLAH ✹ ALLAH ✹ ALLAH ✹ ALLAH ✹ ALLAH ✹ ALLAH

In the name of ALLAH, most Gracious most Merciful

AL-AZHAR
ISLAMIC RESEARCH ACADEMY
Committee of Fatwa

CERTIFICATE OF CONVERSION TO ISLAM

Praise be to Allah, Creator of all, and peace and blessings be upon our Prophet Muhammad, Members of his household and all his companions.

This is to certify that, Mr./Mrs. _Heim Ferdinand_ from : _W—Germany_ follower of Christian Religion and Residing at : _Cairo, Abdel Aziz 39_ came to the headquarters of the Committee of Fatwa (Islamic Committee for Religious Affairs) affiliated to Al-Azhar, where He / She expressed His / Her desire to be converted to the Islamic Religion. In the presnce of the Committee He/She repeated the following Islamic Formula :

« I hereby bear witness that there is no diety but Allah the only God, and that Muhammad is his last Prophet and Messenger, that has been sent by Him untoall mankind as a bearer of good tidings and warner. I believe in Allah, His Angels, His Scriptures, His Messengers, Dooms Day / Resurrection Day and Pre - Destination, good or evil. I have renounced all Religions other than the Religion of Islam, and I hereby bear witness that Jesus Christ is Allah's Servant and Apostle and that Muhammad is the last of all Prophets and Messengers. »

Peace and blessings be upon Muhammad, the illiterate Messenger, upon Members of his household and all his commanions.

The Committee of Fatwa issued this certificate of conversion to the Religion of Islam for bearer to submit to the competent authorities in conformity with legal procedure.

Date : _12. 2. 8_ (Signed) _Heim Ferdinand_

Head of Committee of Fatwa
Al - Azhar

ABOVE: Heim's son Rüdiger visited his father numerous times in his hiding place and kept in touch with him through letters using code names.

LEFT: Aedtner worked with Wiesenthal to continue the search for Heim even after he retired from the police force. But as he grew older, he focused his efforts on archiving the case files from Nazi investigations and giving speeches about the crimes of the Holocaust.

RIGHT: Large money transfers from Rüdiger Heim to his friends Gaetano Pisano and Blandine Pellet in Spain led investigators to wrongly conclude that the couple was harboring the fugitive Nazi doctor. They were later cleared of any involvement.

BELOW: In 2008, the authors used this picture of Heim to track down his friends and acquaintances in Egypt.

ABOVE: The authors recovered a briefcase full of Heim's papers, including medical records and correspondence with his family. Forensic tests and handwriting analysis proved that the briefcase was Heim's and that he had hidden in Cairo for decades.

RIGHT: Now a grown man with his own family, Mahmoud Doma recalled learning English and playing games as a child on the roof of his family's hotel with the man he knew as Uncle Tarek.

Heim on the roof of the Kasr el-Madina in 1990. He is believed to have died in 1992. His body was never discovered.

CHAPTER 44

Aedtner's efforts to secure the testimony of Dr. Wrazlaw Busek, one of the men who kept the list of the dead at Mauthausen, had ended in failure. His letter to Queens, New York, had been returned unopened. It turned out that Dr. Busek was dead. Busek's stepson passed along five new leads, the names and addresses of five Polish survivors. Five men in five cities behind the Iron Curtain—Bydgoszcz, Gdańsk, Grójec, Toruń, and Warsaw—five new chances to find firsthand testimony against Heim.

Wiesenthal began to consider the possibility that Heim, like Eichmann and so many others, had fled to South America. Media reports said that Interpol believed the fugitive doctor was living in Venezuela. Berlin's *Tagesspiegel* reported, "A picture of Heim appeared in all the newspapers in the capital of Caracas." Wiesenthal had also received a tip that Heim might be living on Spain's Mediterranean coast, where a wealthy doctor by the name of Umberto Hahn occupied the Chalet Partida Soria in Alicante.

The letter with the tip included a map with the words "Villa Dr. Hahn" marked in red pen. "Since it would be relatively simple to change the forename 'Aribert' to 'Umberto' and 'Heim' to 'Hahn,' maybe it would be worthwhile trying to learn a little more about this man," Wiesenthal wrote to Aedtner. Their correspondence remained for the most part businesslike, though the younger German police officer's tone was increasingly friendly and at times almost reverential. Their working relationship was deepening into something more, but Aedtner was still just one of many around the world with whom Wiesenthal cooperated.

Wiesenthal also received information that Heim might be on the Spanish island of Ibiza, a popular destination for West German tourists. He was always on the lookout for surrogates he could ask to follow up leads. The Board of Deputies of British Jews put Wiesenthal in touch with an Englishwoman named Gloria Mound who owned an apartment on the island. "We would be very grateful if you could undertake any researches without personal risks," Wiesenthal wrote. "Be sure that we'll handle the whole case most confidentially." She wrote back under her personal letterhead that she could help him but underscored the fact that "discretion is vital."

In the meantime, Aedtner had gotten a hold of a second photograph of Heim, taken in Mannheim in November 1959. Though the picture was already twenty years old, it was more recent than the first photograph he had obtained. The shot appeared to have been taken at a formal event, with Heim in black tie. Aedtner cautioned his colleague not to share the picture with the press. The detective had already shown the photograph to Interpol in Madrid and promised to telephone "as soon as there is any news from Spain."

The picture landed in the media anyway. The Spanish magazine *Interviú* published a long article purporting to follow the doctor's footsteps through Ibiza, which the magazine called the "Island of the Nazis." In his tuxedo, under the spy-novel headline "Heim, the Man with a Thousand Faces," he looked like someone James Bond might cross paths with at the local casino. A German couple was certain they had seen him deep-sea fishing. The myth was outrunning the investigation.

In Venezuela, Wiesenthal worked with a man in Caracas named Hector Gouverneur to determine whether a German immigrant named Werner Ghunter in San Bernardino might actually be the fugitive Heim. The connections were often gossamer thin, but Aedtner dutifully followed up all the leads that Wiesenthal sent him. At one point the detective even forwarded a Spanish translation of an arrest warrant to Wiesenthal's hotel in New York, along with an important new find, a copy of Heim's fingerprints, taken by the U.S. Army when he was a prisoner of war.

With little firm information, the search for Heim focused more and more on the Spanish-speaking world. More publicity and more inquiries led to more tips, in a self-reinforcing cycle that seemed to turn every suspicion into a foregone but unfounded conclusion.

Unbeknownst to either the Nazi hunter or the detective, there was a connection to the case in Latin America, Heim's illegitimate daughter, Waltraut Böser. Growing up without a father in postwar Austria had been difficult. She had longed to know more about him and most of all to see a photograph of him. Waltraut looked nothing like her own mother or her younger brother. They both had dark hair while she was blond. They were on the smaller side and shied away from sports while she was tall, strong, and physically fearless.

Once when she was a girl, while attending an ice hockey game in her hometown of Kitzbühel, Waltraut caught a stray puck that had sailed over the goal and into the cheering crowd at the stadium. She pushed and wriggled her way to the front of the crowd to return it to the goalie from the visiting Viennese team. Waltraut might have expected him to say "thanks" or even hoped for "nice catch" but was unprepared for what he said instead. He looked at her closely and told her, "I played with your father." She was in shock as he skated away. She ran home, missing the rest of the game.

She had inherited her father's athleticism, her mother and her aunt told her, his talent for languages, and his love of travel. Her hopes of becoming an Olympic gold medalist with the Austrian ski team were dashed by a terrible fracture of her lower leg when she was fifteen. She knew that her father had been a doctor, and she developed an interest in medicine, reading and rereading the 1956 book *The Century of Surgeons* and dreaming of one day becoming one.

In the summer of 1962, after graduating from high school, she worked up the courage to visit Heim's mother, the grandmother she had never met. She found Anna Heim and her elder daughter, Hilda, living in Graz. Neither asked who she was. The resemblance must have been such that it was unnecessary. They invited her inside, but the looks her grandmother directed at her gave Waltraut the feeling that she was not welcome.

"I don't want to trouble you, but I'd like to see a photo of my father," she said. Waltraut's father had died in Russia, Heim's mother answered. They did not have any photographs of him. It was clear that the conversation was over. "Thank you and pardon me for barging in on you," Waltraut told the two women. Then she left. In her mind, the matter felt closed.

Before moving to Switzerland, she earned a master's degree in pharmacology at the University of Innsbruck. She worked at a pharmacy in Geneva, where she got a thrill out of celebrity customers like Sophia Loren, who loyally went to Waltraut for her special beauty treatments because the Austrian woman spoke such good Italian.

At the age of thirty-four, she met a man from Chile through a friend in Lausanne, and they fell in love. They married at the Goldenes Dachl in Innsbruck, a local landmark with a golden roof made of thousands of gilded copper tiles for the Holy Roman emperor Maximilian I. On an adventurous road trip from Canada to Costa Rica, Waltraut learned she was pregnant. The couple settled in her husband's native Chile. She was unaware that her father had survived the war. Nor did she realize that she had visited his mother and sister at the same time in 1962 that he was planning his escape from Germany. She was living on the opposite end of the world, her past and her father long behind her.

Waltraut also did not know that she had two half brothers living back in Europe. The elder of the two, Aribert Christian Heim, changed his name to just Christian. Investigators and family members concur that he had little or no contact with his father after he left, never visited him in Egypt as Rüdiger had, and kept his distance from the entire affair.

Rüdiger had not visited his father since the story became public. His residency permit for Denmark, which he had been told was all but complete, was suddenly rejected. He received his passport back with a stamp that read, "Must leave the country within 20 days." He continued to live there illegally, but as the restaurant became more and more successful, he grew frustrated that as an undocumented worker he was unable to buy into the business.

In a letter to Herta, Heim described how he regretted not receiving word from his son. "Unfortunately, I no longer hear from the little one, although it is high time that we talked through everything," Heim wrote in the summer of 1982. "Yet that which has not happened yet can still come to pass."

Although Heim's case was his top priority, Aedtner had other investigations to pursue. In 1981 he traveled to Israel with a young German prosecutor to build a case against a work-detail commander from Auschwitz, Karl Pöllmann. Before leaving Germany, Aedtner had been in a car accident and was forced to wear a neck brace. A little on the vain side even in middle age, he wore an ascot to cover up the unsightly white device. The trip, Aedtner's second to Israel, was for business, but he used the opportunity to see some of the country as well. He was there for nearly a month, from May 16 to June 13, using the Hotel Moriah in Tel Aviv as a base for exploring the ancient land.

An avid reader with an inquisitive mind, Aedtner was fascinated by the country's history. He made friends with an Israeli police officer who every Christmas would send him a crate of oranges. He was photographed on the coast in a white cap and short-sleeved shirt standing beside a camel, and again in his red bathing trunks, slathered in mud from the Dead Sea. But Aedtner did not notice that he was drinking too little water and had become severely dehydrated. He passed out on the beach and might have been in serious trouble if people nearby had not noticed that something was wrong and revived him. It might have been the heat, but the episode might also have been a harbinger of more serious health problems.

He was no longer young, and his health was becoming more fragile. His wife tried to get him to eat a little less, to skip the beers he loved so much, but for the most part he ignored her. All those nights on the road, eating his favorite dishes, roulade, stuffed peppers, and schnitzel, were having an effect. His small paunch had grown to a big belly, and he became diabetic, which likely contributed to his dehydration. Despite his worsening health, his search for Heim continued unabated.

It took more than a year, but between Aedtner, Germany's Federal Criminal Police, Interpol, and the Venezuelan authorities, they managed to track down Wiesenthal's Venezuelan tip. The suspect Ghunter turned out to be Werner Günter Lang, a music teacher of Czech ancestry almost eight years Heim's senior. After comparing his fingerprints with Heim's, they realized they had come to another dead end. The investigation appeared to be stalling. "We haven't heard from one another in quite a while," Aedtner wrote to Wiesenthal, "because not much new has come out in our endeavor." He told Wiesenthal that they were sending undercover investigators to try to find old friends or relatives who might know where Heim was hiding.

By October 1982, Aedtner appeared to be running out of leads. There were "no additional concrete clues about the suspect and no additional criminal-investigative possibilities in the search," he wrote in his case report. He began to focus on Ilse Lamprecht, a friend of Heim's ex-wife. A source told investigators that she received mail from Latin America "presumably from Heim." The prosecutor's office in Baden-Baden requested searches of Lamprecht's mail as well as a phone tap. The court found the surveillance of Lamprecht excessive. It did, however, allow the tapping of Heim's ex-wife's phone.

Three months later Aedtner conceded that his health was so poor he could no longer continue working full-time. He put in for retirement. His colleagues began to plan a farewell party. The invitation had an illustration of Aedtner in profile and a ship plowing through the sea. A colleague had written a few rhyming lines, comparing the hunt for Nazi fugitives to a fishing expedition: "For the catch the old captain no longer sails out. In the future he'll stay there at home in his house . . . He did so very much for our land, even Wiesenthal gave him his hand."

On April 29, 1983, the cantina at state police headquarters was decked out like a restaurant, with white tablecloths, red napkins, and flowers on every table. They even hired a pianist. The guest of honor received bouquets and books. His son came, along with friends and colleagues from Munich and Berlin. Aedtner's predecessor and mentor, Robert Waida, gave a speech, surprisingly somber for the occasion, asking whether too many perpetrators like Aribert Heim had gotten away. "I have the feeling," Waida said, "that we went wrong somewhere."

Wiesenthal, who was unable to attend, telegraphed congratulations. He was sorry he could not be there, but he had already booked a trip to the United States. Perhaps the old Nazi hunter knew what the rest of them did not. Aedtner might have put in for his pension, but he would not be able to quit the search for Heim. Without work to fill his days, Aedtner followed the local daily newspaper, watched the evening news, and kept up with the hardbound volumes of the *Reader's Digest* book club. But after little more than a year he was back at the central office, following up leads about Heim.

CHAPTER 46

Losing the rent money from his apartment building meant that Heim needed to economize, but the move to Port Said Street also meant greater safety. The farther away from downtown he moved, the fewer westerners he would see, reducing the chance of discovery. The Egyptians in the Kasr el-Madina Hotel noticed how the tall foreigner lived a much simpler life than most other Europeans. His small room at the hotel cost him only 7 Egyptian pounds a night.

The floor was tile, with an inexpensive little rug. The walls were painted light green, but the color only went about two-thirds of the way up to the ceiling. The rest was bare, chalky white plaster. He had a steel-frame bed and a simple wardrobe for his clothes. There was a cheap metal office cabinet, a small table, and a single chair, along with an extra stool.

The kitchen, such as it was, consisted of a tin end table with a single gas burner atop it, not unlike a camping stove. Below was a miniature refrigerator. He owned only two plates and two glasses. The bathroom held just a simple white ceramic washbasin, a plastic mirror, and a toilet, along with dozens of plastic bottles filled with water, a reserve for when the pressure was weak and there was no water that high up in the building. There were no private baths, just a common shower room on each floor for the hotel guests.

A degree of chaos crept into Heim's living space simply because the room was so small. Books were piled high wherever there was room, dictionaries and reference books, history books and language studies. Employees at the hotel had never seen so many books, in English, German, and Arabic, including a large copy of the Koran. The foreigner spent a lot of time in his room reading.

Although he hung some photographs taken on the streets of Cairo, there were no family portraits on the walls. Those he kept in the wardrobe, hidden from view. He had photographs of the family, vacation photographs of his ex-wife and children that his sister sent him. He even paid an Egyptian to make paintings of his Friedl and their sons from some of the photographs. He also had a Grundig shortwave radio so he could hear news broadcasts or enjoy Viennese lieder on Austria's public radio. He often sat on the balcony facing the street and watched the busy little shopping street across the way.

Though he told his neighborhood acquaintances he was a businessman, he would often offer minor medical aid. In a sheaf of documents he kept with him in Egypt about Mauthausen, he left a note in the margins that said someone named Ali should take Inderal, a medicine for angina.

His manners were impeccable, never forgetting the formal greeting of "salaam alaikum." He played with the hotel proprietor's children, seeming to love them as if they were his own. He did not talk about where he came from. "You have to respect that there are certain boundaries," was the way Ali al Hussein Ahmed, a porter at the hotel, saw it. "Not everyone wants to talk about his past."

Mahmoud Doma loved growing up in a Cairo hotel as the son of the owner. There was always some new traveler ready to share stories about his native land or a peddler with a suitcase full of whirring toys eager to demonstrate his latest product for the amusement of Mahmoud and his siblings. With its seventy rooms and its location in the heart of old Cairo, the Kasr el-Madina Hotel was usually filled with guests from the Middle East hungry to do business in the bustling city. A few guests called the brown nine-story building home.

The Palestinian with the big, bushy mustache and ink-black hair on the sixth floor was quiet and kept to himself. He left the hotel in the mornings and came back at night hardly saying a word to anyone, though he lived there for years. The portly money changer everyone called Sheikh Taha on the fifth floor talked to everyone. He sat outside on a little wooden chair in front of the hotel chattering away with the merchants hawking clothes and electronics on the ground floor. But the only one who befriended Mahmoud, who taught him English and gave him books to read, was the Austrian who lived next door to his family on the eighth floor, Tarek Hussein Farid.

Mahmoud could not remember exactly when he moved in, but it was when the boy was still little, certainly before he turned ten. "When I opened my eyes, he was there," was how he liked to put it. Mahmoud knew the man he called Amu Tarek, Uncle Tarek, also went by the name Alfred Buediger. He had moved to Egypt because of a problem with his back, which healed in Egypt's warm, dry climate. Mahmoud also knew his friend had a wife and two sons back home in Germany, but they did not come to visit.

Unlike Tarek, Mahmoud himself was hardly ever alone. He was one of twenty-five children from his father's three wives. Mahmoud's mother and her seven children lived in the hotel. Of her four boys and three girls, he was the eldest, but many of his half siblings also came and went, along with the sixteen staff members and of course the guests. Every day people arrived in Cairo from the countryside hoping to better their circumstances in the capital. Centuries earlier the Nile had flowed down what became Port Said Street, and now the street channeled crowds of men and women along the river's former path. It was loud and busy, and it smelled of food, garbage, coal fires, and the sickly sweet smell of human sweat. When the Doma children were bored, they went up to the roof. Uncle Tarek had set up a net there where he taught the children to play tennis, badminton, and Ping-Pong.

Everyone at the hotel laughed in a friendly manner at the foreigner's devotion to exercise. He was in his late sixties but still very strong, and no one could fathom why he would take the stairs all the way up to the eighth floor when the elevator was right there. "Sport!" he would answer and invite them to join him. He walked everywhere, for miles. He would only take a taxi if he was going as far as Giza. He also visited one of the sporting clubs or the university, where he played squash and tennis, swam, and ran track.

Mahmoud would tag along with Uncle Tarek when his chores at the hotel allowed and he thought he could keep up. Sometimes they simply went on errands, to buy pens or film for Heim's camera at the Kodak store. Other times they went to the zoo or even to the pyramids. Uncle Tarek carried his camera with him—he loved to take photographs—but he never wanted to be photographed himself. When he returned from his solitary walks, he would give the children bonbons or Egyptian candies and sit down for a cup of tea with their father. Sometimes he ate with the family.

In the evening they could often hear him pounding away on his typewriter. He wrote letters all the time, mostly in English and German from what Mahmoud could tell. He tried to teach Mahmoud and the other Doma children European languages. He would say a word in Arabic, then say the same word in English and then in French. Finally, he would write down all three. He gave Mahmoud history texts and detective novels. He bought him a book by the Egyptian writer Abbas Mahmoud al-Aqqad, in the hopes of inspiring the boy. He wanted the children to study and to be curious about the world around them.

There was a telephone in the hotel downstairs where he received calls from his own physician and from his Egyptian business associates, Nagy Khafagy and Rifat. Mahmoud was more familiar with Khafagy, who took care of Tarek's more sensitive paperwork. "Dr. Nagy always extended his residency permit," Mahmoud said. "Dr. Nagy was responsible for everything that had something to do with the government." He recalled that Khafagy had power of attorney for bank matters and that he brought Uncle Tarek money from the hotel on Midan Ataba.

Once in a while Heim's younger son would call him. "Why don't your sons come here?" Mahmoud asked. "They are very busy and they don't like Egypt," the Austrian answered.

"I had the impression that he seemed glum," Mahmoud said. "No one checked up on him. No one showed an interest in him." Mahmoud thought that there was some kind of tension within the family, but it was clear that Tarek missed them. Once Mahmoud had seen a black-and-white picture of the man's whole family that he kept hidden in his room.

———

Tarek's Egyptian friends liked to take credit for convincing him to convert to Islam. The Domas recalled how they had bought him a Koran in German at the special German-language bookstore, a holy book that had to be ordered all the way from Saudi Arabia. "When he came to us, he was not a Muslim yet," said Sharif Doma, one of Mahmoud's older half brothers. "Then he started a friendship with my father, and this friendship led to them talking about Islam and the Muslim religion." Not far from the hotel was one of the preeminent mosques in the world. "Any Christian who wants to convert needs to take lessons at the al-Azhar, has to go to al-Azhar," Sharif said, "and the sheikh at al-Azhar has then to confirm that he is a Muslim."

The dentist Dr. Rifai said that it was he who brought his friend to the famous mosque to join the faith. "He came across to me as a man who was very interested in Islam, and therefore I took him to the al-Azhar sheikh," Dr. Rifai said. "There he did his *shahada*." On February 16, 1980, at one o'clock in the afternoon, the sixty-five-year-old Austrian appeared before the officials of the great mosque and said that there was "no god but Allah and Muhammad is his prophet," as he renounced all other faiths and accepted Islam as his religion. "With that his entry into Islam was complete."

The friendly competition to take credit for his decision to convert showed how important it was to the Egyptians that an educated, respected man from the West would not only learn their language but adopt their faith as well. Of great interest to his Muslim friends were the names he selected for himself. "He chose the name Tarek because also my son's name is Tarek," said the dentist, who added that Hussein was the name of the imam who oversaw the conversion.

None of them had considered the possibility that he might have had very different reasons to change his name as well as to convert. "Even his bank account was in his Muslim name," Sharif Doma said. "All the other people then only called him by his new name, his Muslim name." Barely two months after the appeal of the *Spruchkammer* verdict failed, Heim abandoned his birth name for a new Muslim one. The name could be viewed as a relatively good effort at preserving some of the sounds of his German name: with Tarek for Aribert, Farid for Ferdinand, and Hussein for Heim.

CHAPTER 47

When Rüdiger Heim returned to Egypt to visit his father again, the ever-practical Heim asked only for razor blades and Faber-Castell pencils. Rüdiger brought exactly what he was told. He was not, however, fully prepared for what awaited him upon their reunion. The two men could no longer avoid the topic of his father's wartime service and fugitive status as they had during his first visit.

For hours each day, Rüdiger had to relive his father's months at Mauthausen. Heim defined the terms of the discussion with his son. They did not talk about the condition of the inmates brought to the infirmary from the stone quarry. They did not discuss how the patients were treated. Heim tried to reinforce the point that he did not want to work at Mauthausen. "That was something he expressed to me unequivocally: that he did everything he could to get out of this concentration camp as quickly as possible," Rüdiger said. Each day the son dutifully walked from the Scarabee Hotel downtown to listen to hours of lectures on the crimes his father was accused of committing.

The visit was much more of a shock than his previous trip to Cairo and not just because of the civil case. The city was busier, more crowded. Downtown had fallen into disrepair. The country had become more religious, and the girls in miniskirts were gone. Women in modest clothes and head scarves had replaced them. The religious revival was in part due to the rising tide of migrants from more observant villages. But many young people had simply fled their stagnant economy and found jobs thanks to the oil boom in Saudi Arabia and other Gulf states. When they returned with petrodollars in their pockets, they often practiced a stricter Wahhabi form of Islam. Rüdiger realized that along with changing his name to Tarek Hussein Farid, his father had converted to Islam. But this also was a subject they did not discuss.

As in his instructions to Steinacker, Heim talked a great deal about when he was actually at Mauthausen. Witnesses described him working at the camp in 1942 when in reality he left in 1941. *Der Spiegel* magazine said he had committed his crimes between a special room for shooting prisoners in the neck and the gas chamber, when neither existed in 1941.

He spoke very specifically about the charge that he had murdered an older inmate. Heim explained that the patient wanted an operation for his hernia but the doctor determined once he began that the man had not only a hernia but also cancer. That was the reason he had taken the intestines out of the abdomen. "If someone comes in at that point who has never seen an operation, he would say, 'Look, he's tearing out all his intestines,'" he told his son. Rüdiger asked him why he was even there in the first place. His father explained how in order for him to finish his studies, it was necessary for him to enlist in the Waffen-SS. He did not realize that would mean service at concentration camps.

Eventually, Rüdiger could not take it anymore. "The subject isn't pretty, and naturally your head is smoking after two, three hours." His father suggested he spend a week on the Red Sea to recuperate. Rüdiger traveled to Hurghada, where he stayed in a small bungalow on stilts at the edge of the water. He found he could get along quite well on his own and that his few phrases of Arabic were beginning to coalesce into coherent speech. He went for walks and swam. He read extensively about Egypt, which he had not done on his first visit. He enjoyed looking out across the water at the Sinai Peninsula. Upon his return to Cairo, the staff at the Scarabee welcomed him enthusiastically.

When he was not sorting through his father's criminal case, Rüdiger would take a few hours to explore Cairo's markets or eat out by himself. Generally, Mrs. Doma, the hotel owner's wife, cooked for everyone, making stuffed fish, noodle casseroles, and chicken. She was sturdily built with a friendly laugh. Even though Rüdiger only spoke a bit of Arabic and she just a few words of English, they enjoyed talking. She kept her menagerie of children under control and made sure that all of them received a good education. In turn they tried to teach the visiting young man, whom they knew only as Roy, Arabic script. Games with the children became a nightly ritual. Rüdiger would head back to the Scarabee around 9:00 p.m., smoking one of the cigarettes his father detested.

But soon he grew weary of Egyptian manners, the need to say hello "ten times," as he put it, and ask about every family member: " 'How is the dog? How is the cat?' " He made the mistake of complaining to his father, who told him that he needed to develop "a little more tolerance for the fact that people do things differently here." Heim said the Europe of the 1980s that his son described had no appeal to him, as a place to live or even to visit.

After several weeks it was time to say good-bye. Rüdiger left still believing his father was innocent of most of the charges against him. He remembered too how one-sided the trial had seemed, and Heim seemed to have an answer for every allegation. Throughout their discussions his father had been "factual and sober," Rüdiger said, "not emotional." Rüdiger remained uncertain about what had taken place at Mauthausen. He did not believe that his father was wholly blameless after working in a concentration camp. But he also could not believe that Aribert Heim was guilty of the atrocities he was alleged to have committed.

Back in Germany, Rüdiger began trying to help his father. He questioned the state-appointed administrator of the apartment house, which still had not been sold. Heim wanted the building checked out because he suspected that the receiver might have been enriching himself in the process of acting as caretaker. The administrator bluntly told Rüdiger that he was responsible to the district court and not to any relative of Aribert Heim's.

Rüdiger refused to contact Gustav Rieger, who, in Heim's opinion, was one of the key witnesses, if not the key witness, who could prove his innocence. They had worked together daily in the clinic. In his first interview, Rieger claimed he had not seen Heim commit any specific crimes. In his father's view, Rieger could help more but was afraid. That was why he later changed his testimony. Rüdiger feared that getting in touch with Rieger could constitute witness tampering. The dutiful son discovered, like his aunt Herta, that when he did not like a request from his father, he could simply put off answering it indefinitely.

CHAPTER 48

Aedtner had an unconventional notion of the meaning of retirement. In the summer of 1984 he went on what he called his "Spanish holiday," but he did not take his wife or friends. He went alone, on an assignment for Simon Wiesenthal. With the famous Nazi hunter's financial backing he departed for Madrid on June 28, Aribert Heim's birthday, to try to learn more about the man named Umberto Hahn, who was believed to have been a member of the SS. His full name was Umberto Hahn-Stropninsky and he ran a real-estate company in Benidorm called UBAGO and was the chairman or "at the very least a prominent member" of an organization called El Europeo, supposedly made up of former SS officers and their sympathizers. The question was whether Hahn-Stropninsky was in fact Aribert Heim.

From the very beginning the trip did not go as planned. Aedtner was supposed to make contact with an informant he identified as Karmele Marchante, who worked for a local television show. He waited "in vain" for three hours at the Serrano Hotel, but she never showed up. The next day he drove to her office at Televisión Madrid but was still unable to meet with her. He went to the German embassy, where on a previous trip he had gotten to know the vice-consul. Unfortunately, the diplomat had since been transferred back to Bonn.

At the train station that same day a man bumped into Aedtner and spilled something on him. The stranger apologized and tried to help clean up the mess as an accomplice took advantage of the diversion and stole Aedtner's briefcase. Mercifully, the thieves dumped the files he was carrying—a bunch of paperwork in German must have been worthless to them—and the police recovered them. It still must have stung for the retired detective to be conned like a regular tourist.

The following day he met with another of Wiesenthal's colleagues, Max Mazin. Mazin had managed to track down the wayward informant Marchante. "She would not or could not—it was not clear to me—give any additional information," Aedtner wrote to Wiesenthal. She added that she would not be in Madrid in the coming days and had in fact already left for Barcelona. Aedtner would have to rely on Mazin's help to track down Hahn-Stropninsky and UBAGO. The detective had managed to learn that Hahn-Stropninsky had been living in Brazil and had moved to Benidorm in 1947, at a time when Heim was still in detention. "Based on the available information, I am operating under the assumption that we are not dealing with 'our Dr. HEIM' here," Aedtner wrote.

It still seemed worthwhile to continue his investigation in Spain while he was there, but the detective's run of bad luck continued. There was a strike by ground personnel at the nearest airport. "Given that, I decided to break things off there and fly back" as soon as he could, Aedtner wrote. He apologized to Wiesenthal for the delay in getting him the report, but by the time he returned, he had fallen extremely ill. He said that his doctor chalked it up to the hot temperature in Spain. There was no mention of his worsening diabetes.

Wiesenthal wished him a speedy recovery and said that he hoped Aedtner had received the check for 3,800 deutsche marks he had sent to cover the costs of the trip. Wiesenthal promised to work with Mazin to learn more about "this ominous Dr. Umberto Hahn," adding, however, "the fact that he returned to Europe from Brazil in 1947 speaks against a Nazi past." In the meantime, he would also do what he could to learn more about El Europeo.

Since Aedtner had formally left the police force, the relationship between the two men had grown even warmer. In the cover letter to his report on the "Spanish holiday," Aedtner said how much he hoped "for you personally" that Wiesenthal had enjoyed good weather and "beautiful and restful vacation days" on his own holiday.

But there was a valedictory note in Wiesenthal's response, as if the latest bout of illness and Aedtner's decision to break off his investigations early and return home signaled the beginning of the end of their years-long partnership. "I want to send you particularly heartfelt thanks for your total commitment to this matter—and with it to justice," Wiesenthal wrote. "I say that also as a former inmate of Mauthausen whose comrades Dr. Heim killed."

That September, Wiesenthal asked Aedtner for his help in obtaining Heim's file from the Berlin Document Center. More than a month later, Aedtner had to admit that as a pensioned detective he no longer had access to such records. He could usually get a hold of them through his close friend Detective Faller, but Faller had been away for weeks on vacation followed by a business trip to Heidelberg.

Aedtner also thanked Wiesenthal for his "generous help" in another project he had undertaken, working at the federal archive in Ludwigsburg. With Wiesenthal's financial support, the detective had turned his hand from police work to history. He was beginning his transition from hunting Nazis to preserving the memory of their crimes.

On May 31, 1985, West German police searched the home of the Mengele family confidant Hans Sedlmeier. In the past he had been warned about their visits, giving him enough time to hide anything about Mengele's location, but this time the federal police appeared without warning. During their search they found addresses in São Paulo they suspected had a connection to Mengele.

Brazilian police responded quickly, but instead of finding a Nazi doctor in hiding, they discovered Mengele's grave. The highest-profile Nazi fugitive since Adolf Eichmann, Dr. Josef Mengele had drowned on February 7, 1979. Investigators quickly zeroed in on his final resting place and invited reporters along for the very public disinterment. Authors Gerald Posner and John Ware described the scene:

> For nearly an hour three gravediggers with picks and shovels burrowed four feet down before they struck the coffin. Its top was stuck, and the police ordered one of the gravediggers to smash

it open. His pick shattered the wooden lid, revealing shreds of clothing and mud-colored bones. Mengele's arms had been placed at his side, the traditional burial pose for SS men, instead of with hands crossed over the breast, as is the Brazilian custom. Bending down over the open grave, Dr. Jose Antonio de Mello, assistant director of the police forensic laboratory, picked up the skull, then held it high for what surely was one of the world's most grisly photographs.

The five years between Mengele's death and its revelation embarrassed those Nazi hunters who claimed to know where he was hiding. Wiesenthal had made numerous far-fetched pronouncements about the doctor's whereabouts while the war criminal was still alive, at one point placing him on a yacht anchored off a Greek island and another time putting him in a Mercedes with armed guards in Paraguay. More problematic were Wiesenthal's sightings of the doctor after he was dead. On Israeli television the Nazi hunter had confidently stated on December 27, 1980, that Mengele had been spotted in Río Negro, Uruguay, nine weeks earlier. "I think he is contemplating suicide, or has decided to give himself up to a West German Embassy," Wiesenthal had said. At that time Mengele had been dead for nearly two years.

Wiesenthal remained defiant, questioning the legitimacy of the trail that led to Brazil. "This is Mengele's seventh death," he said on ABC's *Nightline* news program. "On one of these occasions, we found the body of a woman. If Mengele really died, then the whole world would have been informed five minutes after, not five years." But as dental records and later DNA tests would prove, it was Josef Mengele.

The Nazi doctor was the inspiration for the villains in the films *Marathon Man* and *The Boys from Brazil*, but the humdrum reality of his final years was nothing like the superhuman Nazi of popular imagination. A flood of Mengele's writings were published, and his life after escaping postwar Germany to South America hardly conformed to the tales of powerful organizations of former Nazis bent on world domination. Mengele was not engaged in the biological engineering of an Aryan superrace or plotting the return of a Fourth Reich. He was supported in part by his wealthy family and lived with a series of Nazi sympathizers, frequently bickering with his hosts and often miserable.

Among the people following the explosion of publicity surrounding Mengele's death was Aribert Heim. The public disinterment, the photographs, the trophy held up for the world press—it was a fate the Mauthausen doctor dearly hoped to avoid.

CHAPTER 49

The black letters X and Y met in the middle of the television screen. The words "Search," "Investigation," and "Prevention" were quickly superimposed one after another. Eduard Zimmermann, host of the popular crime show *Aktenzeichen XY . . . Ungelöst,* welcomed viewers to the first episode of the show's 1986 season. Already in its eighteenth year, the show remained a hit, with a simple format that has been copied by programs like *America's Most Wanted.*

Zimmermann told the audience that a criminal had been arrested not just as a result of the last episode but literally while it was still on the air. With the help of studios and hotlines in Germany, Austria, and Switzerland, Zimmermann brought the viewer an hour's worth of reenactments of murders and robberies. Typewriters and ringing telephones in the background at the studio signaled that it was work as much as entertainment. As Zimmermann began to introduce case number 7, the words "LKA Stuttgart" and the telephone number (0711) 5 06 01 appeared on the screen. This case dealt not with the recent past but with wartime history.

"The grand jury in Baden-Baden, ladies and gentlemen, is pursuing a case of multiple homicides against a man who disappeared twenty-three years ago. The crimes he stands accused of go back even further, more than forty years," Zimmermann said. "The state police in Stuttgart are responsible for the search for the accused fugitive. The man they are looking for is named Dr. Aribert Heim." The photograph of Heim in his tuxedo appeared on the screen. As Aedtner had written to Wiesenthal several years earlier, they were running out of ways to search for Heim. Aedtner's successors turned to television to appeal to the public for assistance. The Justice Ministry of Baden-Württemberg had agreed to double the reward for Heim to 30,000 deutsche marks in time for the program's broadcast.

The previous fall the prosecutors in Baden-Baden had written to Zimmermann. "The accused Dr. Heim managed to escape arrest in the year 1962; it is clearly the case that he is still alive, and the most firmly supported clues available to us point to the assumption that he is currently in Germany or Austria," read the letter. "The grand jury, the district attorney, and the prosecutors' office in Baden-Baden see a search within the framework of the program as the last chance to arrest the accused."

Investigators hoped that even if the viewers were unable to point the finger at Heim's hiding place, the pressure created by the popular program featuring his case would provoke either a call from him to his wiretapped family or a discussion between other family members about whether he was safe in hiding. Detective Faller, handling the matter now that his former colleague Aedtner had retired, had based his request for continuous wiretaps on an anonymous tip from a source in the town of Gaggenau—the same city where Aedtner lived.

Zimmermann gave a description of Heim's crimes at Mauthausen, before telling the audience how the former Nazi doctor had settled in Baden-Baden to work as a gynecologist. "After his past became public, he fled just before his arrest. The state police in Stuttgart have multiple recent signs that he is still alive, but they have not been able to discover his location." He described the fugitive as seventy-one years old, six feet three, possibly speaking with an Austrian accent. "Tips please to the state police in Stuttgart," Zimmermann concluded, before turning his attention to another bank robbery.

Plenty of people phoned in after the program, but none of their tips led to an arrest. Heim remained safely in hiding. The police knew they were running out of chances to find him.

After the discovery of Mengele's body, Simon Wiesenthal suffered a number of other setbacks. His image had been further tarnished over a scandal involving the former United Nations secretary-general and Austria's then president, Kurt Waldheim. Wiesenthal appeared to have supported Waldheim when he lied about his wartime service in areas where Jews were being deported to the camps. At the very least he had been slow to condemn the Austrian politician. The New York–based World Jewish Congress led the campaign against Waldheim. At one point officials there even referred to the Nazi hunter as "Sleazenthal" in an internal memo.

The most severe blow came when he was passed over for the Nobel Peace Prize. The bad publicity over Waldheim probably hurt his chances, and his long-simmering feud with the writer and fellow survivor Elie Wiesel could not have helped. Both had worked to keep the memory of the Holocaust alive, one through literature and the other through prosecution. Wiesenthal's supporters hoped the two men might share the award, but the two Jews disagreed on how much emphasis should be placed on gentile victims at the concentration camps. Wiesenthal argued for a more inclusive position, Wiesel for emphasizing the uniqueness of the Nazi effort to extinguish the Jews. Wiesenthal hurt the chances that they would share the award when he called Wiesel "a superchauvinist." On October 15, 1986, it was announced that Wiesel would receive the award alone. Wiesenthal was crushed.

In the meantime, what little control he might have exercised over the Simon Wiesenthal Center in Los Angeles, which bore his name but operated independently, seemed to have slipped away. He often found himself at odds with the center's leader, Rabbi Marvin Hier. In addition, the donations to his documentation center in Vienna had fallen off significantly. Supporters wrote checks to the center in Los Angeles assuming that they were supporting Wiesenthal, but that was not the case. To prevent a damaging public rift, Hier basically kept the world-famous Holocaust survivor and Nazi hunter on a comfortable but not rich allowance.

It provided Wiesenthal with enough money to play the role of benefactor to Aedtner. His support had proven crucial to getting the detective's historical project off the ground: Aedtner had cataloged thousands of files from the state police investigations of Nazi war crimes into a historical archive for future generations. Aedtner realized that if nothing were done, the files would eventually be thrown out. But in this case, their work included significant primary research into the crimes of the Holocaust, including interviews with perpetrators, witnesses, and survivors. Aedtner received permission to work with an assistant at the State Archive in Ludwigsburg preparing the collection. After the initial support from Wiesenthal, Aedtner managed to secure public funds to continue the project.

The catalog, composed of index cards, written by hand in the neat script of Aedtner's assistant, constituted a frank record of humiliation, torture, and mass murder. Under the heading "Particular Cruelty" was the synagogue in Bialystok, Poland, that the Nazis set on fire with some two thousand men, women, and children inside. Members of Police Battalion 309 shot those who tried to escape. A similar scene served as the opening sequence of the *Holocaust* miniseries.

Every card was like a window into the cruel and complicated Nazi world. A man named Jakob Gorzelezyk was listed as "Jew and inmate at KL-Auschwitz, earlier trainer and sparring partner of German boxing world champion Max Schmeling." German women in Konstanz who slept with Polish men had their heads shaved and were forced to parade through the streets wearing signs that said, "I am a Pole's whore." It was recommended that the Polish men in question be executed, though "milder suggestions" were possible under the law.

CHAPTER 50

Freed from the discretion required by his job as a detective, Aedtner now made public appearances, earning some measure of attention. He published a lengthy article in *Der Spiegel* about his efforts against the members of Police Battalion 322, responsible for the deaths of more than ten thousand people. Called "Shot to Death on the Spot," the article focused on the impediments he and the other investigators faced trying to bring the killers to justice. In spite of well-documented evidence, most of them went unpunished.

A camera crew filmed Aedtner for a documentary aired on German television about his career titled *Alfred Aedtner: A German Fate*. To the sound of lugubrious horn music Aedtner can be seen shuffling to the archive, graffiti sprayed on the front door of the building, the paint on the halls inside peeling. Aedtner puffs away at his cigarette, his mustache turning down at the corners of his mouth in a constant scowl.

The film commended his work and dedication but, like Aedtner's own article in *Der Spiegel,* in the context of "bitter experiences." The film-maker, Yoash Tatari, focused not on how many perpetrators were caught but on the greater number who went free. Too few investigators, too little support, cases sabotaged—it was a litany of futility. The filmmaker visited the state police office in Stuttgart. No one would speak to him on camera. They did show him around and let him film as they flipped through a few files for his benefit. There, in a thick binder, is a glimpse of Heim's photograph and the set of fingerprints Aedtner acquired from the Americans.

The documentary made the retired detective appear uncomfortable. That might have been because he was called into the headquarters in Stuttgart before Tatari recorded his interviews. The implication in the film was that he had been warned not to speak out of turn. Even in spite of the circumstances it was apparent that he did not have Wiesenthal's natural poise in front of a camera or an audience or his talent for spinning yarns. Despite the recent bad publicity, Wiesenthal had lost none of his flair for self-promotion, and another film about him was in the works.

HBO had paid him $350,000 for the right to produce his life story. Unsatisfied with Sir Laurence Olivier's portrayal in *The Boys from Brazil*, Wiesenthal insisted on having a say in casting the actor who would play him, finally agreeing to Ben Kingsley, who had won the Academy Award for *Gandhi*. It was more than just charisma that made Wiesenthal so captivating. He knew how to place hope above despair; death played an important role in his narrative, but it was always followed by rebirth. It helped make him a popular lecturer and author. He was not just a reminder of the Holocaust but an inspirational success story.

Aedtner's largest audiences were composed of small historical societies and students. He lectured to them, bringing along 8-millimeter film reels of mass executions. Had it changed him? the filmmaker asked. "Of course it changed me," Aedtner answered. "You never get away from something like this." His voice was raspy from the cigarettes, and his war-damaged eye sometimes strayed. "You stand before such an abyss with total incomprehension," he said. "All the things a human being can be, on the outside once again a person no one believes could harm anyone, who shoots defenseless old men, women, even infants."

His assistant at the archive confided to Aedtner's wife that he did not seem to have the energy for his work there. "Your husband is declining. By noon every day he's asleep on the table," she said. The documentary ended with Aedtner preparing a finished file for the archives. First he stamped a brown folder with the abbreviation for the state police in Baden-Württemberg, "LKA BW," and the words "Investigative File NS Violent Crimes." He stacked the papers neatly inside, closed the folder, then took a length of white ribbon, tied it into a neat package, and cut the cord.

Around this time memorials were springing up all over West Germany, some built by Jewish groups, others by local governments or groups of German citizens. The West Berlin neighborhood of Moabit built a monument on the site of the demolished Levetzowstrasse synagogue. It was dedicated on November 14, 1988. There was a large statue that depicted a giant ramp and railway car in memory of the synagogue's use as a gathering point for transports to the concentration camps. There was also a plaque dedicated to the city's synagogues, which had been damaged or destroyed on Kristallnacht.

Around the corner from the memorial was the apartment building at Tile-Wardenberg-Strasse 28 that had financed Dr. Aribert Heim's life in hiding. The public paid little attention to the building once it was clear the rent money no longer abetted the Nazi doctor's flight. Heim's lawyer lost his appeal at the end of 1979. But behind the scenes the bureaucratic infighting between the authorities in West Berlin and those in Baden-Baden over who should be handling the Heim case and which office should receive compensation went on for more than eight years.

While the bickering between jurisdictions delayed the sale, the real-estate market did not remain frozen. The price of property in the city rose considerably. When West Berlin finally auctioned off the apartment building to pay Heim's fine, the sale price was 1,710,000 deutsche marks, compared with the city building authority's 1979 estimate of 510,000 marks. But the authorities could legally only take the amount of the fine. The remaining funds still belonged to Aribert Heim, though as a fugitive he was not allowed to touch them. Instead, the fortune of nearly 1.2 million deutsche marks sat in an account at the Landesbank Berlin.

CHAPTER 51

Rüdiger Heim flew to Cairo in the spring of 1990 with 20,000 deutsche marks in a wad of 100- and 500-mark bills stuffed into the front pocket of his jeans. Aunt Herta's message had been urgent. Travel to Egypt and bring money. His father was in the hospital and it was serious.

By 1990, Rüdiger had moved from Denmark to Avignon, France, where he and Tano Pisano had opened another restaurant, this time as partners. Though the restaurant was a success, they gave it up after a couple of years, and from that point on Rüdiger led a wandering existence, migrating at irregular intervals between Germany, France, and Spain, where Pisano had settled to rededicate himself full-time to his art. While his best friend had found a new career, Rüdiger felt adrift.

In some ways he felt as if he were leading a double life. In Germany he was the dutiful son, taking over the management of the family real-estate holdings from his mother. In Spain, by his own admission, he had "dedicated myself rather extravagantly to the nightlife," going out to the nightclubs, having affairs with women, and shooting photographs, without focus, direction, or commitment, "idling in neutral." Once or twice a month he would call his father in Egypt from a pay phone, just to see how he was doing.

But after a conversation with Khafagy, the business associate, Rüdiger knew he had to make the trip quickly. His father had just been operated on, and there was some kind of problem. Rüdiger could not find out the exact diagnosis. He had the impression that Khafagy was trying to make things sound better than they actually were.

The money that he took with him was his own. While a substantial sum, 20,000 deutsche marks was "not an amount that one would have to make an extra big deal to fund," he said. Nor was it as suspicious in those days to take out large quantities of cash. He was not searched either departing Europe or landing in Egypt.

When he arrived in Cairo, he went as usual to the Scarabee Hotel. Once there he contacted Khafagy, and the following morning they drove to Misr International Hospital in the neighborhood of Dokki. "Thank God everything went well," Khafagy said on their way to the leafy side street near the Nile. Rüdiger still could not get a straight answer about the diagnosis.

His father was awake when he entered the room. More than a week had passed since his surgery. The complications had left him in the intensive care unit, but he did not talk about his health problems. He greeted his son warmly, then stood up so that they could walk up and down the hallway together. Heim pointed out the window to a new high-rise going up on the Nile and suggested Rüdiger purchase an apartment there. Egypt, his father reminded him, was a wonderful country, where one could live very well. Rüdiger could buy the place and come for a month or so each year, then rent it out the rest of the time.

It was not until they spoke with a doctor that Rüdiger learned that his father had a cancerous tumor in his rectum. The cancer was already in an advanced stage when it was detected, and it was doubtful that the surgeons had been able to remove all the malignant cells. The seventy-six-year-old Heim had suffered heart complications during the surgery, which was why he was in intensive care. Although he was still wearing a colostomy bag, he would be going home soon. In the coming weeks and months he would need chemotherapy and radiation treatments. Given the grim forecast, Rüdiger decided to stay and help his father through his illness.

Rüdiger had helped nurse his grandmother when she was dying. Caring for his father gave him the sense of direction he lacked in Spain, where he "lived more during the night than the day" and essentially without responsibility.

He cooked whatever he could easily whip together from ingredients he found at the market. His time working in restaurants came in handy. Making the best of the single gas burner, Rüdiger purchased a two-tiered metal pot that allowed him to make couscous or rice on top while stewing meats and vegetables underneath. He took his father's clothes to the dry cleaner and picked up medicine from the pharmacy. All the while Rüdiger pretended he was from Switzerland.

When Heim had a doctor's appointment, they took the subway. Rüdiger once made the mistake of boarding the first car on the train, the one reserved for women. He quickly realized his mistake, but police in black uniforms came running after him yelling. Father and son tried to argue their case to the police, who would not listen. The punishment would have been no more than a small fine, but they feared the attention would reveal Heim's identity. A couple of Cairo residents solved the problem by pulling the two foreigners into the train's second car just as the automatic doors were about to slam shut. The flummoxed policemen were stuck outside watching the train pull away.

At home Rüdiger tried to make his father comfortable. He bought an electric fan, but it only seemed to swirl the hot air. He would then sprinkle water on the balcony to try to lower the temperature through evaporation. He was there in the summer when it was so hot the asphalt was practically melting. At one point Rüdiger noticed that near the market there was a stand selling "measly roses in little earthenware jars." He bought a rosebush along with a small green plant and watered and kept them on the balcony to the joy of the children next door.

Something had changed since his father's surgery. The subject of the trial, which had dominated Rüdiger's previous visit, was largely ignored. Heim described how he felt about not being allowed to practice medicine. He added that the rumor he had worked as a police doctor in Egypt was false. Egyptian universities trained more doctors than could find jobs. At one point he had discussed moving to Libya to work at a clinic there run by a German doctor, but nothing came of it.

Heim had also grown more relaxed about Rüdiger's failure to finish his studies. "Too bad you didn't become a doctor," he told his son, "but at the end of the day it doesn't really make a difference." Rüdiger began to believe that his father wanted a normal and satisfying life for him, and whether he became a doctor or a carpenter was unimportant. Heim related an anecdote from his youth. A friend, the son of an aristocrat, was forced to live in a certain style while the rest of the boys could frolic about as they wished. Heim had felt sorry for him because he was so isolated.

Father and son still played with the children in the evenings, and Rüdiger often bought them sweets as his father once had. Heim explained how their father had passed away the year before and that he was trying to support the children however he could. Mahmoud Doma was now eighteen years old, and Heim said he understood what the young man was going through. His own father had died when he was just fifteen. He did not try to spare the teenager's feelings with false reassurance but spoke to him like an adult. "So it is," Uncle Tarek told him. "We all die." He was there at the burial and said the prayer of the dead for his Egyptian friend. Afterward he had taken Mahmoud to the beach in Alexandria.

Heim told his son how after his own father had been orphaned, his inheritance had been stolen by his great-uncle. As a result Josef Ferdinand Heim could not even afford to go to university, and although he eventually rose high enough in the ranks of the gendarmerie to lead the police in the provincial capital of Radkersburg, his progress beyond the provinces was halted by his lack of education. Rüdiger realized that this was why his own father had pressed his children to finish their education.

By 1990, Heim's remaining assets had dwindled. He lost the rent money first from Berlin and then from the apartment in Alexandria, which a business associate said had been condemned but Heim suspected had been stolen. Worse still, he lost his property in Agamy Beach. His associate in that deal, Rifat, claimed that they had been too slow to develop the land and a rich, politically connected businessman had begun building on the site and there was nothing they could do. As a result of Rifat's actions, Heim accused him in an angry letter, "I became in the last days of my life a beggar."

Heim feared he had been betrayed, his investments slowly taken by confidants as his strength faded. As a fugitive Nazi, he could hardly take Egyptians to court. His partners might have been counting on exactly that. The loss of the beachside property especially stung. Heim had drawn floor plan after floor plan for the layout of the apartments he had wanted to leave to his sons. It was almost all that he could bequeath to them. He was unaware of the 1.2 million deutsche marks accruing interest in the Landesbank Berlin. Khafagy continued to bring money from the Karnak Hotel for the time being, and their relationship persisted.

At least the World Cup was a pleasant distraction. The West Germans were playing in the tournament for the first time since the fall of the Berlin Wall. They won the world championship just a few months before East and West Germany would formally reunify. But Rüdiger noticed that his father was even more excited about the team from Cameroon becoming the first African country ever to reach the quarterfinals.

For the first time Rüdiger considered taking his father's advice and staying in Egypt. He had no restaurant in Copenhagen or Avignon calling him back, no wife or children waiting for him in Europe. But history intervened when Saddam Hussein invaded Kuwait on August 2, 1990. There was talk of war everywhere. The Americans were building up forces in Saudi Arabia, and there was fear in Egypt that as an American ally missiles would be fired against it. With conditions in the Middle East so uncertain, Rüdiger Heim boarded a plane and returned to Europe.

CHAPTER 52

The first word that Aribert Heim had died came in the form of an unsolicited letter to Simon Wiesenthal. In February 1994, a Viennese doctor, Robert Braun, told the Nazi hunter he believed he could save him a little bit of time by striking one name off his list of war criminals. Aribert Heim was dead.

Braun and Heim had become friends at university, where they played sports together. Heim later helped Braun get a job on the medical staff at the Eissport Klub Engelmann, where Heim played ice hockey. According to Braun, Heim was not put off by the fact that Braun was half-Jewish, even inviting him home to Radkersburg to stay with his family during one school vacation. They lost track of each other after the Anschluss. The Brauns were occupied with their struggle to survive. Robert did not hear from his friend and knew nothing about the alleged war crimes.

Decades later, in 1979, he received a letter from Heim's family asking for testimony that the doctor was not anti-Semitic. "I didn't think he could hurt a fly," Braun wrote to Wiesenthal. "Thus one can make mistakes." In the meantime, Braun learned that Heim had died from cancer. He did not say how he had learned it, but added, "I do not doubt that you can close this case and share completely your regret, that this offender was not brought before any court."

For all that the world had changed since Heim fled Germany, the fascination with Nazi crimes showed little sign of abating. In 1993, the United States Holocaust Memorial Museum opened to great fanfare in

Washington, D.C. That same year Steven Spielberg released *Schindler's List*, which played to huge audiences worldwide and swept the Academy Awards in 1994. The German government was planning to build a national Holocaust monument in Berlin, the Memorial to the Murdered Jews of Europe.

In October 1996, a documentary about Nazi physicians called *Doctors Without Consciences* aired on German television, once again featuring Aribert Heim. An employee of the Landesbank Berlin who had seen the show told the police that Dr. Heim had an account at his bank totaling millions of deutsche marks. The tipster did not want to break any privacy laws but hoped it might help the investigation and earn him reward money. After several inquiries investigators realized it was the account set up after the sale of Heim's apartment building with the more than 1 million deutsche marks left over after the fine. As long as Heim was on the run, he could not touch it. As long as he was alive, neither could his heirs.

In Vienna, Wiesenthal was still pursuing Nazis from the cluttered confines of his documentation center. In 1992 he had watched with great satisfaction as the former SS officer Josef Schwammberger, who had been arrested in Argentina, was extradited to Germany. Schwammberger was convicted and sentenced to life in prison. In the meantime, Heim's case remained dormant, not closed, but not exactly active either.

Following the terrorist attacks on September 11, 2001, governments around the world stepped up enforcement against suspicious money transfers. They weren't looking for elderly Nazis in hiding but attempting to identify irregular patterns of financial activity that might turn up terrorist financing. Indeed, employees at Western Union in Germany noticed an unusual pattern of money transfers had taken place between October 11, 2002, and August 18, 2003. Over that period of less than a year, a man named Rüdiger Heim had sent 88,147 euros from Germany to Spain. The sums were all between 950 and 2,500 euros and always to one of two people, Gaetano Pisano or Blandine Pellet, both of whom lived on the Costa Brava. In March 2004, Western Union informed the German authorities about the suspicious transactions.

Investigators quickly realized the information had nothing to do with terrorism. Rüdiger Heim was the younger son of the fugitive Aribert Heim. More than forty years after Heim's disappearance, here was a new impetus to pursue the case. Alfred Aedtner was now in a nursing home, and the case was given to the manhunt unit. Founded in 1996 "for the seizure of fugitive serious criminals," the group was made up of volunteers who were prepared to spend long hours at work and willing to travel abroad. The unit was not concerned with proving Heim guilty. It only cared about the capture.

The members of the unit started over from the beginning, going carefully through the more than forty binders of material on Heim, most of it gathered during Alfred Aedtner's time on the case. Tips still continued to come in and were duly checked out. A great deal of effort had gone into alleged sightings in Uruguay. A former police officer in Wisconsin was certain that he had located Heim in Milwaukee. Dr. Robert Braun of Vienna claimed to have information that Heim had died in 1992, and he had been questioned several times. Unfortunately, with each interview the ninety-four-year-old Braun seemed less certain. They weren't sure whether he was just a confused old man or if he was protecting his old friend.

The investigators were now able to look for Heim in East Germany and found that the Stasi had kept a file on him. It had even spied on West German efforts to locate the fugitive, including a detailed report on the failure of investigators to follow Rüdiger and Friedl on a Swiss vacation. But the Stasi's investigations had also proved fruitless.

The manhunt team focused on the money at the Landesbank. If Heim were dead, the family could claim the fortune that had grown to nearly 1 million euros. The fact that the money was still there was "a very strong indication that he is still alive," said one of the policemen. Meanwhile, the investigators uncovered even more transfers than the initial Western Union report had indicated. Including direct transfers from his own bank account, Rüdiger had sent 289,617.71 euros to Pisano and Pellet between January 2000 and December 2004 and was continuing to send roughly 3,000 to 4,000 euros a month.

Herta, who had forwarded the receipts from the Berlin apartment building to her brother, had passed away in 1997. It appeared that Rüdiger had taken up the responsibility of supporting his father. The investigators suspected Pisano and Pellet of working as his accomplices. Friedl Heim had sent packages to Pisano back in the late 1970s. According to the French National Police, Rüdiger and Pisano had lived together in Avignon. They had a bar on rue Carreterie until around 1990. When Rüdiger returned to Germany, Pisano moved to a home near the Spanish coast with Pellet, a French national. Together they operated an arts and decoration store.

The investigators needed outside help to locate and apprehend Heim. The logical choice would have been Simon Wiesenthal, but he had retired the year before. "My job is done," Wiesenthal said in an interview with the Austrian magazine *Format* in April 2003. "I found the mass murderers I was looking for. I survived all of them." Wiesenthal, now ninety-four, concluded, "Those whom I didn't look for are too old and sick today to be pursued legally."

Fortunately for the manhunt unit, Wiesenthal had an heir apparent in Jerusalem, Efraim Zuroff, the chief Nazi hunter for the Simon Wiesenthal Center. He was already working on his own initiative to apprehend aging Nazis, a project named Operation Last Chance. In late 2004, the Baden-Württemberg state police asked Zuroff for his help in finding Heim.

Efraim Zuroff had been named after his grandfather's brother who was murdered during the war. Yet the Holocaust was not a big part of his upbringing in 1950s America. As a boy growing up in Brooklyn, he was far removed from the deprivation of postwar Europe. Efraim Zuroff dreamed of becoming the first Orthodox Jew to play in the National Basketball Association, though given his highly educated and highly religious family, it was more likely that he would become a rabbi. He was born after World War II, in 1948. In any event he had scant knowledge of the Holocaust.

Then, in 1961, his mother made him watch Eichmann's trial on television. The Nazi was not wearing his SS uniform. Sitting behind bulletproof glass, he looked more like an accountant than a mass murderer. Eichmann's expression remained impassive as witnesses testified to inconceivable crimes at places like Chelmno, Sobibor, Treblinka, and Auschwitz.

But the reality of the Nazi effort to exterminate the European Jews did not really sink in for Efraim until the eve of the 1967 war. He was looking at a map in the *New York Times* about the coming conflict. The map listed the number of troops each Arab army had at its disposal. Zuroff realized that Israel was surrounded and outnumbered. "There's going to be another Holocaust," the eighteen-year-old thought.

Instead, the Israeli military swiftly defeated its opponents in what became known as the Six-Day War, capturing new territory, including the Sinai Peninsula, the Gaza Strip, the West Bank, the Golan Heights, and East Jerusalem. As a college student Zuroff spent a year abroad in the young country flush with its triumphs and decided to make his home in Israel.

Rather than pursuing rabbinical studies, he began graduate school at Hebrew University's Institute of Contemporary Jewry, focusing on the Holocaust. He had gone on to work at Yad Vashem, Israel's official memorial to the Holocaust, before moving with his wife and young children to Los Angeles to work at the Simon Wiesenthal Center. Simon Wiesenthal's first meeting with Zuroff did not go smoothly. Wiesenthal began speaking in German, assuming Zuroff spoke the language, which he did not. "Nicht gut, nicht gut," the old Nazi hunter said when he learned that he didn't, "not good, not good." It was a bumpy start, but Zuroff respected Wiesenthal and dedicated himself to furthering the older man's work.

After a few years with the center, Zuroff took a job with the U.S. Justice Department's newly formed Office of Special Investigations. The work was in Israel, where so many of the historical documents relating to the Nazi genocide were kept and so many of the survivors still lived. Zuroff quickly went from looking for eyewitness accounts to searching for the perpetrators themselves. He became the Simon Wiesenthal Center's representative in Jerusalem. Zuroff described the job of putting together a Nazi war-crimes investigation as "similar to putting together an extremely large and complicated jigsaw puzzle."

In spite of what he called "the aura of adventure and drama" associated with Nazi hunting, the work consisted of "meticulous, detailed research . . . Yet it is precisely this very prosaic and often monotonous work which yields positive and, at times, spectacular results."

Zuroff specialized in the Nazis' on-site accomplices from countries like Latvia, Lithuania, Ukraine, Hungary, and Croatia. Without their local knowledge the extermination of the Jews would not have been nearly as brutally effective. Zuroff put particular emphasis on the collaborators who had fled, not just to the United States, but also to Canada, Britain, and Australia. Wiesenthal liked to say that when he met Holocaust victims in the afterlife, he would tell them, "I did not forget you." Zuroff made that his mantra.

Alerted to the bank transfers by Heim's son, the German manhunt team wanted to know if Zuroff would include Dr. Aribert Heim in the German rollout of Operation Last Chance. On January 26, 2005, Zuroff offered a 140,000-euro reward, nearly $200,000, for information leading to Heim's capture.

I n his Gaggenau nursing home, unaware of these developments, Alfred Aedtner was dying. Diabetes ravaged his extremities. First the doctors had to cut off his toes. Then they amputated one of his feet. While he still had one leg, his wife, Lore, had been able to keep him at home and care for him. Once they removed his other leg, the doctor asked if she had anyone to help care for him. When she told the doctor that she was alone, he advised her to put her husband in a nursing home. She sadly but dutifully complied and sat with him every day. The surgeons kept operating, higher and higher up. Why didn't they just take it all at once and spare him the constant operations? his wife and his son asked. That was against the rules, the doctors answered. Soon it didn't matter. The patient no longer knew where he was. On the afternoon of April 2, 2005, Alfred Aedtner passed away. He was seventy-nine years old. He died largely in anonymity.

Two months after Aedtner's death the president of Austria, Heinz Fischer, appeared at Simon Wiesenthal's apartment in Vienna to present him with the Gold Medal for Services to the Republic of Austria, one of the highest civilian honors the country could give. The year before, the queen of England had named Wiesenthal knight commander of the Order of the British Empire. There was a growing acknowledgment that the chances to recognize his service while he was still alive were running out. His wife, Cyla, whom he had married in 1936, had died in 2003 at the age of ninety-five. Wiesenthal's health was finally declining. He died at home on September 20, 2005. He was ninety-six years old. In addition to his daughter, Wiesenthal was survived by three grandchildren and seven great-grandchildren, all of whom lived in Israel. His final wish was that he be buried in the Holy Land, and three days later he was laid to rest north of Tel Aviv at a service attended by hundreds of mourners and covered by the international media.

Around this time investigators went to see Dr. Braun again, to question him about his assertions that Heim was dead. The elderly doctor admitted that it was Heim's younger sister, the late Herta Barth, who had passed on the news. Under intense questioning he changed his story and said that after her first call, she called back declaring, "Aribert lives!" In their report the investigators wrote their conclusion that "the hint that Dr. Heim was dead was a test of Dr. Braun's reliability." They asked for permission to search the old man's home and tap his phone and were refused.

But the court said that the Baden-Württemberg state police could once again wiretap the Heim family's phones. In one conversation Heim's niece, Birgit, and ex-wife, Friedl, mentioned media reports that the fugitive had been spotted in Austria. "And then it also says that he sat somewhere in Austria having a grand old time," Friedl told her niece. "And—what does one eat in Austria—and had dumplings or whatever to eat and something to drink."

"That must have been in *Spiegel*," Birgit answered.

"Grinning and laughing," Friedl said. "Could be. I wasn't there. I mean I don't want to . . ."

"Well, I did not get a card at any rate," Birgit said, "from the Austrian visit." The police requested a search warrant for her premises.

Investigators also overheard Rüdiger and his brother, Christian, discussing the investigative efforts brought to bear on the family. "Die wissen gar nichts," Rüdiger said of the police. "They don't know anything."

Tano Pisano and his companion Blandine Pellet were preparing to depart from an exhibition in Italy when Rüdiger proposed that they stay a while longer. They told him thanks but no thanks, loaded up their little Fiat Multipla, and started back to the Costa Brava. They spent the night in a small town near the French-Italian border and spoke to Rüdiger again, this time by phone. Once again he suggested, insisted really, that they dally there for a while instead of heading home. Once again they told him they needed to get back.

As Pellet drove home, they discussed their friend's strange insistence that they linger in Italy or France. While traveling for the exhibition, they had not kept up with the news. They had not seen the article about a fugitive Nazi hiding in Spain. Even if they had, they would not have connected it to their friend, much less themselves.

The next morning there was a loud banging at their front door. Pellet answered and found two men waiting outside. They identified themselves as plainclothes police officers and said that she and Pisano had to come to the station. "Don't talk to anybody. Don't call anybody. Just come."

Two more senior investigators had traveled from Barcelona to question the couple. They kept asking if they had read the article on Heim in the Spanish daily newspaper *El Mundo*. They said they had not. One of the policemen told them to go outside, buy a paper, and come back. Don't speak to anyone, just read it. It was a strange way to interrupt an interrogation. When they stepped outside, a photographer started snapping their pictures. It felt like a setup. Once they got a hold of the newspaper, they saw the story about the Nazi war criminal and the Italian man living in Palafrugell who had helped to hide and support him.

"Is this a joke?" Pisano asked.

In reply, one of the policemen asked if he knew Rüdiger Heim. Pisano answered that he did. "Why is he sending you money?" Pisano explained that Rüdiger was buying a lot of his artwork, acting almost as a patron, and holding the pictures as a guarantee. "I'm sorry, but if your friend is a real friend, he will tell the truth," said the investigator.

The police explained that Rüdiger's father was a wanted Nazi war criminal. Pisano was stunned. He said he thought Rüdiger's father was dead and insisted that he needed to talk to his friend to clear everything up. With the officer still in front of him, he called his friend at home.

"It's me," Pisano said. "I'm at the police station, and they're saying here your father is a Nazi."

"It is true," Rüdiger answered. Their conversation ended quickly, although Pisano had many unanswered questions.

"This is crazy," he told the police officer. "What do we all have to do with this?"

They were allowed to leave. The police warned them that the media attention was going to get worse. When they got home, Pisano called Rüdiger again, and the two friends of nearly thirty years fought. Pisano asked him to tell his father to come out and admit he and Pellet had nothing to do with it. Rüdiger said there was nothing he could do. He had not seen his father since he was a little boy and did not know where he was.

The next day, Pisano picked up the newspaper and saw his face across from Aribert Heim's with a photograph of Jewish concentration camp victims in between. Soon he realized he was not just in the Spanish press but in papers all over the world. Friends from as far away as South Africa and Australia were calling to ask them if they were hiding a Nazi war criminal. They decided to hold a press conference to declare their innocence. They asked Rüdiger to come, but he did not show up.

Pisano sat at his computer entering "Gaetano Pisano" into Google. Instead of paintings and ceramics, the search results showed page after page of stories about decapitated concentration camp inmates, the vivisection of living patients on the operating table, and lethal injections of gasoline to the heart. There were articles from Italy, where he was born, from Denmark and France, where he used to live, from Spain, where he had made his home. His exhibitions were canceled, and orders for his artworks slowed dramatically.

Shortly thereafter officials told Pisano and Pellet that their accounts had checked out. The money sent by Rüdiger Heim had not flowed to his father in hiding but been used for art supplies, food, and gasoline. His name had been cleared. Pisano even had a letter from the government saying as much. But when he entered "Gaetano Pisano" into Google again, the search results still showed page after page of atrocities.

CHAPTER 54

Heim's illegitimate daughter, Waltraut Böser, still lived in Chile, half a world away from her native Austria. She had her husband and now three children. She played tennis and basketball. She had learned to speak Spanish, which came easily to her, as languages always did. Her father was far from her thoughts on the morning in 2006 when she looked at the newspaper and finally saw a picture of the man she had spent years hoping to catch a glimpse of and believed was dead. Aribert Heim's photograph was in the newspaper sitting on her kitchen table. He might be alive. Then she read about his alleged crimes and began to feel dizzy and sick.

"Why did your mother never tell you about him?" her husband wanted to know. Gertrud had since passed away. Waltraut tried to remember everything her mother had told her about her father. She had been told nothing of this catalog of atrocities. Still, many of her talents had been inherited from him, her love of sports, her interest in medicine, her ability at languages. She spoke not only German and Spanish but also French and English and a smattering of Italian and Russian, and she was now trying to learn the Chilean Indian language of Mapuche, the local language of where she spent her summers. If the newspapers were right, all the qualities her father bequeathed to her had come from a sadistic killer.

Reporters and photographers spent days on her front lawn. For five nights she could not sleep. Her father had not died in the war. He had been alive and could have visited her the way that her brother's father visited him. She had missed knowing the man the newspapers described as a war criminal. And she was accused of hiding him.

The manhunt unit was not prepared to dismiss a possible connection between Heim and his illegitimate daughter as Aedtner had. Her presence in Latin America fit the pattern of other high-profile fugitives. Like Brazil and Argentina, Chile had its own past with Nazis. Most notably, the country had provided refuge to Walther Rauff, who had designed mobile gas vans used for executions. After immigrating to Latin America, he had worked as an agent of the West German intelligence service—even though the spy service was aware of his past. Wiesenthal and Beate Klarsfeld had both pressed unsuccessfully for Rauff's extradition. In 1984 he died of natural causes in Santiago.

The refusal to extradite Rauff "was always in the back of my mind," said Efraim Zuroff. Learning of Waltraut's residence in Chile, he decided to launch a version of Operation Last Chance there. The presence of Heim's illegitimate daughter tantalized him. He believed she was "the key to the mystery, the person who would lead us to the fugitive." The problem was that "this fugitive happened to be her father."

Zuroff had an informant he called Juan B. who said that he had bumped into Böser's husband carrying bags of groceries to an old relative living on the island of Chiloé, south of Puerto Montt. The informant stated that Böser's husband did not have any elderly relations living on the island, raising Zuroff's suspicion that the groceries were intended for Heim.

He organized a press conference complete with a wanted poster of the fugitive. The reward for information leading to his capture had risen to just under half a million dollars. Zuroff had raised the profile and the urgency of the hunt for Heim significantly in 2008 by declaring him the most wanted Nazi war criminal in the world. The Holocaust organizers and death camp commandants were dead, as were most of those old enough to have occupied leadership positions in the Third Reich. More than six decades after the war, Heim had risen from obscurity to the top of the list.

Zuroff went "with several journalists to the home of [Waltraut]

Böser, for what would basically be a staged encounter for the benefit of the media." A German shepherd was barking behind the gate. The group arrived "in a driving thunderstorm," according to the *Newsweek* correspondent Joe Contreras, who was traveling with Zuroff. The Nazi hunter asked the reporters to try the front door to see if anyone was in. "A visibly nervous man in a white beard and green ski parka [opened] the door a crack" and told the reporters that Böser and her husband were out of town. Zuroff was not so sure. Smoke billowed from the chimney, and two cars belonging to the owners of the house were parked outside the home. It was "astonishing behavior on the part of people who claimed to have done nothing wrong. We left the scene with the disappointed journalists in tow."

As Zuroff suspected, Waltraut was doing her best to avoid the reporters. Off and on for two years now, cameramen, photographers, and reporters had waited outside her house, called at all hours, followed her, and, most disconcerting, followed her children. Earlier that year she had been driving in a neighborhood she described as "not exactly the safest" when she turned her car around in a cul-de-sac. An unfamiliar vehicle that had been following her came to a halt in front of her car, blocking her in. It was a television crew filming a documentary.

When the documentary aired on German television, the footage showed Böser's Volvo turning in to a side street as the narrator explained that the crew hoped she would lead them to Heim, "if we only observe her long enough." When she stopped her car, a man with a camera rushed up to her and began questioning her.

"You can follow me forever," Böser told the reporter. "You'll never find my father, because I don't know him."

The reporter continued to interview her through the window of her car, a blurry rectangle placed over her eyes in postproduction to give her a small measure of anonymity. Her face was round and looked weathered. "I have no idea."

"Can it be that you don't know him but do know where he is?"

"No, I also don't know where he is."

"Are you in contact with your half brother in Baden-Baden?" he asked.

"I have no idea who they are," she said. "I don't know anyone."

The documentary implied that this was a lie, replaying part of an interview with a man who worked for the family. "Once a year she visits her brother," the man said. Without commenting on the apparent contradiction, or mentioning that she had a maternal half brother, Peter, she had grown up with in Austria, the scene switched back to the interview in Chile.

"It is a fact that in Berlin there is an account with roughly a million euros," the reporter said. "You would inherit a large share of it if he's not alive."

"Yes, but . . . what should I say . . . ," she stammered. "I'm going to say . . . Money—" The interviewer interrupted her.

"Everyone can use money," he said.

"Everyone can use money," Böser repeated, "but I'm not interested in the money. What I'm interested in is that people finally believe that what I say is true and that I'm left in peace. I don't know him and I don't need any money." The reporter said if she didn't know anything, she should tell the police, not just in Chile, as she claimed she had, but in Austria as well.

"Why was she so sure we wouldn't find him? Does she know that he has powerful assistance?" the narrator of the film intoned. "It spoke either for the involvement of a secret service abetting his flight or for a really good hiding place."

The next time she was in Austria, Waltraut gave a statement to the police. The German manhunt unit believed the Austrians "treated her far too gently," according to Zuroff. In September 2008, she and Peter, with whom she was raised and whom she actually visited each year in Austria, sat down with Zuroff and his German colleague, the historian Stefan Klemp, in Innsbruck.

"I have never set eyes on my father," she stated.

"If your father walked in this door right now, what would you say to him?" Zuroff asked her.

"Where have you been all this time?"

The answer neither satisfied his curiosity nor stilled his skepticism. "Very touching perhaps," he wrote later, "but I was not convinced by her version of the events." The key question for Zuroff was how her mother, after multiple interviews with police, could not have told her daughter that her father was a mass murderer.

"I could not believe, for example, that many years previously when the Austrian police came to question her mother about Heim, and she was in the house at the time (claiming to be ill, which is why she was not present at the questioning), she never asked her mother why the police had come to speak to her," Zuroff said. "In short, we did not receive convincing answers for many of the questions we posed." Yet there was a plausible and relatively simple explanation, of a mother trying to protect her daughter.

In August 2008, Rüdiger welcomed a reporter named Burkhard Uhlenbroich from *Bild am Sonntag,* the Sunday edition of the popular German tabloid, to his family's home for an interview. When the reporter arrived at eleven o'clock in the morning as arranged, Rüdiger told him he was "punctual as a Swiss watch." As he walked into the house, Uhlenbroich marveled at the twelve-foot ceilings, the antique furniture, and the oil paintings, all purchased by Rüdiger's maternal grandparents, the Bechtolds, who made successful real-estate investments before World War II.

The pleasantries dispensed with, they began to talk about his father. "I cannot even remember when I last saw him," Rüdiger told Uhlenbroich. "I do not know where he lives, nor am I financing his flight. If he is dead, I do not know where he is buried." Had the family really never heard from Dr. Heim after he fled? the interviewer asked. "Between 1962 and 1967, two notes appeared in our mailbox. Each contained a single sentence, 'I am doing well,'" Rüdiger said. "Whether those letters really came from my father, I do not know." When Uhlenbroich asked Rüdiger what he would do if he knew where his father was living, he declared, "I would shout it out to the entire world that he should turn himself in and answer to the terrible accusations.

"My father's past is a part of my life," Rüdiger said. "To deny this would be pointless." He revealed precisely what he wanted without necessarily answering the questions he was asked. Rather than saying when he last saw Aribert Heim, he simply told a story about two anonymous letters.

The burden on Heim's family and acquaintances was rising. In the same television documentary whose crew had cornered Waltraut Böser in the cul-de-sac, long-lensed cameras peered into Heim's old house in Baden-Baden. The Heim family, like Böser, chafed under the investigative pressure, but the difference was they were actually complicit, having hidden and financially supported Heim. The legal protections afforded to relatives meant they were not guilty of any crime, but they were involved in exactly the ways that the police believed they were.

For Pisano and Pellet, their innocent association with Rüdiger made them victims of overzealous journalists as well as law enforcement. All this distress had a purpose, however: to break the silence surrounding Heim's whereabouts. Because he was the most wanted Nazi war criminal in the world, the attention to Heim's case had grown exponentially, and with it the incentive for someone to bring it to a conclusion. In the end, the public pressure had the intended effect.

The break came in the form of a tip not to law enforcement but to a journalist. "I can't tell you on the phone, but I need to see you in person," said the caller. "It's important." For several years he had been a reliable source for Souad. "I'm flying via Frankfurt tomorrow and will have some time around noon," he told her. They agreed on a place near the city's famous Hauptwache plaza.

The source produced a file with a photograph of a middle-aged man in a suit and tie. In the lower left-hand corner, part of a stamp with markings in Arabic was visible. "Do you know who this man is?" he asked. She said she did not. "Aribert Heim, they also call him Dr. Death." After extracting a promise of anonymity, the tipster revealed where the Nazi fugitive had fled when he left Germany in 1963.

Just as the neighbors had whispered in the wake of his departure and as Simon Wiesenthal had suspected in 1967, the trail led not to the Costa Brava or a Chilean island but to Cairo's Kasr el-Madina Hotel and to the Doma family that used to run it. The evidence of Aribert Heim's hideout was uncovered in a storage space in Cairo's Nasr City neighborhood, in a clothing store owned by the Doma brothers, filled with women's blue jeans, skirts, and blouses and one leather attaché case with rusty clasps.

"This is the briefcase of Amu," said Ahmed Doma, Mahmoud's younger brother, as he set it down on the table. "We haven't opened it for the last fifteen, maybe sixteen years," he said. Sharif, their older half brother, undid the clasps. Inside were hundreds of pieces of paper, some sealed in yellowed envelopes with handwritten titles that read "Bills" or "Documents." He took out a page.

"Here is a hotel bill of his from Alexandria," Sharif said. To the incessant sound of city traffic they read aloud the letters, written in blue ink on yellowish paper, as they were pulled from the briefcase. There were black-and-white photographs of athletes training, brochures and articles on the tourism industry, dozens of letters and medical prescriptions, bills, and other paperwork inside.

"He loved reading," Ahmed said. He described how Uncle Tarek would go to the famed Groppi café, once among the finest Western locales in the city, by 2008 a run-down shadow of itself like much of Cairo's old European quarter. "He would bring cake for us sometimes, and he would play Ping-Pong and other sports on the roof with us children."

The papers inside the case were mostly written in German and English and some in French and were therefore indecipherable to the Domas. Uncle Tarek tried to teach them all three languages, but they forgot much of what they learned, except for the English they used in commercial transactions. Mahmoud in particular regretted that he had forgotten so much of what Uncle Tarek taught him.

In addition to the many defenses Heim had composed about his criminal case and the report about anti-Semitism and the Khazars, there were a great number of medical records among the papers, including more than a dozen urinalysis reports, as well as careful sketches in colored pencil of his urinary, digestive, and reproductive systems, apparently drawn by Dr. Heim himself. On one envelope he wrote the names of two doctors. Next to one was the word "treatment," next to the other, "inoperable." One paper said "Pathology Report" at the top and dealt with a "rectal carcinoid." Another was labeled "Biological Tumor Markers," and the referral was from Dr. Mohsen Barsoum, a professor of radiotherapy at the cancer center of Cairo University.

When we visited Dr. Barsoum at his practice in the Cairo neighborhood of Dokki, he instantly recognized his former patient from the photograph. "He was a peculiar case," Dr. Barsoum said. "In your career, some people have special features." He said that Heim had spent a year under his observation and that the cancer was advanced. After looking at a copy of a prescription he had written, found in Heim's briefcase, he said, "I'm sure he was stage 4. It was not an early case."

Many other people recognized Heim from the photograph. The dentist Abdelmoneim el Rifai and his family remembered Heim. Abu Ahmad, who used to help out at the Kasr el-Madina, explained simply, "He always stood out in the crowd." Downstairs in the building a seller of cheese, peppers, and olives took one look at the photograph and before he was even asked about it offered, "That was the foreigner upstairs." Everyone in the neighborhood remembered the day that he died, the cheese seller recalled. Wrapped in white cotton for a traditional Muslim burial, he was still recognizable because of his height as they carried him out of the building.

It was a rainy and cold January morning in 2009 when Rüdiger Heim welcomed us into his home. He was a gracious and polite host, offering drinks and snacks as a crew set up a camera and lights in the living room and hooked him up to a microphone. He spoke quietly and slowly as if a single false word would be held against him, which in some cases it had been.

His skin was pale from spending too much time indoors, his hair graying, yet he looked younger than his fifty-three years. His large glasses were at least a decade out of fashion, but his appearance did not seem to interest him much. He tended to wear faded blue jeans and T-shirts, a vest or a sweater if it was cold. The family had money, but he drove an old Opel rather than a fancy car.

Now it was time for Rüdiger to tell his story, once and for all. If for no other reason, he could do it for the sake of his friends in Spain. If he remained silent, there was no sign that the pursuit of his father would ever cease. Silence had only made his legend grow.

"Mr. Heim," Souad said, "do you know the person in this photograph?" It was the same picture the source had handed over, the same one identified by the friends, acquaintances, and physicians in Egypt.

"Yes, that is my father," Rüdiger said.

"Do you know where this photograph comes from?" she asked.

"It must be from an Egyptian document, probably my father's residency permit."

"That means your father lived in Cairo?"

"Yes," Rüdiger answered. "My father lived in Cairo."

CHAPTER 56

Rüdiger had returned to Egypt in July 1992 for what he expected to be his last visit. Father and son spoke regularly, with Rüdiger calling from pay phones so that their conversations could not be tapped. In the first few months after Rüdiger returned to Europe, his father would say, "It would be nice if you came." Finally, as his illness worsened, Heim had simply said, "It is time now for you to come."

By that point Aribert Heim did not leave the Kasr el-Madina. A nurse visited each day to check on him and to change his colostomy bag. His room was next to Mahmoud Doma's, and if he needed something, he would knock on the wall. Mahmoud was twenty-two years old by then and studying engineering at the university. Heim became more candid as his life slipped away. His cover story with so many Egyptian friends— Alfred Buediger, the owner of a demolition company—was gone, and he told Mahmoud that he had been a doctor who used to study women's cancer. "He said he was very famous and a very good doctor," Mahmoud said. Heim never told him anything about his military service.

Toward the end he asked his young friend, "Can I donate my body after I die so that the university can use it for tests?" Mahmoud said it was because his uncle Tarek had an unusual illness and hoped that before he was buried the students at the medical school could learn from his body. "I told him that our Islamic beliefs did not allow you to donate your body. It is a sin."

"All right," Heim said. "If that is so, then it does not have to happen."

When Rüdiger entered his father's room in the Kasr el-Madina, the lights were off, and Heim was sitting in a wheelchair. Rüdiger greeted his father.

His father returned his greeting, then immediately turned to practical matters. "We have to decide now if I'm going to remain in this chair for my final days or if I'm going to lie in the bed." He refused to discuss recovery, remission, or improvement. Rüdiger learned most of what he needed to know just by looking at the weakened state of his father's once-powerful body. Moving from the wheelchair to the bed to sleep at night had become an excruciating ordeal. Heim finally said, "From now on I will be in the bed."

The following day Rüdiger helped his father lie down. "He was a moribund, doomed person, slowly rotting from the inside," Rüdiger said. His pain was compounded by a return bout of kidney stones. At one point the agony was so overpowering he demanded that Rüdiger give him all the painkilling medication they had at once.

For nourishment, he took only warmed milk. "Milk has everything in it that the body needs, and I don't need any more than that now," Heim said.

Father and son spent much of the time watching the Barcelona Olympics. When the Olympics were not on, they tuned to coverage of the war in Bosnia. On the matter of his own criminal case, the dying man expressed conflicting wishes. He said at one point that he wanted "the truth to come to light," but at another he told his son, "Don't worry about this nonsense anymore."

At a certain juncture his pain was so great that Heim could no longer roll over to urinate, and short of taking him to a hospital for a catheter to be inserted, Rüdiger had to help him pee every two or three hours. When Rüdiger made a mistake, the bed would be soaked in urine, and it became a major production to move his father to change the sheets. Rüdiger had taken to massaging his father's arms and legs because he noticed that it helped with the pain.

"I also caught myself thinking that the suffering actually had to end, that it was too much, that it was outrageous," Rüdiger said. "And one discovers, too, in oneself, the weakness to hope that it stops, and it is actually a shameless thought, a terrible thought," thinking ahead to his father's death. At one point, Rüdiger went to the bathroom and wept. He was sure that in Europe no one would have to die like that.

Heim's voice gave out several days before he passed away. Rüdiger blamed himself for dallying in Europe before coming to Egypt. He had lost his last chance to ask the lingering questions he had about his father's past.

On August 9, 1992, Aribert and Rüdiger Heim watched the closing ceremonies of the Olympics. Dr. Heim fell asleep at around 10:00 p.m. Instead of going back to the Scarabee to sleep, Rüdiger now had a thin mattress that he rolled out in front of the balcony. Around one o'clock in the morning he noticed that his father's breathing was slowing. Over the course of hours, his father had *"hinüber gedämmert"* ("faded across").

"There was no exact time of death, but at some point he had stopped breathing," Rüdiger said. He spoke to him, checked to make sure his father was not still alive, and placed his hand over his father's head. When it was clear he had died, Rüdiger took a piece of white cloth and ran it under his father's chin, tying it at the top of his head. He had learned when his grandmother died that this was necessary so that rigor mortis would not leave his mouth hanging open.

"One says good-bye in a very personal way," Rüdiger said. He smoked a cigarette on the balcony, staring out into the Cairo streets. Then he went downstairs and notified the hotel's night porter that his father was dead. The porter reached Mahmoud, who had been away in Alexandria. The young man arrived with his mother and one of his brothers within a few hours. The hotel also notified the authorities. A representative from the German embassy came to Heim's deathbed, as well as the Egyptian official who filled out the death certificate.

Ever wary of the authorities, Rüdiger gave them his Danish driver's license as identification. He also put down a false birthday for his father, to further throw off anyone trying to find Aribert Heim. Rüdiger said Heim did not want investigators to bother his family and he did not want trouble for the Domas.

Some time after sunrise, two men came to bathe his father one final time. They took the body out into the hall, where they had set up a table. They took off his clothes, removed the colostomy bag, and began to wash him according to Islamic ritual. Mahmoud didn't want Rüdiger to watch, but the Egyptian man cleaning his father said, "Come, look at this. This is your father." When they were done with the washing, they wrapped him in long white winding sheets.

It is Muslim tradition to bury the body as quickly as possible, without embalming or autopsies. Mahmoud wanted to inter Uncle Tarek in the same tomb with his own father. Rüdiger wanted to honor Heim's wish that his cadaver be used for medical research. Mahmoud tried to explain that it would be simplest if he were buried according to local custom, but the son refused. The man from the German embassy, an Arab who spoke German, finally told Mahmoud that as the son Rüdiger had certain rights in deciding what would happen to the body. Mahmoud did not like it, but he remembered his uncle Tarek's request and reluctantly went along.

The body was carried downstairs to a waiting mortuary van, where it was laid out on a wooden bier in the back. Mahmoud cried. "He was like a father. He loved me and I loved him. He was the same as my father."

Mahmoud and Rüdiger, the son Mahmoud knew only as Roy, drove to several hospitals, but none of them wanted to take the corpse. It was an unusual request with possible legal repercussions. The orderlies told them that they could not accept corpses for donation. After several hours Rüdiger began to wonder if his father's body was beginning to putrefy. Mahmoud said finally, "That's enough. We can't go on like this. Let's first of all put him in a refrigerator. You're more than welcome to keep looking, but I'm tired."

They eventually found a man at one of the hospitals who was willing to take the body. The details were sketchy. He might have been bribed or simply offered to do them a favor by keeping Heim's body overnight. Either way the two men left his body there. Rüdiger believed that the body had been accepted according to his father's last wishes. Mahmoud described the arrangement as more temporary.

When the two returned to the Kasr el-Madina, they sorted through Heim's belongings, packing his papers into the old leather briefcase and a hard-shell Samsonite case. Once this was done, Rüdiger told Mahmoud to watch his father's effects and said he would soon return for them. He did not give his address or any way to contact him. Mahmoud found it strange at the time but did not ask any questions. He might have had an ulterior motive in helping to speed Rüdiger's departure, for, once the son left, Mahmoud went back to try to claim Heim's body so that it could be interred in his family tomb, as he had wanted to do in the first place. The hospital told him that he might have called the man uncle but that did not make him a legal relative. Corpses were not just given out to anyone who wanted them.

In the end, Tarek Hussein Farid was buried in a common crypt like an Egyptian pauper.

CHAPTER 57

Rüdiger in the meantime had returned to Germany, where the news began to travel in the very small circle of the family. He called his cousin Birgit and asked her to come down to Baden-Baden, afraid that the phone had been tapped. Rüdiger broke the news to her in the car, where they thought they were least likely to be eavesdropped upon by the police. Birgit in turn drove home and told her mother. They kept the secret for close to seventeen years.

In February 2009, the *New York Times* and ZDF German television reported that Dr. Aribert Heim, the Simon Wiesenthal Center's most wanted Nazi war criminal, had lived in Egypt as a convert to Islam and that he had died there in 1992. Reporters descended in droves on the Kasr el-Madina Hotel. Mahmoud and the other sources quoted in the story were dragged in for harsh and lengthy questioning by Egyptian state security.

Without the actual body, Efraim Zuroff did not believe a Nazi fugitive should be declared dead. He had precedent in this. One of Simon Wiesenthal's most important contributions to Eichmann's capture had been to prevent Eichmann's wife from having her husband declared dead shortly after the war. If he had been, investigators would have stopped looking for him. In Heim's case, "there are too many question marks," said Zuroff. "The scenario is almost too perfect to be believed . . . No body, no grave, no DNA, the most important test there is."

Meanwhile, Heim's briefcase was transferred to the state police in Baden-Württemberg. Experts checked the authenticity of its contents. They compared the handwriting on the documents with older writing samples and confirmed that Heim was their author. The dust in the case included a form of lime that is found in Egypt. Certain microorganisms also supported its authenticity. "The extensive criminal technical analyses of the documents from the briefcase lead us to the conclusion that it actually came from Aribert Heim," said the police in a statement. But the death certificate bore the name Tarek Hussein Farid and gave a false birth date.

It took four more years to confirm his death to the satisfaction of the German courts. Additional documents surfaced from the second bag Rüdiger and Mahmoud had packed up when he died. The Samsonite case was too useful to leave idle, and at some point over the years someone had taken it, stashing the loose papers in one of the Doma brothers' homes. Those papers included documentation of his name change and his conversion to Islam. The court in Baden-Baden finally declared Heim dead. Life slowly went back to normal for the Doma family. The house on Maria-Viktoria-Strasse in Baden-Baden remained much as it was.

Yet questions still lingered about the veracity of his death. Zuroff asked, couldn't one final escape have been possible, to Chile maybe, or Spain, or back to his native Austria? Had his accomplices wound a living Aribert Heim in white sheets like a corpse, carried him out in broad daylight for a maximum number of witnesses? Had they sworn the Doma family to secrecy and left the papers behind for the day when his pursuers came uncomfortably close to his hiding place?

When the war ended, Heim was essentially a nobody, one of tens of thousands of perpetrators. It would have been impossible for the Allies, both logistically and politically, to round up all the concentration camp guards, to imprison every SS officer, to remove every member of the Nazi Party from public life. The willingness to find and prosecute war criminals grew precisely as their numbers dwindled.

Today, German politicians and officers of the law don't have to worry about Nazi-era skeletons in their closets. Far from the mark of shame it bore in the early postwar years, the contemporary German state possesses a moral authority that stems in part from its image as a country that dealt with its past head-on, a nation that accepted its guilt and rose above it, paying reparations to survivors, providing health insurance in their old age, and generally succoring those their forebears tormented. One important way to underscore that has been to stick with the legal pursuit of the war criminals.

From the Nuremberg trials to this day, a pattern has emerged of using the criminal-justice system as a tool for teaching about the Holocaust. Deniers could not easily explain away Adolf Eichmann sitting behind bulletproof glass, or the parade of eyewitnesses describing Nazi atrocities, or the documents entered into evidence. That is one reason prosecutors have continued to put older and older defendants in the dock. Many of them are now dying as they await their verdicts or appeals, as in the case of the retired autoworker John Demjanjuk.

Demjanjuk, a Ukrainian immigrant to the Cleveland area, was wrongly accused of being Ivan the Terrible, one of the worst guards at Treblinka. He was tried in Israel and sentenced to death, only to be partially exonerated. Demjanjuk was not Ivan the Terrible, it turned out, but he had been a guard at Sobibor. No one but him knows what he did there, but he was sent to Germany and tried using a novel prosecution theory. Merely by serving at a death camp, he was considered an accessory to the murder of everyone killed while he was stationed there. Demjanjuk might have been bloodthirsty, or he might have helped people escape. That, combined with his advanced age, made many people uncomfortable, as he lay in a hospital bed set up in the courtroom.

Heim, by comparison, remained in our imaginations a worthy adversary, with his mocking half smile in the photograph in which he is wearing a tuxedo. Eyewitnesses accused him of murdering with his own hands. There could be no qualms about searching for him. By eluding capture for so long, Heim became the eternal Nazi in the minds of those who had sworn never to forget.

No number of final-hour prosecutions could ever do justice to the crimes committed in the Holocaust. Reading through Alfred Aedtner's index cards, even a researcher jaded by constant exposure to the machinery of death feels overwhelmed again by the specific cruelties. But the pursuit of Nazi war criminals is not just a dwindling exercise. It has also set a precedent for genocide victims everywhere.

With each passing year, Heim's complaint that only Nazis were singled out for war-crimes prosecution has become increasingly untrue. The ethnic cleansing of the Bosnian War, which Rüdiger and Aribert watched unfold on CNN, led to the creation of the International Criminal Tribunal for the Former Yugoslavia. The likes of Ratko Mladić, Radovan Karadžić, and Slobodan Milošević were delivered to The Hague for trial. Perpetrators of the genocide in Rwanda were put before the International Criminal Tribunal for Rwanda. On July 1, 2002, a permanent sitting court, the International Criminal Court, was created to prosecute war criminals from all nations.

The Department of Justice's Office of Special Investigations, dedicated to the pursuit of Nazi war criminals, was combined with the Domestic Security Section in 2010 to create the new Human Rights and Special Prosecutions Section, with a mandate to prosecute "violators for genocide, torture, war crimes, and recruitment or use of child soldiers."

The hunt for Nazi war criminals might have been fitful and incomplete, as in the search for Heim even beyond the grave, but it established a worthy model. Famous men like Simon Wiesenthal and unknown ones like Alfred Aedtner left a legacy beyond their pursuit of the criminals of the Holocaust, a new standard of justice amid the violent injustice of war.

EPILOGUE

In a surviving black-and-white photograph, Max Heftmann is dressed like a grown man in a suit and tie, but his bright grin for the camera betrays his youth. The oldest of three sons, he worked at a lightbulb factory in Vienna. He was a member of a Zionist youth club called Blau Weiss, or Blue White, and had a passion for skiing and water sports.

At the end of 1937, with Nazi Germany's annexation of Austria approaching, Heftmann decided to immigrate to Holland. He worked in Amsterdam as an electrician at Werkdorp, a training center for would-be immigrants to Palestine. There he met a young Dutch woman named Ray Soesman. The two wanted to marry, but Max could not get the necessary documents from Austria.

The Nazis invaded Holland in May 1940. They shut down Werkdorp the following year. Heftmann was deported to Mauthausen in 1941. Ray was sent to the Westerbork camp and then to Theresienstadt. She received three letters from her fiancé. In the first two letters he implored her to write him back. In the third and final letter she received, he did not. Somehow it sounded to Ray like a good-bye.

In 1941, when Aribert Heim performed surgery on him to remove, according to the operation book, necrotic skin tissue from his right foot, Heftmann was just twenty-eight years old. Heim was twenty-seven. Heftmann's entry in the death book states that he passed away ten days later from an infection in his lower left leg.

Heim was at Mauthausen as Jews from Holland were systematically killed, but those receiving lethal injections were not included in the operation book. The details in the death book, including the precise dates and causes of death, were frequently altered to cover up for executions, as Ernst Martin testified at the trial in Dachau, making it difficult to determine who might have been Heim's victims.

Another young Austrian discovered Max Heftmann's story almost seven decades later. Andreas Kranebitter is part of the small but dedicated staff on the top floor of the Austrian Interior Ministry in Vienna who keep up the Mauthausen archive and are responsible for the exhibits at the concentration camp, which today is both a memorial and a teaching institute. Like many of the staffers, he started out volunteering there as part of his national civil service and stayed.

Kranebitter's grandfather was also an SS doctor. Like Aribert Heim's brother, Josef, he served with the paratroopers for the offensive in Crete. Kranebitter thinks the two doctors might have known each other. Rather than a reason to avoid the history of Nazism in his native Austria, Kranebitter saw it as all the more reason to investigate the subject.

Rüdiger Heim embodies the more fitful reckoning many Germans have with their past. He both recognizes and deplores the terrible atrocities committed by Nazi Germany in the Holocaust but believes his father is wrongly accused of the crimes he was alleged to have perpetrated. A gap exists for many people between collective guilt, which is easier to accept, and individual responsibility. It often feels in Germany as though there were many more Nazis than descendants of Nazis, when just the opposite is the case.

There is little question that Heim served a harsher sentence—thirty years in exile—than he would have received in Germany in the 1960s, where capital punishment had already been abolished and prison terms in Nazi cases were often surprisingly short. That is assuming he was convicted in the first place. Instead of relieving his family of embarrassment by fleeing to Egypt, he inflicted far greater and far more lasting suffering on them, through decades of surveillance and questioning by law enforcement and the media alike.

His story does not provide an easy sense of closure. If it were a movie, Aribert Heim would have been caught by Alfred Aedtner after a chase through Cairo, his arrest announced by Simon Wiesenthal. Heim would have had his day in court with the international media there to hear his defense. But his story was not a movie, and for many of those involved, the effects lingered long after his death and its revelation.

Waltraut Böser still travels each summer to Austria to visit her half brother Peter. Lately she has found her way to neighboring Germany on those visits, where she has struck up a warm friendship with her cousin Birgit Barth. On a recent trip Waltraut brought old photographs, pictures of her mother and of herself as a young woman at around the time that she impulsively hitchhiked to see Elvis, from a downhill competition after her youthful prime where she became the ski champion of pharmacists.

Birgit in turn shared photographs of the Heim family in Radkersburg and a poetry album, in which a young Aribert implored his elder sister, Hilda, "Wanderer, learn in a faraway place," and "Speak as your heart speaks with itself." In his own family, Heim is still remembered as the dutiful son, brother, and father, their personal experiences of the man trumping all the outside accusations. Waltraut was happy to learn about the sides of her father she never read about in the newspaper, though the sadness at never meeting him remains.

"He lived his whole life beside me, and I never saw him," Waltraut said. "For me that was the worst part—that I never saw him." Like Rüdiger, she did not believe that he was guilty. "I quite simply could never believe that he did it," Waltraut said. "I was not at Mauthausen, and I can't know, but purely on instinct I can't believe it."

She had inherited so many of her traits, talents, and interests from him. The possibility that he also had it within himself to commit gruesome murders was just too distressing for her. Heim impregnated and abandoned her mother, yet Gertrud told Waltraut only stories about the wonderful young man her father had been, never letting a bad word about him pass her lips.

"She only said good things about him," Waltraut said. "For me he was a role model."

ACKNOWLEDGMENTS

From its inception to its conclusion, this book has been the product of many people's labor. Elmar Thevessen was an integral part of the original story about Aribert Heim for ZDF Television and cannot be thanked enough as a journalist, colleague, and friend for his many contributions.

Christine Kay and Matt Purdy from the investigative team at the *New York Times* helped drive the reporting and shape the writing of the article about Heim's hideaway in Cairo. Bill Keller was an unwavering supporter of this project and many others in his time as executive editor.

Almut Schönfeld was a steadfast researcher and a brilliant guide through the warrens and nooks of Germany's archives. Chris Cottrell was an extraordinary fact-checker, bringing verve and curiosity to his work.

Not enough can be said about the team at the Mauthausen Archive at the Austrian Ministry of Interior, in particular Andreas Kranebitter, Gregor Holzinger, and Doris Warlitsch, who were equally adept at pulling out the perfect file as they were at doling out advice over a beer.

Carter Dougherty and the Mekhennet family helped with the storage and movement of the dusty old briefcase that formed the backbone of our early work on Heim's story. Stefan Pauly spent a sleepless night scanning page after yellowed page of Heim's correspondence, medical records, and clippings, finding invaluable documentaries and archival materials on his own time and initiative that would inform both the article and the book. Victor Homola gave logistical and research support throughout the process. The ZDF documentary would not have been possible without the brilliance of Christian Deick. Jihan Rushdy-Koydl of ZDF was instrumental on the ground in Egypt. Nagi al Adawi was more than a driver, always there with insight and a warm smile. Luc Walpot, the former Egypt correspondent for ZDF, gave us generous assistance.

Our stays in Egypt would have been immeasurably less enjoyable and significantly less comfortable without the generosity and kindness of Alexandra Rydmark, Hans Grundberg, JoAnna Pollonais, Frederik Matthys, and Matt Bradley, whose rooftop in Dokki, gone but not forgotten, was a clearinghouse for journalist gossip in Cairo, before and after the start of the Egyptian Revolution in 2011.

Several people worked to free us from detention for reporting during the revolution. Our thanks go to Elizabeth O. Colton from the United States embassy, the journalist Claudia Sautter, Philipp Ackerman from the German foreign ministry, and Ambassador Michael Bock from the German embassy. Others in Morocco and Germany who prefer not to be named were equally instrumental in our release and we thank them as well.

This book would not have been possible without the patience of Aribert Heim's living relatives. Rüdiger Heim suffered through interminable and often repetitive interviews. Birgit Barth brought a sharp sense of humor and acute memory to our discussions. Waltraut Böser overcame her resistance to speaking with journalists and sacrificed time during her summer vacation in Europe to share her story. Friedl Heim relived painful memories time and again but was always a kind hostess, may she rest in peace. Khalid Habouchi made us feel most welcome in Baden-Baden.

Gaetano Pisano and Blandine Pellet shared their story as well as providing deep insights into Rüdiger Heim's life in Italy, Denmark, France, and Spain.

Lore Aedtner shared memories and mementos of her late husband. Harald Aedtner spoke at length about his father. Agnes Haag shared the story of Fritz Haag, who helped young Alfred restart his life after the war.

Fritz Steinacker welcomed us to his office repeatedly to share memories of his client and allow us access to otherwise inaccessible depositions and court records.

Mahmoud Doma gave his time unstintingly as he shared memories of his Amu Tarek. He and his family endured difficult questioning after the initial story broke and suffered on the business side in the glare of publicity. We thank Sharif, Ahmed, and the rest of the Doma family for their assistance.

Kamal Gabala at *Al-Ahram,* Mahmoud Salah at *Akhbar el-Hawadeth,* and Gamal al Ghitany at *Akhbar el Yom* helped us navigate fifty years of Egyptian history.

We would like to thank the Jewish community of Morocco and in particular Rachel Muyal, former director of the Librairie des Colonnes bookshop, who took time to explain the fascinating history of the Jewish community in Tangier. Soraya Sebti and Abderrahim Sabir were also a great help and comfort.

It is hard to say enough about Germany's brilliant network of libraries and archives, from small towns to the capital of Berlin. Thanks in particular to Wolfgang Läpple at the Stadtarchiv Ludwigsburg and Garnisonmuseum Ludwigsburg, Tobias Herrmann at the Aussenstelle Ludwigsburg Bundesarchiv, Brigitte Faatz at the Stadtarchiv Bad Nauheim, Lutz Schneider at the Stadtarchiv Friedberg, Günther Berger at the Heidelberg City Archives, Gisa Franke at the Archiv der Hansestadt Rostock, Werner Renz at the Fritz Bauer Institute, and Stephan Kühmayer at the Deutsche Dienststelle (WASt).

Kurt Schrimm at the Central Office in Ludwigsburg has taken more than a few sudden calls on his cell phone asking for information and never been anything but gracious and forthcoming. The LKA Baden-Württemberg could not always be open about an ongoing investigation, but Joachim Schäck and others always did their best.

In Austria, Beatrix Vreca in the Bad Radkersburg shed important light on the Heim family history. Dr. Marianne Enigl of *Profil* magazine helped a great deal with the Anschluss. Herbert Posch at the Institut für Zeitgeschichte at the University of Vienna was instrumental in finding documentation about Aribert Heim's academic record and on his own initiative found a letter from Josef Heim in the archives that confirmed several old Heim family stories. Michaela Vocelka at the Simon Wiesenthal Archive is a fine hostess and runs a tight ship at the Nazi hunter's former office. His successor, Efraim Zuroff, brought a healthy skepticism that challenged numerous assumptions and made our work more rigorous.

In the United States, the United States Holocaust Memorial Museum library was an essential resource. William H. Cunliffe at the National Archives at College Park is a national treasure himself. Eli Rosenbaum at the Justice Department is a knowledgeable source on the history of American Nazi hunting.

Representing Canada, Tomaz Jardim's work on the Mauthausen trials is indispensable. In France, Dominique Dreyer at the Cernay Archive helped fill in answers to questions about the end of the war for Aribert Heim.

The documentary filmmaker Yoash Tatari performed a great service to history by filming Alfred Aedtner at work on his archive and telling the story of just one of the men and women dedicated to bringing Nazi war criminals to justice.

Gary Smith of the American Academy in Berlin provided guidance and insightful comments from before the article had even begun its evolution into the book. Christine Kay helped a great deal with the early stages of the manuscript. Rachel B. Doyle provided support and assistance throughout the writing process. Rachel, Elmar Thevessen, Jörg Müllner, Christoph Niemann, Andreas Kranebitter, Almut Schönfeld, Melissa Eddy, Chris Cottrell, and Professor Steffen Burkhardt were insightful readers as it neared completion.

Thanks to our agents, Marly Rusoff and Kirby Kim, for their help from start to finish with the project. Phyllis Grann at Doubleday believed in this project from the very beginning. Kristine Puopulo shared her vision and carried it forward. Dan Meyer kept us on the straight and narrow so the book was polished and ready to go.

Lastly, none of this would have been possible without the support of our friends and family over the past five years. Thank you all.

NOTES

PROLOGUE

4 "In the inner compartment": Baz, *Secret Executioners*, p. 94.

CHAPTER 1

7 There were caravans of displaced persons: Bessel, *Germany 1945*, p. 68.

7 Central Registry of War Criminals and Security Suspects: Ryan, *Klaus Barbie and the United States Government*, p. 22.

7 By some estimates 160,000 people: Bascomb, *Hunting Eichmann*, p. 65.

7 The Americans alone had to deal with some 7.7 million: Bessel, *Germany 1945*, p. 200.

8 One clue as to who was who: Sher and Rosenbaum, *In the Matter of Josef Mengele*, pp. 37–38.

8 Seventeen people named Josef Mengele: Ibid., p. 25.

8 The U.S. Third Army: Ibid., p. 37.

8 the British sent home some 300,000 Germans: Bessel, *Germany 1945*, p. 348.

8 The telecommunication network, postal service, highways: Ibid., p. 63.

8 If a soldier was discharged: Sher and Rosenbaum, *In the Matter of Josef Mengele*, pp. 37–38.

9 Though a prisoner, he continued to serve as a doctor: Edward S. Jones, letter, September 26, 1946.

9 The Red Cross inspector found the conditions: Copie conforme Archive du CICR (Comité International de la Croix-Rouge), France, Hôpitaux Dépendant de la Base de Normandie (en mains américaines), Visites par le Dr. Rossel du 10 au 17 Mai 1945.

9 "had been excellent": Jones, letter, September 26, 1946.

9 "practiced his medicinal arts": Werner Ernst Linz, attestation, November 15, 1947.

10   Just eight days after the first American soldier: Knopp, *Die Befreiung Kriegsende im Westen*, p. 236.

CHAPTER 2

11   A writer by profession: Arthur Alexander Becker, file from International Tracing Service, Bad Arolsen.

11   "mostly shell-shocked tank officers": Benjamin Ferencz, interview with Jardim, in *The Mauthausen Trial: American Military Justice in Germany*, p. 64.

11   The enormity of the task: Jardim, *Mauthausen Trial*, p. 62.

12   The investigative team Becker worked for: Ibid., p. 110.

12   Gas, electricity, and telephone services were disrupted: MacDonogh, *After the Reich*, pp. 278–94.

12   As an adult, he was bald: Photograph of Josef Kohl, Republik Österreich, BMI Archiv P/19/10/09.

12   After the Nazis absorbed Austria: Marsalek, "Er hat jedem geholfen."

13   That meant that, according to the Nazis' own rating: Le Chêne, *Mauthausen*, p. 36.

13   That year more than half: Marsalek, *Mauthausen*, p. 125, quoted in Jardim, *Mauthausen Trial*.

13   Now he was free: Transcript of questioning, Josef Kohl, War Crimes Investigating Team 6836, Republik Österreich, BMI IV/7 Archiv V/3/9.

13   "What do you know about the abuse": Josef Kohl, interview by Special Investigator Dr. Alexander Becker, January 18, 1946, Republik Österreich, BMI IV/7 Archiv V/3/9.

CHAPTER 3

15   A new sign hung over the entryway: *Prozess Mauthausen: Das Urteil*, Welt im Film, http://www.youtube.com/watch?v=HHNA9YyJh94.

15   There were also more than fifty SS doctors: Freund, "Der Mauthausen-Prozess," p. 107.

15   "a throw of the dice": Paul Guth, interview by Joshua Greene, Lafayette, La., February 24, 2001, four cassette tapes, Denson Papers, series 5, Audiovisual Materials, 1918–2004, boxes 46–49, quoted in Jardim, *Mauthausen Trial*.

16   "ranged in age from twenty-one": Jardim, *Mauthausen Trial*, pp. 103–04. See also Freund, "Der Mauthausen-Prozess," p. 104.

16   "The material was so large": U.S. v. Altfuldisch et al., case 000-50-5, Hauptverhandlung, Ernst Martin, testimony, vol. 1, p. 153. See also "Die Totenbücher des K.L. Mauthausen," Republik Österreich, BMI IV/7 Archiv St/9/1.

16   If the SS had realized what he was doing: U.S. v. Altfuldisch et al., Hauptverhandlung, Martin, testimony, vol. 1, pp. 153–54. See also "Die Totenbücher des K.L. Mauthausen."

16   He had also preserved the operation book: U.S. v. Altfuldisch et al., Hauptverhandlung, Martin, testimony, vol. 1, pp. 195–200.

17   At his trial, under intense questioning: Verhandlung gegen Mauthausen SS, Special Investigator Dr. A. Becker, Republik Österreich, BMI IV/7 Archiv P/19/11.

17   **"It is the same with people"**: Translation of statement of Eduard Krebsbach, P-79A Republik Österreich, BMI IV/7 Archiv.

17   **"degenerate and perverse practices"**: U.S. v. Altfuldisch et al., Hauptverhandlung, Josef Podlaha, testimony, vol. 2, p. 247; see also *Medical Science Abused: German Medical Science as Practised in Concentration Camps and in the so-called Protectorate, reported by Czechoslovak doctors* (Prague: Orbis, 1946), p. 62.

17   **"for different diseases"**: U.S. v. Altfuldisch et al., Hauptverhandlung, Podlaha, testimony, vol. 2, p. 255.

17   **But the prosecutor asked Kohl no questions**: U.S. v. Altfuldisch et al., Hauptverhandlung, Bl. 1110–2359, vols. 5–8.

17   **Nor had Heim's name been on the list**: Cohen, Report of Investigation of Alleged War Crimes, pp. 11–16.

18   **Three days later, a little over a hundred miles away**: Reimann, "Der Weg ins Leben," p. 8.

CHAPTER 4

19   **The rent and basic expenses**: Levy, Wiesenthal File, pp. 79–80.

20   **Less than three weeks after being rescued**: Wiesenthal Archive, http://www.simon -wiesenthal-archiv.at/01_wiesenthal/01_biographie/c04_linz.html.

20   **He was so light-headed**: Levy, Wiesenthal File, p. 71.

20–21 **There, Wiesenthal lived just a few doors down**: Ibid., pp. 71–72.

21   **As Hungarian survivors told him**: Segev, Simon Wiesenthal, p. 77.

21   **Some forty thousand of the nearly quarter million**: Ibid., p. 68.

21   **On September 5, 1946, Simon and Cyla added**: Levy, Wiesenthal File, p. 77.

22   **What had he—or she—done?**: Segev, Simon Wiesenthal, p. 70.

22   **Before computers Wiesenthal had to**: Levy, Wiesenthal File, p. 80.

22   **In Vienna another survivor, named Tuviah Friedman**: Walters, Hunting Evil, pp. 148–49; "Tuviah Friedman, Tireless Pursuer of Nazis, Dies at 88," *New York Times*, February 5, 2011.

22   **He was recaptured but got hold of a bayonet**: Tuviah Friedman, The Hunter, pp. 72–73, cited in Walters, Hunting Evil, p. 148.

22   **Friedman and Wiesenthal exchanged nearly two hundred letters**: Segev, Simon Wiesenthal, pp. 108–10.

23   **Wiesenthal was interested in the collaboration**: The book is Simon Wiesenthal, Grossmufti: Grossagent der Achse (Salzburg, Austria: Ried, 1947).

CHAPTER 5

25   **"We won't lose the war"**: Gottfried Montag, interview with authors.

25   **They seized Aspach-le-Bas**: Archives Départementales du Haut-Rhin, 3, rue Fleischhauer 68026 Colmar.

25   **He was carried from a first-aid station**: Krankenbuchlager Berlin, K Nr. 417/18 des Reserve Lazaretts H.V.Pl. Isenheim, Landesamt für Gesundheit und Soziales Berlin. Eleonore Aedtner, interview with authors.

25 **Both wore the gray uniform:** Eleonore Aedtner and Agnes Haag, interviews with authors.

26 **Overzealous SS officers summarily executed deserters:** Bernstein, "Germans Still Finding New Moral Burdens of War."

27 **Aedtner had no work:** Eleonore Aedtner, interview with authors.

CHAPTER 6

29 **By the time Heim got there a decade later:** Läpple, *Schwäbisches Potsdam*, pp. 40–42.

29 **Men worked at the shoemaker, watchmaker, or bookbinder:** Stadtarchiv Ludwigsburg, J 168/2 Bü 1.

30 **"most notably the young":** "Eishockey: Ein Probespiel unsrer Nationalmannschaft," *Sport-Tagblatt*, January 15, 1936.

31 **Aribert's older brother, Josef, was brave but impetuous:** Stadtamt Radkersburg, August 23, 1932, Bad Radkersburg Stadtarchiv, 586/32/1.

31 **There he underwent military training:** Josef Heim to the Dekan der medizinischen Fakultät, Universität Graz, April 28, 1939, University Archive, Graz.

31 **Back in Vienna, the zealous Nazi anatomist:** Promotionsprotokoll, Medizinische Fakultät, Universität Wien (MF 472), Nr. 4892.

32 **The official cause of death:** WASt, Deutsche Dienststelle, Berlin GZ V 2-677, 1.12.2010.

32 **Captain John D. Austin signed and stamped:** Release processing form, Aribert Heim, December 4, 1947, Landesarchiv Baden-Württemberg, Staatsarchiv Ludwigsburg, EL 902/12 Bü 20793.

32 **In the same month, the Dachau court:** Bögeholz, *Die Deutschen nach dem Krieg*, p. 71.

CHAPTER 7

34 **The product was introduced to the market in 1907:** Persil German Web site, http://www.persil.de/ueber-persil/historie.html.

35 **They were checked out with the American military government:** Beisitzer für Spruchkammer Jagstfeld, October 22, 1946, Landesarchiv Baden-Württemberg, Staatsarchiv Ludwigsburg, EL 900/12 II Bü 12.

35 **Officials sent each candidate's questionnaire:** Ministerium für politische Befreiung Württemburg-Baden, Beisitzer für die Spruchkammer Jagstfeld, November 27, 1946, Landesarchiv Baden-Württemberg, Staatsarchiv Ludwigsburg, EL 900/12 II Bü 12.

35 **The pharmacist was rejected:** Office of Military Government, Liaison and Security Office H-28 SK & LK Heilbronn, Land Wuerttemberg-Baden, First Military Government Battalion (SEP) APO 154 U.S. Army, KOHLER, Adolf, July 26, 1947, Landesarchiv Baden-Württemberg, Staatsarchiv Ludwigsburg, EL 900/12 II Bü 12.

35 **"to a complete standstill":** Spruchkammer Heilbronn-Land to the Bezirksbauamt Heilbronn, May 27, 1947, Landesarchiv Baden-Württemberg, Staatsarchiv Ludwigsburg, EL 900/12 II Bü 2.

36 **The staff arrived at their new offices:** Spruchkammer Heilbronn-Land to the

Bezirksbauamt Heilbronn, July 21, 1947, Landesarchiv Baden-Württemberg, Staatsarchiv Ludwigsburg, EL 900/12 II Bü 2.

36 **"Everything else," the invitation promised:** Spruchkammer Heilbronn-Land, Einladung, May 9, 1947, Landesarchiv Baden-Württemberg, Staatsarchiv Ludwigsburg, EL 900/12 II Bü 12.

36 **Some thirteen million people reported:** Bögeholz, *Die Deutschen nach dem Krieg*, p. 46.

36 **"the son of German parents":** Aribert Heim, statement, March 20, 1948, Landesarchiv Baden-Württemberg, Staatsarchiv Ludwigsburg, EL 902/12 Bü 20793.

37 **"As a result of the events of war":** Dr. Aribert Heim, Lebenslauf, March 4, 1947, Landesarchiv Baden-Württemberg, Staatsarchiv Ludwigsburg, EL 902/12 Bü 20793.

37 **Mrs. Weinaug affirmed the truth of her statement:** Herta Weinaug, Zur Vorlage bei der Spruchkammer, April 8, 1947, Landesarchiv Baden-Württemberg, Staatsarchiv Ludwigsburg, EL 902/12 Bü 20793.

37 **"spent a great deal of time":** Ursula Kraft, Eidesstattliche Erklärung, April 15, 1947, Landesarchiv Baden-Württemberg, Staatsarchiv Ludwigsburg, EL 902/12 Bü 20793.

37 **"I learned through conversations":** Werner Ernst Linz, attestation, November 15, 1947.

38 **"The investigations undertaken did not yield":** Klageschrift Dr. Aribert Heim, Spruchkammer Neckarsulm, March 4, 1948, Landesarchiv Baden-Württemberg, Staatsarchiv Ludwigsburg, EL 902/12 Bü 20793.

CHAPTER 8

39 **The catalog was moved to Berlin:** Kellerhof, "Das Erbe der NSDAP sind 10,7 Millionen Namen"; http://www.bundesarchiv.de/oeffentlichkeitsarbeit/bilder _dokumente/00757/index-11.html.de.

39 **It was the birth of the Berlin Document Center:** Ryan, *Klaus Barbie and the United States Government*, p. 10.

39 **The personnel files of the Reich:** Raim, "NS-Prozesse und Öffentlichkeit," p. 35.

39 **The document center contained files:** http://www.bundesarchiv.de /fachinformationen/01001/index.html.de.

40 **And from June 19 to July 14:** Ministry for Political Liberation, Int. Lager 77, October 14, 1947, Landesarchiv Baden-Württemberg, Staatsarchiv Ludwigsburg, EL 902/12 Bü 20793.

40 **"purely nominal membership":** Meldebogen 1, Spruchkammer 26 Heilbronn, Landesarchiv Baden-Württemberg, Staatsarchiv Ludwigsburg, EL 902/12 Bü 20793.

41 **"The civilian populace embraced him":** Mayor of Offwiller, attestation, translated copy, Landesarchiv Baden-Württemberg, Staatsarchiv Ludwigsburg, EL 902/12 Bü 20793.

41 **"because the populace had remained":** Dr. Franz Niedner, Eidesstattlich Versicherung, February 22, 1947, Landesarchiv Baden-Württemberg, Staatsarchiv Ludwigsburg, EL 902/12 Bü 20793.

41 **"The entire community":** Friedrich Schauly, letter, April 10, 1947, translated copy, Landesarchiv Baden-Württemberg, Staatsarchiv Ludwigsburg, EL 902/12 Bü 20793.

41   "what esteem the person concerned": Dr. Hans Frank reply to the Spruchkammer
      Neckarsulm, March 19, 1948, Landesarchiv Baden-Württemberg, Staatsarchiv
      Ludwigsburg, EL 902/12 Bü 20793.

41   "that would document his humane": Ibid.

41   Heim's hearing on March 20, 1948: Bögeholz, *Die Deutschen nach dem Krieg,*
      p. 74.

42   "the swiftest possible conclusion": Spruchkammer Heilbronn-Land to Amts-
      gerichtsdirektor Dr. Schrempf, May 27, 1947, Landesarchiv Baden-Württemberg,
      Staatsarchiv Ludwigsburg, EL 900/12 II Bü 2.

42   The Soviet Military Administration in Germany: Bögeholz, *Die Deutschen nach
      dem Krieg,* p. 73.

42   Dr. Heim answered group 4: Meldebogen 1a, Spruchkammer 26 Heilbronn, Landes-
      archiv Baden-Württemberg, Staatsarchiv Ludwigsburg, EL 902/12 Bü 20793.

42   "The person concerned has credibly proved": Spruchkammer Neckarsulm,
      Spruch, March 22, 1948, Landesarchiv Baden-Württemberg, Staatsarchiv Lud-
      wigsburg, EL 902/12 Bü 20793.

42   The Spruchkammer Neckarsulm office closed: Spruchkammer Neckarsulm, June
      1948, Landesarchiv Baden-Württemberg, Staatsarchiv Ludwigsburg, EL 900/12 II
      Bü 1.

43   "The chamber hopes and wishes": Chairman of the Spruchkammer Neckarsulm
      to Robert Henne, July 8, 1948, Landesarchiv Baden-Württemberg, Staatsarchiv
      Ludwigsburg, EL 900/12 II Bü 12.

43   It was not stamped as received: Office of Military Government for Germany
      (U.S.) Document Center NSDAP Records Request for Aribert Heim, February 6,
      1948, Landesarchiv Baden-Württemberg, Staatsarchiv Ludwigsburg, EL 902/12
      Bü 20793.

CHAPTER 9

44   "Pardon me for my sincere inquiry": Records of the High Commissioner for Ger-
      many, Extradition Board, Austria, case 102-33, RG 466, National Archives.

44   The association staffer included a note: Copy of a letter from the Austrian
      Ice Hockey Association, February 24, 1948, Records of the High Commissioner
      for Germany, Extradition Board, Austria, case 102-33, RG 466, National
      Archives.

45   The American Military Police had to pull: Bachmann, Gebhard, and König, *Höl-
      lenspass & Höllenqual,* p. 15; Gruppe für Design, Fotografie und Werbung, *Vau
      Eff Ell.*

45   But the games were: Bachmann, Gebhard, and König, *Höllenspass & Höllenqual,*
      p. 17.

46   "He's afraid," teammates whispered: Albert Molitor, interview with ZDF Tele-
      vision, 2009.

46   "could write a novel": Karl Kaufmann to Wiener Eishockey Verband, February 4,
      1948.

46   He described Heim as: Karl Kaufmann, witness questioning, April 14, 1948.

47   Still, in May 1948: Eissport Klub Engelmann to the Landgericht für Strafsachen,
      Vienna, May 28, 1948.

CHAPTER 10

48   **On her way home:** Eleonore Aedtner and Agnes Haag, interviews with authors.

49   **Heim had given up his position:** Bescheinigung, Dr. Luft, Leitender Arzt, Sanatorium Hahn, for Dr. Aribert Heim, October 27, 1949.

49   **"He ran the ward":** Dr. Wilhelm Kramer, Facharzt für Chirurgie, Chefarzt des Bürgerhospitals Friedburg/Hessen.

49   **The Americans printed and shipped:** Bavendamm, *Amerikaner in Hessen*, p. 61.

49   **The new currency was an instant success:** Wiedemann, "Zwischen Kriegsende und Währungsreform," doc. 3.66.

50   **In May 1949, Karl Kaufmann:** Karl Kaufmann, report, May 11, 1949.

50   **Rupert Sommer appeared before:** Rupert Sommer, witness questioning, June 24, 1949.

50   **Karl Lotter was interviewed:** Karl Lotter, witness questioning, July 6, 1949.

51   **the concentration camp Sachsenhausen:** The KZ Oranienburg closed in 1935 and was replaced by Sachsenhausen in 1936.

52   **The public safety division:** Haftbefehl, March 28, 1950, Records of the High Commissioner for Germany, Extradition Board, Austria, case 102-33, RG 466, National Archives.

52   **They even had a correct date:** Ibid.

52   **"By night and fog the doctor":** Bachmann, Gebhard, and König, *Höllenspass & Höllenqual*, p. 16.

CHAPTER 11

53   **She grew up across:** Friedl Heim, interviews with authors.

53   **She was raised in a stately:** Landesdenkmalamt Baden-Württemberg, Liste der Kulturdenkmale, Stadtkreis Heidelberg.

54   **Prospects for even an educated:** Bessel, *Germany 1945*, p. 273.

55   **On March 28, 1950, with Friedl Heim:** Haftbefehl, March 28, 1950, Records of the High Commissioner for Germany, Extradition Board, Austria, case 102-33, RG 466, National Archives.

56   **In May the American military approved:** Bernard Gufler to J. R. Rintels, May 8, 1950, and letter from W. R. Rainford, May 26, 1950, Records of the High Commissioner for Germany, Extradition Board, Austria, case 102-33, RG 466, National Archives.

56   **Heim had been hired:** Dr. Wilhelm Kramer, Facharzt für Chirurgie, Chefarzt des Bürgerhospitals Friedburg/Hessen.

56   **Other members of the staff:** Hess. Landeskriminalamt Abt. V/Sonderkommission, Wiesbaden, December 11, 1962.

56   **"You are advised that Heim cannot be located":** High Commissioner for Germany, Extradition Board, to the Office of the U.S. High Commissioner for Austria, December 21, 1950, Ext. Bd. 1527c, Records of the High Commissioner for Germany, Extradition Board, Austria, case 102-33, RG 466, National Archives.

CHAPTER 12

57   "It is felt that his value": Ryan, *Klaus Barbie and the United States Government*, p. 40.

58   He set sail on March 23: Ibid., p. 155.

58   He had sympathized with the Croatian fascists: Klee, *Persilscheine und falsche Pässe*, pp. 30, 37, 44.

58   He promised to pursue the worst: Fröhlich, "Der 'Ulmer Einsatzgruppen-Prozess' 1958," p. 244.

59   After convicting some seventy thousand: Schmeitzner, "Unter Ausschluss der Öffentlichkeit?," p. 154; Werkentin, "Die Waldheimer Prozesse 1950," p. 230.

59   Leading politicians argued: Fröhlich, "Der 'Ulmer Einsatzgruppen-Prozess' 1958," p. 237.

59   Dr. Hans Eisele: Weindlin, *Nazi Medicine and the Nuremberg Trials*, p. 95.

59   According to an American colonel: Fisk, "Butcher of Buchenwald in an Egyptian Paradise."

60   Like Wiesenthal, he was obsessed: Segev, *Simon Wiesenthal*, pp. 117, 137.

60   In Wiesenthal's telling: Wiesenthal Archive, http://www.simon-wiesenthal-archiv .at/02_dokuzentrum/01_geschichte/e01_history.html; *Yad Vashem Bulletin*, no. 1 (April 1957).

60   After a few years on the police force: Eleonore Aedtner, interviews with authors.

CHAPTER 13

62   When the repairs were finished: The description of the Heims' home life is based on multiple interviews with Friedl Heim and Rüdiger Heim as well as photographs and letters from the Heim family papers.

CHAPTER 14

64   The first handful of German military advisers: "Deutsche Militärberatergruppe in Aegypten," Auswärtiges Amt, 708-83.40 Betreff Deutsche Militärberater in Ägypten, December 31, 1956, 18967.

64   The nineteenth-century reformer Muhammad Ali: Marsot, *History of Egypt from the Arab Conquest to the Present*, p. 67.

65   "Contact with the German military advisers": Auslieferung des deutschen Staatsangehörigen Ernst-Günther Gerhartz, January 15, 1957, Politische Archiv, Auslandsvertretungen, Auswärtiges Amt, Botschaft der Bundesrepublik Deutschland Kairo, Betreff RK Einzelfälle, Band 25 1956–1965, Forts. Band: 26, 10745, V5, 88/8223, V5 88/8505.

65   "Right now Mr. Gerhartz": Ibid.

65   If pressed, Gerhartz might: Embassy of the Federal Republic of Germany in Cairo, Auslieferung des deutschen Staatsangehörigen Ernst-Günther Gerhartz aus Ägypten nach Deutschland, May 7, 1957, Politische Archiv, Auslandsvertretungen, Auswärtiges Amt, Botschaft der Bundesrepublik Deutschland Kairo, Betreff RK Einzelfälle, Band 25 1956–1965, Forts. Band: 26, 10745, V5, 88/8223, V5 88/8505.

65–66   Gerhartz offered his resignation: Embassy of the Federal Republic of Germany in Cairo, Aktenvermerk, June 7, 1957.

66   **He was known for making life difficult:** http://www.berlin.de/sen/inneres
      /innensenatoren/lipschitz.html.

66   **Under the law, the *Spruchkammer*:** "Entnazifizierung/Prominenten Vermogen";
      E.U., SenInn to Simon Wiesenthal, November 2, 1978, Landesarchiv Berlin, B Rep.
      031-02-01, Nr. 12713, Band 1.

67   **The staircase was made of oak:** Scherf, from Der Senator für Bau- und Wohnungs-
      wesen, "V bA 6—6537/02.97 /4," March 16, 1979, Landesarchiv Berlin, B Rep.
      031-02-01, Nr. 12713, Band 6.

67   **Heim purchased the building:** Antrag auf Eröffnung eines Sühneverfahrens,
      March 29, 1979, Landesarchiv Berlin, B Rep. 031-02-01, Nr. 12713, Band 1.
      Merten, Rechtsanwältin, office of Dr. Hildegard Stahlberg, to Senatsrat, Senator
      für Inneres, September 12, 1979, Landesarchiv Berlin, B Rep. 031-02-01, Nr. 12713,
      Band 1.

CHAPTER 15

69   **Rather than accept that his past:** Böhmer, "Sie konnten sich an nichts erinnern."

69   **Their trial opened on April 28:** Mix, "Als Westdeutschland Aufwachte."

70   **Chilling dispatches appeared:** Fröhlich, "Der 'Ulmer Einsatzgruppen-Prozess'
      1958," p. 244.

70   **By that time the story:** "Kollegen," Der Spiegel.

70   **Then a sympathetic individual:** "Deutsche Raketen für Nasser," Der Spiegel.

71   **By the end of the first month:** Heiner Lichtenstein, "NS-Prozess—viel zu spat und
      ohne System," in Aus Politik und Zeitgeschicte, p. 7.

71   **On July 23:** Der Spiegel, "Ohne Schelle im Wald," August 12, 1959.

71   **He thought it would probably take:** Tatari, Ein deutsches Schicksal.

71   **He heard how new:** Aussage des Zeugen Aedtner betreffend den Angeklagten
      Stark, Mitschrift, 130, Verhandlungstag, January 25, 1965.

71   **These cases had to be solved:** Tatari, Ein deutsches Schicksal.

CHAPTER 16

73   **Shinar promised that Israel:** Bascomb, Hunting Eichmann, pp. 98–100.

73   **"Any second-class policeman":** Ibid., p. 124.

74   **"I must inform the Knesset":** Web site of the Knesset: http://www.knesset.gov.il
      /lexicon/eng/aichman_eng.htm.

CHAPTER 17

76   **Word traveled quickly that Dr. Heim:** Ursula Schlewitz (former patient), interview
      with authors.

76   **In the summers Heim's mother:** Rüdiger Heim and Birgit Barth, interviews with
      authors.

77   **He received one of the highest:** Schreiber, "Der Anwalt des Bösen."

78   **"an honorable job as well":** Fritz Steinacker, interview with authors.

78   **He believed that even:** Aribert Heim, letter, March 19, 1979.

79   **"Long live Germany":** Arendt, Eichmann in Jerusalem, p. 252.

79   **Eichmann's sentence was complete:** Bascomb, Hunting Eichmann, pp. 320–21.

CHAPTER 18

80   "This was found": LKA Baden-Württemberg, Vernehmungsniederschrift, December 9, 1965, Helene Possekel.

81   The couple's increasingly frequent: Landeskriminalamt Baden-Württemberg, "Vernehmungsniederschrift: Ursula Karcher, geb. Kammerer," July 23, 1965.

81   When he was home: Rüdiger Heim, interviews with authors.

CHAPTER 19

83   "They carried on": Landeskriminalamt Baden-Württemberg, "Vernehmungsniederschrift: Ursula Karcher, geb. Kammerer," July 23, 1965.

84   "Compared with his otherwise normally calm": Ibid.

84   "especially on account of the children": Ibid.

84   It was not unusual: Birgit Barth, interviews with authors.

85   A police investigator rang: Landeskriminalamt Baden-Württemberg, Sonderkommission Zentrale Stelle, report, February 21, 1963.

85   Instead, he gave her: "Hinten raus," Der Spiegel.

86   "disappeared unexpectedly": Hess. Landeskriminalamt Abt. V/Sonderkommission, Wiesbaden, December 11, 1962.

CHAPTER 20

87   Rather than drive an hour: Eleonore Aedtner and Harald Aedtner, interviews with authors.

88   "You can't fix": Tatari, Ein deutsches Schicksal.

88   The enormity of the task: Schüle, Erwin. "Die Zentrale der Landesjustizverwaltungen zur Aufklärung nationalsozialistische Gewaltverbrechen in Ludwigsburg," Juristenzeitung, no. 8, April 19, 1962.

88   His superiors had: Dietrich Strothmann, "Was habe ich den Schlimmes getan?" Die Zeit, February 26, 1965.

88   But after the Soviets: "Schüle: Die Ermittlung," Spiegel, November 17, 1966.

88   "Isn't it time": "Verjährung: Gesundes Volksempfinden," Spiegel, November 11, 1965.

89   Still Aedtner remained single-minded: Karl-Heinz Weisshaupt, interview with authors, March 16, 2012.

89   "The accused was very willing": Aussage des Zeugen Aedtner betreffend den Angeklagten Stark, Mitschrift, 130, Verhandlungtag, January 25, 1965.

CHAPTER 21

92   A hulking, scar-faced: Walters, Hunting Evil, p. 218.

92   Ms. Kammerer recalled: Landeskriminalamt Baden-Württemberg, "Vernehmungsniederschrift: Ursula Karcher, geb. Kammerer," July 23, 1965.

92   "Where thousands of years: "Deutsche Raketen für Nasser," Der Spiegel.

93   "The German government cannot sit": Ibid.

94   On July 7, 1962: Ibid.

94 **In September, a German businessman:** "Heidi und die Detektive," *Der Spiegel.*
94 **Two Israeli agents:** Ibid.
94 **Five Egyptian workers:** Elten, "Militärhilfe für Israel, Raketen für Nasser."
94 **Dr. Carl Debouche's only connection:** Fisk, "Butcher of Buchenwald in an Egyptian Paradise."
94 **The bomb failed:** "Deutsche Raketen für Nasser," *Der Spiegel.*

CHAPTER 22

95 **One afternoon in 1964:** Birgit Barth, interviews with authors.
97 **Underneath the family's stylish:** The description of the Barth family is based on several interviews with Birgit Barth, Herta's daughter, and Rüdiger Heim, Aribert's son.
98 **"What does that have to do with me?":** Landeskriminalamt Baden-Württemberg, report, August 22, 1966.

CHAPTER 23

99 **One weekend around:** Harald Aedtner, interview with authors.
99 **The Nazi hunters had moved:** Kurzchronik, Gebäude Schorndorfer Strasse 58, Zentrale Stelle Ludwigsburg.
100 **Aedtner was traveling so much:** Eleonore Aedtner, interviews with authors.

CHAPTER 24

102 **"In contrast to Nazi criminals":** Invitation to a press conference, June 7, 1967, Aegypten (Pressekonferenz) File, Wiesenthal Archive.
102 **"SS-Hauptsturmführer Dr. Heribert Heim":** Flüchtige Naziverbrecher im Nahen Osten und Ihre Gegenwärtige Rolle, June 7, 1967, Aegypten (Pressekonferenz) File, Wiesenthal Archive.
102 **Adalbert Rückerl:** Rückerl to Wiesenthal, August 23, 1967, Aegypten (Pressekonferenz) File, Wiesenthal Archive.
102 **Wiesenthal decided to check:** Wiesenthal to Jacques Givet, April 17, 1968, Aegypten (Pressekonferenz) File, Wiesenthal Archive.
103 **And the aforementioned Heribert:** Invitation to a press conference, June 7, 1967.
103 **"The person concerned":** Zusammenstellung, Zentrale Stelle der Landesjustizverwaltungen, August 22, 1967, Aegypten (Pressekonferenz) File, Wiesenthal Archive.
103 **State Institute for War Documentation:** It changed its name to the Netherlands Institute for War Documentation in 1999.
103 **By that time he had:** Wiesenthal to Ben A. Sijes, October 6, 1969, Aribert Heim File (1), Wiesenthal Archive.
103 **He also appealed:** Rückerl to Wiesenthal, November 4, 1969, Aribert Heim File (1), Wiesenthal Archive.
103 **The man's name was:** Anonymous letter to Wiesenthal on Kleinwalsertal, Aribert Heim File (1), Wiesenthal Archive.
103 **He even wrote:** Letter to Ambassador Hans Georg Steltzer, February 5, 1973. The name he sent the report under is cut off in the copy of the letter remaining in his briefcase. Presumably it was an alias.

103 **In his absence:** Friedl Heim, interviews with authors.
104 **Both said they did not know:** Landeskriminalamt Baden-Württemberg, report, December 6, 1966.
104 **The inspector did not:** Ibid.
104 **"The respondent [had] told the plaintiff":** Dr. Klaus Froebel, divorce suit on behalf of Frau Dr. med. Friedl Heim-Bechtold versus Dr. med. Aribert Heim, February 22, 1967.
105 **He intended to stay:** Fritz Steinacker, notes from meeting with Aribert Heim, June 5, 1971.
105 **"Herr Dr. H. informed me":** Steinacker to Käthe Bechtold, June 28, 1974.

CHAPTER 25

106 **The extreme elements:** For a thorough accounting of the group and its activities see Stefan Aust, *Der Baader-Meinhof-Komplex* (Munich: Goldmann Verlag, 1998).
106 **The Red Army Faction seized:** *Der Spiegel,* "Mein Instinkt sagt mir: Nicht nachgeben," April 28, 1975.
106 **"His goal was to hunt down":** Karl-Heinz Weisshaupt, interview with authors.
107 **"I had seen Dr. Heim already":** Vernehmungsniederschrift, Gustav Rieger, July 14, 1975, Landeskriminalamt Baden-Württemberg, Dez. 831, Gz 130/61 Az.
108 **"a large but as of yet undetermined":** Haftbefehl, September 12, 1962, Staatsanwaltschaft Baden-Baden, 1 Js 1383/62.
109 **Franz Powolny, who reportedly:** Landeskriminalamt Baden-Württemberg, report, Alfred Aedtner, August 13, 1975.
109 **"The analysis of the audiotapes":** Ibid.

CHAPTER 26

110 **He remembered little:** Rüdiger Heim, interviews with authors.
110 **"above all in arithmetic":** Rüdiger Heim to Aribert Heim, May 3, 1964.
110 **Heim stressed the importance:** Aribert Heim to Christian Heim, n.d.
111 **His body was found:** UPI, "Israeli Aide Is Linked to Killing of Latvian Nazi in Montevideo."
112 **Lotz even attended parties:** Lotz, *Champagne Spy,* p. 61.
112 **his fluent German led the Mossad:** "Champagne Spy," *Time.*
112 **In 1968 she publicly slapped:** "Den Bundeskanzler Misshandelt," *Der Spiegel.*
112 **In 1971 they unsuccessfully:** Chronology at www.klarsfeldfoundation.org.
112 **The following year:** "Graue Maus," *Der Spiegel.*
113 **"definitely worked for some group":** Aribert Heim, note in personal files.

CHAPTER 27

114 **"the odds are":** Kriminalrat Textor to Ministerialrat Bundesministerium für Inneres, July 23, 1975.
114 **Sommer identified Heim:** Alfred Aedtner, report on trip to Austria, September 26, 1975.
115 **"no longer had his powers":** Ibid.

115 **"Somehow the name":** Vernehmungsniederschrift, Ernst Martin, September 11, 1975.

115 **"awakens no memory":** Vernehmungsniederschrift, Alois Madlmayr, September 10, 1975.

115 **Maršálek said he arrived:** Aedtner, report on trip to Austria, September 26, 1975.

115 **At seventy-three Karl Lotter:** Karl Lotter, witness questioning, September 15, 1975.

CHAPTER 28

118 **Rüdiger Heim arrived in Egypt:** Rüdiger Heim, interviews with authors.

121 **Heim had purchased:** Aribert Heim to Rifat, January 19, 1990.

CHAPTER 29

123 **"shoot drugs in the heroin capital":** Ruether, "Man Who Came from Hell."

123 **Then, rather than being handed over:** Berlin Wall Memorial, Berlin Wall, Fatalities, 1975, http://www.berliner-mauer-gedenkstaette.de/en/1975-323,438,2.html.

124 **"No indications came":** III B 21—0334/612, February 13, 1979, Vermerk, Ermittlungen in einer NSG-Strafsache, questions from Herr Magen, Landesarchiv Berlin, B Rep. 031-02-01, Nr. 12713, Band 1.

124 **"The suspicion arises":** Finanzamt Offenbach-Land to Finanzamt Baden-Baden, April 20, 1976.

125 **"Over the course of time":** Vernehmungsniederschrift, Rolf Gallner, February 26, 1976.

125 **He, Gallner, and an officer:** Report to the Staatsanwaltschaft Baden-Baden, April 6, 1976.

125 **The old coal boiler:** Ibid.

125 **In all, Gallner estimated:** https://www.destatis.de/DE/ZahlenFakten/Gesam twirtschaftUmwelt/VerdiensteArbeitskosten VerdiensteBranchen/Tabellen/ LangeReiheFB_1913.html. In 2012 dollars that would be nearly $40,000 a year.

126 **Or Heim could pass:** Landeskriminalamt Baden-Württemberg, report, July 26, 1976.

CHAPTER 30

128 **"There is definitely":** Alfred Aedtner, Bericht an der Staatsanwaltschaft bei dem Landgericht, November 25, 1976.

128 **"For me the man":** Interview with Johann Payerl, July 22, 1976.

128 **Back in Austria:** Alfred Aedtner, investigation report, May 31, 1977.

128 **Her entire family contracted:** Waltraut Böser, interviews with authors.

129 **She never saw him again:** Die Sicherheitsdirektion für das Bundesland Tirol, Österreich, Gertrud Böser, Ausforschung, July 2, 1976.

129 **"Gertrud Böser enjoys":** Austrian police report on Waltraut Böser, 11-II/7/NS; Sicherheitsdirektion für das Bundesland Tirol, Innsbruck, July 2, 1976, 11.057/ 9-II/7/NS.

129 **Aedtner said he was pursuing:** Bericht, Befragung Gertrud Böser, Innsbruck, April 26, 1977, 11.057/14-II/7/NS/77.

130 **By the end of the meeting:** Aedtner, investigation report, May 31, 1977.

CHAPTER 31

131 **"had reassured me":** Rüdiger Heim to Aribert Heim, January 22, 1976.

131 **An upcoming exhibition:** Rüdiger Heim to Aribert Heim, November 15, 1976.

132 **"Some days I feel terribly miserable":** Rüdiger Heim to Aribert Heim, January 31, 1977.

132 **Buses were so overcrowded:** McLaughlin, "Infitah in Egypt."

132 **The population of the Cairo:** Timothy M. Phelps, "Egypt: The Poverty of One Man's Family," *New York Times,* February 7, 1977.

132 **Some 200,000 newcomers:** Raymond, *Cairo,* p. 343.

133 **For 1,760 deutsche marks:** Rechnung, Flug + Touristik Service, March 23, 1977; Reisekostenabrechnung, April 2, 1977.

CHAPTER 32

134 **Heim was thinner:** Fritz Steinacker, interviews with authors.

135 **"already well cultivated":** Aribert Heim, unlabeled document, Briefcase.

135 **Captives were paraded:** Schmidt, "Arab Shells Rock City of Jerusalem."

135 **Within three days:** Greenhouse, "Only Man Convicted for My Lai."

136 **Titled "Counterfeit Semites":** El Dakhakhni, "Counterfeit Semites."

136 **Although members of his family:** Lebrecht, "Tragedy of Koestler."

136 **"While this book deals":** Koestler, *Thirteenth Tribe,* pp. 223–26.

CHAPTER 33

138 **At 6 deutsche marks:** Dipl.-Ing. Rambald von Steinbüchel-Rheinwall, Architekt BDA. & Partner, invoice, May 26, 1977.

138 **They all waited:** Landeskriminalamt Baden-Württemberg, report, November 25, 1976.

139 **From his vantage point:** Alfred Aedtner, investigation report, May 31, 1977.

139 **He was on his way to work:** *Der Spiegel,* "Das Attentat: Mord nach Fahrplan," April 18, 1977.

139 **The state police asked colleagues:** Landeskriminalamt Baden-Württemberg, report, July 26, 1976.

140 **She insisted that she:** Landeskriminalamt Baden-Württemberg, report, November 25, 1976.

140 **Aedtner was convinced:** Landeskriminalamt Baden-Württemberg, report, July 26, 1976.

140 **Police in Holland:** "Das Attentat," *Der Spiegel.*

140 **"The news just came on":** Rüdiger Heim to Aribert Heim, October 18, 1976.

CHAPTER 34

142 **There was Herta Barth's address:** Wiesenthal, note, Aribert Heim File (1), Wiesenthal Archive.

142 **Aedtner sent Wiesenthal:** Aedtner to Wiesenthal, August 4, 1977, Aribert Heim File (1), Wiesenthal Archive.

143   **"one of the most sadistic":** Wiesenthal to Harald Salzmann, May 3, 1977, Aribert Heim File (1), Wiesenthal Archive.

143   **Wiesenthal's office was:** Wiesenthal Archive, http://www.simon-wiesenthal-archiv .at/02_dokuzentrum/01_geschichte/e01_history.html.

144   **"The fugitive SS camp doctor":** Wiesenthal to Galinski, September 25, 1978, Landesarchiv Berlin, B Rep. 031-02-01, Nr. 12713, Band 1.

145   **Wiesenthal had Galinski forward:** Galinski to Jürgen Brinkmeier, October 5, 1978, Landesarchiv Berlin, B Rep. 031-02-01, Nr. 12713, Band 1.

145   **"We don't know whether Dr. Heim":** Wiesenthal to Vogel, October 18, 1978, Landesarchiv Berlin, B Rep. 031-02-01, Nr. 12713, Band 1.

145   **After they talked:** Notes on telephone conversation between Wiesenthal and Höhne, November 30, 1978, Aribert Heim File (1), Wiesenthal Archive.

CHAPTER 35

146   **"I killed you Jews once before":** "Holocaust: Die Vergangenheit kommt zurück," *Der Spiegel,* May 1979.

147   **"sterile collection of wooden characters":** O'Connor, "TV Weekend."

147   **"untrue, offensive, cheap":** Wiesel, "TV View."

147   **"I say no because 'Holocaust' ":** Vinocur, " 'Holocaust' TV Series, Criticized, Is Sidelined by West Germans."

147   **Public critiques of the program's:** Ibid.

148   **"The problem will be":** Vinocur, "Germans Buy TV 'Holocaust.' "

148   **One station, Westdeutscher Rundfunk:** Dreisbach, "*Holocaust* in America and West Germany."

149   **After the program:** Vinocur, "Germans Hard Hit by TV 'Holocaust.' "

CHAPTER 36

150   **Tano Pisano never expected:** Gaetano Pisano, interviews with authors.

151   **The unassuming little gatekeeper's:** http://www.cottagerne.dk/den-gule-cottage /den-gule-cottage/historien-om-huset.aspx?lang=en.

152   **His idea was to move:** Rüdiger Heim, interviews with authors.

152   **"people from every corner":** Rüdiger Heim to Aribert Heim, September 4–10, 1978.

152   **"Here and there I had small romances":** Ibid.

152   **"I'm afraid this is not a long letter":** Rüdiger Heim to Aribert Heim, Copenhagen, January 22–25, 1979.

152   **He did not know that packages:** Leitender Oberstaatsanwalt investigative file, undated.

153   **"When Gretel awoke one morning":** Rüdiger Heim to Aribert Heim, February 27, 1979, March 3 and 5, 1979.

CHAPTER 37

154   **One week after the national:** "Hinten raus," *Der Spiegel.*

157   **"Soon bombs are going":** Dr. Klaus Frobel to Oberstaatsanwalt Dr. Haehling von Lanzenauer, March 13, 1979.

157   **Steinacker personally visited:** Fritz Steinacker, interviews with authors.

157   **Rüdiger drove down:** Rüdiger Heim, interviews with authors.

CHAPTER 38

158   **"I can't believe that":** "Flüchtiger KZ-Arzt bezieht Einkünfte aus Mietshaus," *Der Tagesspiegel.*

158   **"We want to speak with an attorney":** "Riesenaufregung um ein Haus in Tiergarten," *B.Z.*, Landesarchiv Berlin, B Rep. 031-02-01, Nr. 12713, Band 1.

158   **"a new owner":** "Eine Hausgemeinschaft kämpft gegen unselige faschistische Vergangenheit," *Wahrheit.*

159   **The vandal left a note:** Berlin police report, February 27, 1979, Landesarchiv Berlin, B Rep. 031-02-01, Nr. 12713, Band 1.

159   **Even state television:** Message, Landesarchiv Berlin, B Rep. 031-02-01, Nr. 12713, Band 1.

159   **"the house be placed immediately":** "Offener Brief an die Parteien und Verbände," Die Mieter des Hauses Tile-Wardenberg-Str. 28, February 27, 1979, Landesarchiv Berlin, B Rep. 031-02-01, Nr. 12713, Band 1.

159   **"Countless Jewish fellow citizens":** Wurche to Senator Ulrich, March 6, 1979, Landesarchiv Berlin, B Rep. 031-02-01, Nr. 12713, Band 1.

159   **"The authorities have been aware":** Siegried Thiemert (Beauftragter der Mietergemeinschaft, Tile-Wardenberg-Str. 28) to Innensenator, March, 14, 1979, Landesarchiv Berlin, B Rep. 031-02-01, Nr. 12713, Band 1.

159   **The former minister:** http://www.berlin.de/sen/inneres/innensenatoren/lipschitz.html.

159   **Under it, the independent panel:** E.U., SenInn (could be Brinkmeier, Wiesenthal writes back to Brinkmeier), to Wiesenthal, November 2, 1978, Landesarchiv Berlin, B Rep. 031-02-01, Nr. 12713, Band 1.

160   **The head of Berlin's Jewish:** Heinz Galinski to Brinkmeier, October 5, 1978, Landesarchiv Berlin, B Rep. 031-02-01, Nr. 12713, Band 1.

160   **"He immediately smelled":** Ernst R. Zivier, interview with authors.

161   **He learned that Heim:** I B 2—0258 23754/78 Vermerk: Betr.: Dr. med. Aribert Heim, geb. 28.6.1914, Landesarchiv Berlin, B Rep. 031-02-01, Nr. 12713, Band 1.

161   **Magen's first instinct:** Konzentrationslager Mauthausen Kommandatur to Frau Dorothea Schifftan, November 10, 1941, Landesarchiv Berlin, B Rep. 031-02-01, Nr. 12713, Band 1.

161   **"the results of their investigation":** Magen to the Staatsanwaltschaft Baden-Baden, November 1, 1978, Landesarchiv Berlin, B Rep. 031-02-01, Nr. 12713, Band 1.

161   **"I regret once again":** Oberstaatsanwalt Wieser to Senator für Inneres Berlin, November 30, 1978, Landesarchiv Berlin, B Rep. 031-02-01, Nr. 12713, Band 1.

161   **"I am under the impression":** Wiesenthal to Brinkmeier, November 21, 1978, Landesarchiv Berlin, B Rep. 031-02-01, Nr. 12713, Band 1.

161   **Then the Heim case broke:** "Flüchtiger KZ-Arzt soll nicht mehr von Mieteinnahmen leben," *Frankfurter Rundschau.*

CHAPTER 39

162   **"goal of the procedure":** E.U. to the Landgericht Linz, February 13, 1979, Landes-archiv Berlin, B Rep. 031-02-01, Nr. 12713, Band 1.

162   **It came to the conclusion:** Office of the Senator für Finanzen to the Senator für Inneres, May 4, 1979, Landesarchiv Berlin, B Rep. 031-02-01, Nr. 12713, Band 1.

162   **It sent inspectors:** Scherf, from Der Senator für Bau- und Wohnungswesen, "V bA 6—6537/02.97 /4," March 16, 1979, Landesarchiv Berlin, B Rep. 031-02-01, Nr. 12713, Band 6.

163   **He assessed the value:** Ibid.

163   **"They fear that evidence":** "Hinten raus," *Der Spiegel.*

163   **The Berlin authorities appealed:** E.U. to Dr. Heinz Eyrich (Justizminister des Landes Württemberg), February 9, 1979, Landesarchiv Berlin, B Rep. 031-02-01, Nr. 12713, Band 1.

163   **"reason to believe":** "Simon Wiesenthal jagt SS-Arzt aus der Tile-Wardenbergstrasse 28," *Berliner Morgenpost.*

163   **"I hope as soon as possible":** Brinkmeier to Wiesenthal, February 16, 1979, Landesarchiv Berlin, B Rep. 031-02-01, Nr. 12713, Band 1.

163   **City authorities filed:** Antrag auf Eröffnung eines Sühneverfahrens, March 29, 1979, Landesarchiv Berlin, B Rep. 031-02-01, Nr. 12713, Band 1.

163   **"The personal appearance":** Spruchkammer Berlin I B—0258 (Dr. Heim) SprKa 124/79, April 27, 1979, Landesarchiv Berlin, B Rep. 031-02-01, Nr. 12713, Band 1.

163   **"definitely still alive":** Aedtner to Busek, April 12, 1979, LKA Kapitel 14, p. 9.

163   **The moment Fritz Steinacker submitted:** Letter from Referat 906, Gutzsche, May 7, 1979.

164   **There was no evidence:** Untersuchungsbericht, LKA Baden-Württemberg, May 17, 1979.

164   **As if to prove:** "15 000 Mark Belohnung," *B.Z.*

164   **Although there had been:** Landgericht Baden-Baden Strafkammer III, Beschluss, June 13, 1979.

164   **Then, under severe political pressure:** Klemp, *KZ-Arzt Aribert Heim,* p. 169.

164   **"A trip to Berlin is impossible":** Rieger to the Senator für Inneres, March 10, 1979, Landesarchiv Berlin, B Rep. 031-02-01, Nr. 12713, Band 1.

164   **"I would like to answer":** Payerl to the Senator für Inneres, March 15, 1979, Landesarchiv Berlin, B Rep. 031-02-01, Nr. 12713, Band 1.

165   **"judge what decision":** Magen to Payerl, March 20, 1979, Landesarchiv Berlin, B Rep. 031-02-01, Nr. 12713, Band 4.

165   **"Imagine for a moment":** Payerl to the Senator für Inneres, March 23, 1979, Landesarchiv Berlin, B Rep. 031-02-01, Nr. 12713, Band 1.

165   **"As a witness in the criminal matter":** Lotter to the Senator für Inneres, April 24, 1979, Landesarchiv Berlin, B Rep. 031-02-01, Nr. 12713, Band 1.

CHAPTER 40

166   **The large room on the eleventh floor:** Spruchkammer Berlin, Ladung, May 3, 1979, Landesarchiv Berlin, B Rep. 031-02-01, Nr. 12713, Band 1.

166   **"No," the defense attorney answered:** Voss-Dietrich, "Untergetauchter SS-Arzt Verliert Sein Miethaus in Moabit."

166 **Although lawyers from:** Ernst R. Zivier, interview with authors.

166 **"part of the enforcement clique":** Voss-Dietrich, "Untergetauchter SS-Arzt Verliert Sein Miethaus in Moabit."

167 **The witness statements:** "Teil der Vollstreckungsclique um Hitler," *Der Tagesspiegel.*

167 **"deadly silent":** Voss-Dietrich, "Untergetauchter SS-Arzt Verliert Sein Miethaus in Moabit."

167 **"26 to 30 prisoners incapable":** Karl Kaufmann, testimony, Bezirksgericht, Linz, Austria, May 18, 1949.

167 **"Countless Jews were liquidated":** Ibid.

167 **Only then would he give:** Josef Kohl, testimony, October 28, 1949.

167 **"a markedly perverse mass murderer":** Karl Lotter, testimony, July 6, 1949.

167 **"taking the air away":** "Alles 'Latrinengerüchte,'" *Die Tageszeitung.*

168 **A former member of the SS:** Vernehmungsniederschrift, Otto Kleingünther, April 12, 1962.

168 **Lotter and Kaufmann both remembered:** Antrag auf Eröffnung eines Sühneverfahrens, March 29, 1979, Landesarchiv Berlin, B Rep. 031-02-01, Nr. 12713, Band 1.

168 **"All testified in agreement":** Voss-Dietrich, "Untergetauchter SS-Arzt Verliert Sein Miethaus in Moabit."

168 **Steinacker did not answer:** "Teil der Vollstreckungsclique um Hitler," *Der Tagesspiegel.*

168 **"Dr. Heim rejects all":** "KZ-Arzt verurteilt!," *Bild.*

168 **"Based on the information":** Voss-Dietrich, "Untergetauchter SS-Arzt Verliert Sein Miethaus in Moabit."

168 **Heim's name appeared:** Kranebitter, "Aribert Heim, Lagerarzt im KZ Mauthausen," pp. 87–88.

168 **Referring to a handwritten letter:** "NS-Verb Rechen," *Der Spiegel.*

169 **"a medium was speaking":** Ibid.

169 **Considering that several:** Voss-Dietrich, "Untergetauchter SS-Arzt Verliert Sein Miethaus in Moabit."

169 **"polemical and not precise":** "Teil der Vollstreckungsclique um Hitler," *Der Tagesspiegel.*

169 **Many witnesses described events:** Ibid.

169 **"picked apart" the statements:** "Alles 'Latrinengerüchte,'" *Die Tageszeitung.*

169 **Legally, his client's fortune:** "NS-Verb Rechen," *Der Spiegel.*

169 **By the time the decision:** Voss-Dietrich, "Untergetauchter SS-Arzt Verliert Sein Miethaus in Moabit."

169 **"The crimes we heard":** "Ex-SS Doctor Is Fined $255,000 in Germany for the Killing of Jews," *New York Times.*

169 **"because it was no movie":** "Geldstrafe im Verfahren gegen Heim," *Frankfurter Allgemeine Zeitung.*

169 **It levied a fine:** "Ex-SS Doctor Is Fined $255,000 in Germany for the Killing of Jews," *New York Times.*

170 **"The *Spruchkammer* announces the verdict":** "Alles 'Latrinengerüchte,'" *Die Tageszeitung.*

CHAPTER 41

171 **Rifai hoped that after:** Abdelmoneim el Rifai, interviews with authors.

171 **Buediger had sent his report:** Report on Anti-Semitism, distribution list, December 1977–April 1978.

172 **"Till now, the mass":** Report on Anti-Semitism, English version, p. 12.

172 **"the accurate and true justice":** Ibid., p. 13.

172 **"It was understood":** Tarek Abdelmoneim el Rifai, interview with authors.

172 **"I remember that when Egypt":** Mrs. Abdelmoneim el Rifai, interview with authors.

173 **"absolute dominator of all German agencies":** Aribert Heim, Response, March 19, 1979.

173 **"my school-age children":** Aribert Heim to Lothar Späth, unsent letter, July 26, 1979.

173 **"Greuelpropaganda":** Ibid.

173 **"the only one constantly informed":** Ibid.

174 **"into contact with athletes":** Ibid.

174 **Heim also highlighted:** Pauline Kuchelbacher, Erklärung an Eides-Statt, n.d.

174 **"Only through athletic occupation":** Heim to Späth, unsent letter, July 26, 1979.

174 **"I lost eight years to war":** Ibid.

174 **"try to accomplish a dissection":** Ibid.

175 **"No one can deny":** Ibid.

175 **"The little man alone":** Ibid.

175 **"the citizen must be prepared":** Aribert Heim, unlabeled document page.

CHAPTER 42

176 **The postcards were sent to Chancellor:** Segev, *Simon Wiesenthal,* p. 352.

176 **The head of the Simon Wiesenthal Center:** Ibid., p. 354.

177 **"There should be absolutely":** Walters, *Hunting Evil,* p. 513.

177 **On July 3, the Bundestag:** Vinocur, "Bonn Parliament Vote Abolishes Time Limit on War-Crime Cases."

177 **"During the debate":** Aribert Heim, unlabeled document page.

177 **The family could feel cold stares:** Friedl Heim and Rüdiger Heim, interviews with authors.

177 **"In my letter from March 12":** Magen to Bechtold, September 11, 1979, Landesarchiv Berlin, B Rep. 031-02-01, Nr. 12713, Band 1.

178 **"completely taken aback":** Dr. Klaus Froebel and Dr. Uta Schueler, Rechtsanwälte, to the Senator für Inneres Berlin, September 14, 1979, Landesarchiv Berlin, B Rep. 031-02-01, Nr. 12713, Band 1.

178 **"Don't worry about":** Rüdiger Heim to Aribert Heim, October 28–30, 1979.

CHAPTER 43

180 **The rules had changed:** Fritz Steinacker, filing to the Berufungsspruchkammer, "Aufhebung des Urteils der Spruchkammer Berlin vom 13. 6. 1979," December 3, 1979, Landesarchiv Berlin, B Rep. 031-02-01, Nr. 12713, Band 2.

180 **Steinacker then asked:** "Anwalt forderte 'faires Verfahren' gegen untergetauchten KZ-Arzt," *Tagesspiegel.*

180 **"At least three cases":** Protokoll, Öffentliche Sitzung der Berufungsspruchkammer Berlin, Az.: BerKa 157/79, Landesarchiv Berlin, B Rep. 031-02-01, Nr. 12713, Band 2.

180 **The penalty of 510,000:** "KZ-Arzt erneut verurteilt," *Frankfurter Rundschau.*

180 **On March 7, 1980:** Office of the Senator für Inneres to Steinacker, March 7, 1980; Finanzamt für Erbschaft- und Verkehrsteuern, May 13, 1988, Landesarchiv Berlin, B Rep. 031-02-01, Nr. 12713, Band 8.

181 **"in the territory of the Federal Republic":** Landgericht Baden-Baden Strafkammer III, Beschluss, June 13, 1979.

181 **"twitching and convulsing":** Hans Wolter to Oberstaatsanwalt von Lanzenauer, July 4, 1979.

181 **At the Lübeck South police precinct:** Vernehmungsniederschrift, Erwin Balczuhn, August 24, 1979, Steinacker file.

182 **The doctor had probably:** Vernehmung in der Ermittlungssache gegen Dr. Heim, December 19, 1979, Steinacker file.

182 **"countless pictures of the accused":** Ibid.

182 **His Austrian colleagues sent:** Bundesministerium für Inneres, April 8, 1980, Aribert Heim File (2), Wiesenthal Archive.

CHAPTER 44

183 **Aedtner's hopes for:** Aedtner to Busek, April 12, 1979, Aribert Heim File (1), Wiesenthal Archive.

183 **Five men in five cities:** Simon Wiesenthal to Aedtner, September 6, 1979, Aribert Heim File (1), Wiesenthal Archive.

183 **"A picture of Heim appeared":** "KZ-Arzt Heim offenbar in Caracas," *Der Tagesspiegel.*

183 **"Since it would be":** Wiesenthal to Aedtner, November 11, 1979, Aribert Heim File (2), Wiesenthal Archive.

184 **"We would be very grateful":** Wiesenthal to Mound, June 18, 1980, and Mound to Wiesenthal, June 23, 1980, Aribert Heim File (2), Wiesenthal Archive.

184 **The detective had already:** Aedtner to Wiesenthal, March 6, 1980, Aribert Heim File (2), Wiesenthal Archive.

184 **At one point the detective:** Aedtner to Wiesenthal, November 3, 1980, Aribert Heim File (2), Wiesenthal Archive.

185 **Growing up without a father:** Waltraut Böser, interviews with authors.

186 **"Unfortunately, I no longer hear":** Aribert Heim to Herta Barth, August 11, 1982.

CHAPTER 45

187 **In 1981 he traveled to Israel:** Aedtner to Simon Wiesenthal, March 25, 1981, Aribert Heim File (2), Wiesenthal Archive.

187 **He passed out:** Harald Aedtner, interview with authors.

188 **"We haven't heard from one another":** Aedtner to Wiesenthal, October 6, 1982, Aribert Heim File (2), Wiesenthal Archive.

188 "no additional concrete clues": Alfred Aedtner, Aktenvermerk, Aribert Heim case, October 8, 1982, Aribert Heim File (2), Wiesenthal Archive.

188 A source told investigators: Ibid.

188 The prosecutor's office: Anträge auf Postbeschlagnahme und Telefonüberwachung, November 18, 1982, Aribert Heim File (2), Wiesenthal Archive.

188 It did, however, allow: Beschluss in der Strafsache gegen Dr. Aribert Heim, December 13, 1982, Aribert Heim File (2), Wiesenthal Archive.

189 "I have the feeling": Tatari, *Ein deutsches Schicksal.*

CHAPTER 46

190 The floor was tile: Rüdiger Heim and Mahmoud Doma, interviews with authors.

191 The foreigner spent: Ali al Hussein Ahmed, interview with authors.

191 A few guests called: Mahmoud Doma and Sharif Doma, interviews with authors.

194 "He came across": Abdelmoneim el Rifai, interviews with authors.

194 "With that his entry": Certificate of Conversion to Islam, original document.

CHAPTER 47

195 When Rüdiger Heim returned: Rüdiger Heim, interviews with authors.

195 "That was something he expressed": Rüdiger Heim, interview with authors.

196 *Der Spiegel* magazine said: "Hinten raus," *Der Spiegel.*

CHAPTER 48

198 His full name was Umberto: Alfred Aedtner, "Report on Enquiries into Dr. Aribert Heribert Ferdinand Heim," July 16, 1984, Aribert Heim File (2), Wiesenthal Archive.

198 He waited "in vain": Ibid.

199 It still must have stung: Lore Aedtner and Harald Aedtner, interviews with authors.

199 "this ominous Dr. Umberto": Wiesenthal to Aedtner, July 20, 1984, Aribert Heim File (2), Wiesenthal Archive.

200 That September, Wiesenthal: Wiesenthal to Aedtner, September 5, 1984, Aribert Heim File (2), Wiesenthal Archive.

200 With Wiesenthal's financial support: Aedtner to Wiesenthal, October 15, 1984, Aribert Heim File (2), Wiesenthal Archive.

200 On May 31, 1985, West German police: Posner and Ware, *Mengele,* pp. 199, 314–15.

200 "For nearly an hour": Ibid., p. 319.

201 More problematic were: Walters, *Hunting Evil,* p. 523.

201 "I think he is contemplating": "Nazi Found in Uruguay, Wiesenthal Tells Israelis," *New York Times.*

201 "This is Mengele's seventh death": Simon Wiesenthal, interviewed on ABC's *Nightline,* June 7, 1985, quoted in Posner and Ware, *Mengele,* p. 318.

CHAPTER 49

203 Eduard Zimmermann, host: *Aktenzeichen XY,* episode first broadcast January 17, 1986.

204   **The Justice Ministry:** Justizministerium Baden-Württemberg to Oberstaatsanwalt Baden-Baden, December 23, 1985.

204   **"The accused Dr. Heim":** Schwurgericht Baden-Baden, Strafkammer 4, to Eduard Zimmermann, September 23, 1985.

204   **Investigators hoped that even:** Staatsanwaltschaft Baden-Baden, request to the Landgericht Baden-Baden, October 29, 1985.

205   **At one point officials:** Segev, *Simon Wiesenthal*, p. 374. See also Rosenbaum, *Betrayal*.

205   **Wiesenthal hurt the chances:** Segev, *Simon Wiesenthal*, p. 377.

205   **Wiesenthal was crushed:** Ibid., p. 378.

206   **Members of Police Battalion:** Erschließung von Akten des Landeskriminalamts über NS-Verbrechen durch ehrenamtliche Mitarbeit von 1. Kriminalhauptkommissar Alfred Aedtner; Fortsetzung der Arbeit im Werkvertrag, 1982–1990.

CHAPTER 50

208   **It was more than just charisma:** Segev, *Simon Wiesenthal*, p. 356.

208   **"Of course it changed me":** Tatari, *Ein deutsches Schicksal*.

209   **When West Berlin finally:** Karlheinz Sendke to the Landgericht Baden-Baden, May 31, 1988.

CHAPTER 51

210   **Rüdiger Heim flew:** Rüdiger Heim, interviews with authors.

213   **"So it is":** Mahmoud Doma, interviews with authors.

213   **"I became in the last days":** Aribert Heim to Rifat, January 19, 1990.

CHAPTER 52

215   **The first word that Aribert:** Dr. Robert N. Braun to Simon Wiesenthal, February 11, 1994.

216   **The tipster did not want:** Landeskriminalamt Baden-Württemberg Dettling to Hertweck, October 21, 1996.

216   **The sums were all:** Rechtshilfeersuchen from the Landgericht Baden-Baden to the Ministerio di Justicia, March 29, 2005, EA Bd 6, p. 5.

217   **Founded in 1996:** www.lka-bw.de/LKA/UeberUns/Seiten/historie.aspx.

217   **It had even spied:** MfS—HA IX/11, RHE 9/79 DDR, Eigenermittlungen zum KZ-Arzt Heim.

217   **If Heim were dead:** Landeskriminalamt Baden-Württemberg to Staatsanwaltschaft Baden-Baden, January 26, 2005.

217   **The fact that the money:** Joachim Schäck (Leiter der Inspektion Zielfahndung, LKA), interview with authors.

217   **Including direct transfers:** Rechtshilfeersuchen des Landgerichts Baden-Baden to Ministerio de Justicio, May 12, 2005.

218   **They had a bar:** Ibid.

218   **"My job is done":** Quoted in "Nazi Hunter Wiesenthal to Retire," BBC News Web site, April 18, 2003, http://news.bbc.co.uk/2/hi/europe/2959591.stm.

219   **"There's going to be another":** Zuroff, *Occupation: Nazi-Hunter*, p. 6.

219 "Nicht gut, nicht gut": Zuroff, *Operation Last Chance*, p. 29.
219 "similar to putting together": Zuroff, *Occupation: Nazi-Hunter*, p. 47.
219 "the aura of adventure and drama": Ibid., p. 45.

CHAPTER 53

221 In his Gaggenau nursing home: Eleonore Aedtner, interviews with authors.
222 His wife, Cyla: Van der Nat, "Cyla Wiesenthal."
222 "the hint that Dr. Heim": Landeskriminalamt Baden-Württemberg to Staatsanwaltschaft Baden-Baden, report, July 20, 2006.
222 The police requested: Ibid.
222 "They don't know anything": Ibid.
223 As Pellet drove home: Blandine Pellet and Gaetano Pisano, interviews with authors.

CHAPTER 54

225 Heim's illegitimate daughter: Waltraut Böser, interviews with authors.
226 "was always in the back": Zuroff, *Operation Last Chance*, p. 200.
226 "the key to the mystery": Ibid., p. 199.
227 "A visibly nervous man": Contreras, "Doctor of Death."
227 "astonishing behavior": Zuroff, *Operation Last Chance*, p. 203.
227 "if we only observe her": Helm, *Die Jagd nach Dr. Tod*, 40:00 mark. The narrator says that Ms. Böser "had nothing against" being asked the questions and that she later told them, "You're only doing your job." Ms. Böser said she felt ambushed and went to the police precinct later in the day to try to file a complaint.
228 "treated her far too gently": Zuroff, *Operation Last Chance*, p. 204.
229 "I could not believe": Ibid., p. 205.

CHAPTER 55

230 As he walked into: Uhlenbroich, "Zum ersten Mal spricht sein Sohn Rüdiger Heim (52)."
232 "This is the briefcase": Ahmed Doma, interviews with authors.
232 "Here is a hotel bill": Sharif Doma, interviews with authors.
232 Mahmoud in particular: Mahmoud Doma, interviews with authors.
232 On one envelope: Medical records, Dr. Aribert Heim's briefcase.
233 "He was a peculiar case": Dr. Mohsen Samy Barsoum, interview with authors.
233 "That was the foreigner": Hicham Shabaka, interview with authors.
233 It was a rainy and cold: In addition to the authors, Elmar Theyessen from ZDF German television was part of the original report on Heim's fate.
234 "Yes, that is my father": Rüdiger Heim, interview with authors.

CHAPTER 56

235 Rüdiger had returned: Rüdiger Heim, interview with authors.
235 He said he was: Mahmoud Doma, interview with authors.

CHAPTER 57

240 **He called his cousin:** Rüdiger Heim, interview with authors.

240 **"there are too many question marks":** Kulish, "Germans Corroborate Reports of Nazi Doctor's Death in Egypt."

241 **"The extensive criminal technical":** Kulish and Mekhennet, "Police Confirm Cairo Link to Fugitive Nazi."

241 **The court in Baden-Baden:** Kulish, "Hunt Ends for a Nazi Now Believed to Be Dead."

243 **The Department of Justice's Office:** U.S. Department of Justice, http://www.justice.gov/criminal/hrsp/.

EPILOGUE

244 **He was a member:** Kranebitter, "Aribert Heim, Lagerarzt im KZ Mauthausen," pp. 88–89.

245 **Kranebitter's grandfather was:** Andreas Kranebitter, interviews with authors.

246 **He lived his whole life:** Waltraut Böser, interviews with authors.

BIBLIOGRAPHY

ARCHIVES AND LIBRARIES

Archiv der Hansestadt Rostock (Archive of the Hanseatic City of Rostock)

Archives Départementales du Haut-Rhin, Colmar, France (Upper Rhine State Archive)

Archiv Stadt und Kreis Lauban, Königslutter (City Archive, Lauban, Königslutter)

Bad Radkersburg Stadtarchiv, Museum im alten Zeughaus (City Archive, Bad Radkersburg, Museum in the Old Zeughaus)

BStU, MfS, Der Bundesbeauftragte für die Unterlagen des Staatssicherheitsdienstes der ehemaligen DDR, Berlin (Office of the Federal Commissioner for Preserving the Records of the Ministry for State Security of the former GDR)

Bundesarchiv, Berlin (Federal Archive, Berlin)

Bundesarchiv, Aussenstelle Ludwigsburg (Federal Archive, Branch Archive Ludwigsburg)

Deutsche Dienststelle (WASt) für die Benachrichtigung der nächsten Angehörigen von Gefallenen der ehemaligen deutschen Wehrmacht, Berlin (German Bureau [WASt] for the notification of next-of-kin of members of the former German Wehrmacht who were killed in action)

Fritz Bauer Institut, Frankfurt (Fritz Bauer Institute, Frankfurt)

Fritz Steinacker, legal archive

Heidelberg Stadtarchiv (City Archive, Heidelberg)

Heim family papers

ITS International Tracing Service, Bad Arolsen

Krankenbuchlager, Landesamt für Gesundheit und Soziales Berlin (Medical Records, Office for Health and Social Affairs, Berlin)

Landesarchiv Baden-Württemberg (State Archive, Baden-Württemberg)

Landesarchiv Berlin (State Archive, Berlin)

Ludwigsburg Stadtarchiv, Ludwigsburg (City Archive, Ludwigsburg)

Mauthausen Archiv, Republik Österreich Bundesministerium für Inneres, Vienna (Mauthausen Archive, Republic of Austria, Interior Ministry, Vienna)

Politisches Archiv, Auswärtiges Amt, Berlin (Political Archive, Foreign Office, Berlin)

Simon Wiesenthal Archive, Vienna

Staatsarchiv Freiburg (State Archive, Freiburg, Baden-Württemberg)
Staatsarchiv Ludwigsburg (State Archive, Ludwigsburg, Baden-Württemberg)
Stadtarchiv Bad Nauheim (City Archive, Bad Nauheim)
Stadtarchiv Friedberg (City Archive, Friedberg)
United States Holocaust Memorial Museum
United States National Archives at College Park

AUTHOR INTERVIEWS

Eleonore Aedtner
Harald Aedtner
Ali al Hussein Ahmed
Dr. Mohsen Barsoum
Birgit Barth
Waltraut Böser
Ahmed Doma
Mahmoud Doma
Sharif Doma
Kamal Gaballa
Gamal al-Ghitany
Agnes Haag
Friedl Heim
Rüdiger Heim
Gottfried Montag
Dr. Sharif Omar
Blandine Pellet
Gaetano Pisano
Abdelmoneim el Rifai
Tarek Abdelmoneim el Rifai
Mahmoud Salah
Joachim Schäck
Ursula Schlewitz
Kurt Schrimm
Hicham Shabaka
Fritz Steinacker
Karl-Heinz Weisshaupt
Ernst R. Zivier
Efraim Zuroff

BOOKS, ARTICLES, AND OTHER MEDIA

Aciman, André. *Out of Egypt: A Memoir*. New York: Picador, 1994.
Aedtner, Alfred. *Erschließung von Akten des Landeskriminalamts über NS-Verbrechen durch ehrenamtliche Mitarbeit*. Ludwigsburg: Landesarchiv Baden-Württemberg, Staatsarchiv Ludwigsburg, 1982–1990.
Amin, Galal. *Egypt in the Era of Hosni Mubarak, 1981–2011*. Cairo: American University in Cairo Press, 2011.

Arendt, Hannah. *Eichmann in Jerusalem: A Report on the Banality of Evil*. New York: Penguin Books, 2006.

Armbrust, Walter. *Mass Culture and Modernism in Egypt*. Cambridge, U.K.: Cambridge University Press, 1996.

Auschwitz Trial Transcript. Aussage des Zeugen Aedtner betreffend den Angeklagten Stark, Mitschrift, 130. Verhandlungstag, January 25, 1965.

Bachmann, Markus, Yvonne Gebhard, and Thomas König. *Höllenspass & Höllenqual: 60 Jahre Rote Teufel*. Advantage Printpool, 2007.

Bascomb, Neal. *Hunting Eichmann: Chasing Down the World's Most Notorious Nazi*. London: Quercus, 2010.

Bavendamm, Gundula. *Amerikaner in Hessen: Eine besondere Beziehung im Wandel der Zeit*. Hanau: CoCon, 2008.

Baz, Danny. *The Secret Executioners: The Amazing True Story of the Death Squad That Tracked Down and Killed Nazi War Criminals*. London: John Blake, 2010.

BBC. "Nazi Hunter Wiesenthal to Retire." *BBC News*, April 18, 2003. news.bbc.co.uk /2/hi/europe/2959591.stm.

Berliner Morgenpost. "Simon Wiesenthal jagt SS-Arzt aus der Tile-Wardenbergstrasse 28." February 13, 1979.

Bernstein, Richard. "Germans Still Finding New Moral Burdens of War." *New York Times*, May 8, 2005.

Bessel, Richard. *Germany 1945: From War to Peace*. London: Simon & Schuster, 2009; Pocket Books, 2010.

Bild. "KZ-Arzt verurteilt! Mord mit Benzinspritze ins Herz." June 14, 1979.

Bögeholz, Hartwig. *Die Deutschen nach dem Krieg, eine Chronik*. Reinbek bei Hamburg: Rowohlt, 1995.

Böhmer, Willi. "Sie konnten sich an nichts erinnern." *Südwest-Presse*, February 9, 2008.

Burk, Heinrich. *Das Hunderttage-Stadion*. Bad Nauheim: Stadt Bad Nauheim, Giessen Druck, 1999.

B.Z. "15 000 Mark Belohnung: Wo ist der KZ-Arzt?" March 19, 1979.

———. "Riesenaufregung um ein Haus in Tiergarten: Besitzer soll ein ehemaliger KZ-Arzt sein: 'Wir zahlen doch keine Miete an einen KZ-Mörder.'" February 7, 1979.

Cesarani, David. *Arthur Koestler: The Homeless Mind*. New York: Free Press, 1998.

Cohen, Major Eugene S. Investigating Officer. *Report of Investigation of Alleged War Crimes*. Office of the Judge Advocate General, U.S. Third Army, 1945.

Contreras, Joe. "Doctor of Death: Inside the Search for the World's Most-Wanted Nazi: An On-Scene Report." *Newsweek*, July 16, 2008.

Dreisbach, Tom. "*Holocaust* in America and West Germany." *Penn History Review* 16, no. 2 (2009).

Drescher, Bettina, Karl Stocker, and Beatrix Vreca. *Museum im alten Zeughaus Bad Radkersburg: Museumführer*. Bad Radkersburg: Stadtgemeinde Bad Radkersburg, 1999.

Eichmüller, Andreas. "Die Strafverfolgung von NS-Verbrechen seit 1945: Eine Zahlenbilanz." In *Vierteljahrshefte für Zeitgeschichte* no. 4 (2008).

El Dakhakhni, Mamdouh. "Counterfeit Semites." *Egyptian Gazette*, September 19, 1976.

Elten, Jörg Andrees. "Militärhilfe für Israel, Raketen für Nasser." *Stern*, January 1, 1965.

Fisk, Robert. "Butcher of Buchenwald in an Egyptian Paradise." *Independent,* August 7, 2010.

Forsyth, Frederick. *The Odessa File.* New York: Bantam Books, 1995.

Frankfurter Allgemeine Zeitung. "Geldstrafe im Verfahren gegen Heim." June 15, 1979.

Frankfurter Rundschau. "Flüchtiger KZ-Arzt soll nicht mehr von Mieteinnahmen leben." June 13, 1979.

———. "KZ-Arzt erneut verurteilt." December 18, 1979.

Freund, Florian. "Der Mauthausen-Prozess: Zum amerikanischen Militärgerichtsverfahren in Dachau im Frühjahr 1946." *Dachauer Hefte,* December 1997.

Fröhlich, Claudia. "Der 'Ulmer Einsatzgruppen-Prozess' 1958: Wahrnehmung und Wirkung des ersten grossen Holocaust-Prozesses." In Osterloh and Vollnhals, *NS-Prozesse und deutsche Öffentlichkeit.*

Greenhouse, Linda. "The Only Man Convicted for My Lai: William Laws Calley, Jr." *New York Times,* September 26, 1974.

Gruppe für Design, Fotografie und Werbung. *Vau Eff Ell: Eishockey in Bad Nauheim.* Bad Nauheim, 1967.

Helm, Ingo. *Die Jagd nach Dr. Tod: Protokoll einer Fahndung,* 2008.

Herf, Jeffrey. *Nazi Propaganda for the Arab World.* New Haven, Conn.: Yale University Press, 2010.

Höhne, Heinz. *The Order of the Death's Head: The Story of Hitler's S.S.* New York: Ballantine Books, 1971.

Jardim, Tomaz. *The Mauthausen Trial: American Military Justice in Germany.* Cambridge, Mass.: Harvard University Press, 2012.

Judt, Tony. *Postwar: A History of Europe Since 1945.* London: Pimlico, 2007.

Kellerhof, Sven Felix. "Das Erbe der NSDAP sind 10,7 Millionen Namen." *Die Welt,* December 15, 2010.

Klee, Ernst. *Persilscheine und falsche Pässe: Wie die Kirchen den Nazis halfen.* Frankfurt: Fischer, 1992.

Klemp, Stefan. *KZ-Arzt Aribert Heim: Die Geschichte einer Fahndung.* Münster/Berlin: Prospero, 2010.

Knopp, Guido. *Die Befreiung Kriegsende im Westen.* Munich: Ullstein, 2004.

Koestler, Arthur. *The Thirteenth Tribe.* New York: Random House, 1976.

Kranebitter, Andreas. "Aribert Heim, Lagerarzt im KZ Mauthausen, im Spiegel der Dokumente." In *KZ-Gedenkstätte Mauthausen/Mauthausen Memorial 2008.* Vienna: Bundesministerium für Inneres, 2008.

Kulish, Nicholas. "Germans Corroborate Reports of Nazi Doctor's Death in Egypt." *New York Times,* February 5, 2009.

———. "Hunt Ends for a Nazi Now Believed to Be Dead." *New York Times,* September 21, 2012.

Kulish, Nicholas, and Souad Mekhennet. "Police Confirm Cairo Link to Fugitive Nazi." *New York Times,* August 13, 2009.

Lagnado, Lucette. *The Man in the White Sharkskin Suit: A Jewish Family's Exodus from Old Cairo to the New World.* New York: Harper Perennial, 2008.

Läpple, Wolfgang. *Ludwigsburg in den ersten Jahren nach dem 2. Weltkrieg— dargestellt anhand von Quellen des Stadtarchivs.* Ludwigsburg: Historischen Verein für Stadt und Kreis Ludwigsburg e.V., 1991.

———. *Schwäbisches Potsdam: Die Garnison Ludwigsburg von den Anfängen bis zur Auflösung.* Ludwigsburg: Stadt Ludwigsburg, 2009.

Lebrecht, Norman. "The Tragedy of Koestler." *Evening Standard,* September 26, 2005.

Le Chêne, Evelyn. *Mauthausen: The History of a Death Camp.* London: Methuen, 1971.

Levy, Alan. *The Wiesenthal File.* Grand Rapids, Mich.: William B. Eerdmans, 1994.

Lichtenstein, Heiner. "NS-Prozess—viel zu spat und ohne System." In *Aus Politik und Zeitgeschicte, Beilage zur Wochenzeitung das Parlament.* Bonn: Bundeszentrale für politische Bildung, 1981.

Lifton, Robert Jay. *The Nazi Doctors: Medical Killing and the Psychology of Genocide.* New York: Basic Books, 2000.

Lotz, Wolfgang. *The Champagne Spy: Israel's Master Spy Tells His Story.* London: Corgi Books, 1972.

MacDonogh, Giles. *After the Reich: The Brutal History of the Allied Occupation.* New York: Basic Books, 2007.

Marsalek, Hans. "Er hat jedem geholfen: Unserm Pepi Kohl zum Gedenken." *Der neue Mahnruf.* RÖ BMI IV/7 Archiv R/1/1.

Marsot, Afaf Lutfi al-Sayyid. *A History of Egypt from the Arab Conquest to the Present.* Cambridge, U.K.: Cambridge University Press, 2008.

McLaughlin, Gerald T. "Infitah in Egypt: An Appraisal of Egypt's Open-Door Policy for Foreign Investment." *Fordham Law Review* 46, no. 5 (1978).

Medical Science Abused: German Medical Science as Practiced in Concentration Camps and in the So-Called Protectorate, Reported by Czechoslovak Doctors. Prague: Orbis, 1946.

Mitchell, Richard P. *The Society of the Muslim Brothers.* Oxford: Oxford University Press, 1993.

Mix, Andreas. "Als Westdeutschland Aufwachte." *Spiegel Online,* November 18, 2009. http://einestages.spiegel.de/static/topicalbumbackground/1853/als_westdeutschland_aufwachte.html.

New York Times. "Ex-SS Doctor Is Fined $255,000 in Germany for the Killing of Jews." June 14, 1979.

———. "Nazi Found in Uruguay, Wiesenthal Tells Israelis." December 28, 1980.

O'Connor, John J. "TV Weekend." *New York Times,* April 14, 1978.

Osman, Tarek. *Egypt on the Brink: From Nasser to Mubarak.* New Haven, Conn.: Yale University Press, 2010.

Osterloh, Jörg, and Clemens Vollnhals. *NS-Prozesse und deutsche Öffentlichkeit: Besatzungszeit, frühe Bundesrepublik und DDR.* Göttingen: Vandenhoeck & Ruprecht, 2011.

Posner, Gerald L. *Hitler's Children: Inside the Families of the Third Reich.* London: William Heinemann, 1991.

Posner, Gerald L., and John Ware. *Mengele: The Complete Story.* New York: Cooper Square Press, 2000.

Raim, Edith. "NS-Prozesse und Öffentlichkeit: Die Strafverfolgung von NS-Verbrechen durch die deutsche Justiz in den westlichen Besatzungszonen, 1945–1949." In Osterloh and Vollnhals, *NS-Prozesse und deutsche Öffentlichkeit.*

Raymond, André. *Cairo: City of History.* Cairo: American University in Cairo Press, 2007.

Reimann, Viktor. "Der Weg ins Leben." *Salzburger Nachrichten,* May 18, 1946.

Rodenbeck, Max. *Cairo: The City Victorious.* New York: Vintage Departures, 2000.

Rosenbaum, Eli. *Betrayal: The Untold Story of the Kurt Waldheim Investigation and Cover-Up.* With William Hoffer. New York: St. Martin's Press, 1993.

Rückerl, Adalbert. *NS-Verbrechen vor Gericht: Versuch einer Vergangenheitsbewältigung.* Heidelberg/Karlsruhe: C. F. Müller Juristischer Verlag, 1982.

———. *Die Strafverfolgung von NS-Verbrechen, 1945–1978: Eine Dokumentation.* Heidelberg/Karlsruhe: C. F. Müller Juristischer Verlag, 1979.

Ruether, Tobias. "The Man Who Came from Hell." *032c,* no. 12 (Winter 2006/2007).

Ryan, Allan A., Jr. *Klaus Barbie and the United States Government: A Report to the Attorney General.* Washington, D.C.: U.S. Department of Justice, Criminal Division, 1983.

Schmeitzner, Mike. "Unter Ausschluss der Öffentlichkeit? Zur Verfolgung von NS-Verbrechen durch die sowjetische Sonderjustiz." In Osterloh and Vollnhals, *NS-Prozesse und deutsche Öffentlichkeit.*

Schmidt, Dana Adams. "Arab Shells Rock City of Jerusalem." *New York Times,* April 11, 1948.

Schreiber, Jürgen. "Der Anwalt des Bösen." *Die Zeit,* November 1, 2009.

Schrimm, Kurt, and Joachim Riedel. "50 Jahre Zentrale Stelle in Ludwigsburg: Ein Erfahrungsbericht." *Vierteljahrshefte für Zeitgeschichte,* 4/2008.

Segev, Tom. *1967: Israel, the War, and the Year That Transformed the Middle East.* London: Abacus, 2008.

———. *Simon Wiesenthal: The Life and Legends.* New York: Doubleday, 2010.

Shapiro, T. Rees. "Tuviah Friedman, Credited with Helping to Find Adolf Eichmann, Dies at 88." *Washington Post,* January 20, 2011.

Sher, Neal M., and Eli Rosenbaum. *In the Matter of Josef Mengele: A Report to the Attorney General of the United States.* Washington, D.C.: U.S. Department of Justice, Criminal Division, Office of Special Investigations, 1992.

Sims, David. *Understanding Cairo: The Logic of a City Out of Control.* Cairo: American University in Cairo Press, 2010.

Der Spiegel. "Das Attentat: Mord nach Fahrplan." April 18, 1977.

———. "Den Bundeskanzler Misshandelt." November 11, 1968.

———. "Deutsche Raketen für Nasser." May 8, 1963.

———. "Entnazifizierung/Prominenten Vermogen: Sie soll alles erben." July 20, 1955.

———. "Es geht mir gut." August 29, 2005.

———. "Graue Maus." February 28, 1972.

———. "Heidi und die Detektive." March 27, 1963.

———. "Hinten raus." February 5, 1979.

———. "Kollegen." December 17, 1958.

———. "NS-Verb Rechen: Speziellen Note." June 18, 1979.

Strauss, Christof. "Zwischen Apathie und Selbstrechtfertigung: Die Internierung NS-belasteter Personen in Württemberg-Baden." In *Kriegsende und Neubeginn: Die Besatzungszeit im schwäbisch-alemannisch Raum,* edited by Paul Hoser and Reinhard Baumann. Konstanz: UVK, 2003.

Der Tagesspiegel. "Anwalt forderte 'faires Verfahren' gegen untergetauchten KZ-Arzt." December 15, 1979.

———. "Flüchtiger KZ-Arzt bezieht Einkünfte aus Mietshaus." February 6, 1979.

———. "KZ-Arzt Heim offenbar in Caracas." February 23, 1980.

———. "Teil der Vollstreckungsclique um Hitler." June 14, 1979.

Die Tageszeitung. "Alles 'Latrinengerüchte.'" June 15, 1979.

Tatari, Yoash. *Ein deutsches Schicksal: Kriminalkommissar Alfred Aedtner.* 44' BetaSP, BRD, 1987.

Time. "The Champagne Spy." November 23, 1970.

Uhlenbroich, Burkhard. "Zum ersten Mal spricht sein Sohn Rüdiger Heim (52)." *Bild am Sonntag*, August 25, 2008.

UPI. "Israeli Aide Is Linked to Killing of Latvian Nazi in Montevideo." *New York Times*, March 10, 1965.

Van der Nat, Dan. "Cyla Wiesenthal." *Guardian*, November 14, 2003. www.guardian .co.uk/news/2003/nov/14/guardianobituaries.

Vinocur, John. "Bonn Parliament Vote Abolishes Time Limit on War-Crime Cases." *New York Times*, July 4, 1979.

———. "Germans Buy TV 'Holocaust.'" *New York Times*, April 28, 1978.

———. "Germans Hard Hit by TV 'Holocaust.'" *New York Times*, May 9, 1979.

———. "'Holocaust' TV Series, Criticized, Is Sidelined by West Germans; No Longer a National Event." *New York Times*, July 3, 1978.

Voss-Dietrich, Valeska. "Untergetauchter SS-Arzt Verliert Sein Miethaus in Moabit." *Berliner Morgenpost*, June 14, 1979.

Wahrheit. "Eine Hausgemeinschaft kämpft gegen unselige faschistische Vergangenheit." March 23, 1979.

Walters, Guy. *Hunting Evil: How the Nazi War Criminals Escaped and the Hunt to Bring Them to Justice.* London: Bantam Books, 2010.

Weindlin, Paul Julian. *Nazi Medicine and the Nuremberg Trials: From Medical War Crimes to Informed Consent.* New York: Palgrave Macmillan, 2004.

Werkentin, Falco. "Die Waldheimer Prozesse 1950." In Osterloh and Vollnhals, *NS-Prozesse und deutsche Öffentlichkeit.*

Wiedemann, Andreas. "Zwischen Kriegsende und Währungsreform: Politik und Alltag in Landkreisen Friedberg und Büdingen, 1945–1949." *Wetterauer Geschichtsblätter: Beiträge zur Geschichte und Landeskunde* 43, pt. 2 (1994).

Wiesel, Elie. "TV View; Trivializing the Holocaust: Semi-fact and Semi-fiction." *New York Times*, April 16, 1978.

Zuroff, Efraim. *Occupation: Nazi-Hunter.* Southampton, U.K.: Ashford Press, 1988.

———. *Operation Last Chance.* New York: Palgrave Macmillan, 2009.

INDEX

Ackermann, Johannes, 28, 48
Adenauer, Konrad, 58, 66, 74, 175
ADN, 88
Aedtner, Alfred:
  Auschwitz trial testimony of, 90
  background of, 24–25
  Balczuhn interviewed by, 181–82
  commitment to Nazi hunting of, 100–101
  dandyish habits of, 87–88
  death of, 221
  in discussion with tax authorities, 138–39, 141, 159
  documentary on, 207–8
  drinking by, 89–90, 188
  Gallner interviewed by, 124–25, 155
  German hostility to, 89
  Gertrud Böser interviewed by, 129–30
  health problems of, 187–88, 199, 200
  Heim obsession of, 106–7
  Heim's investments investigated by, 124, 127
  Heim's letter investigated by, 164
  Holocaust videos of, 99–100
  injury of, 25–26
  Israel visit of, 187
  legacy of, 243
  Lotter interviewed by, 115–17
  made detective, 87
  Magen and Zivier's meeting with, 160
  marriage of, 48–49
  Martin interviewed by, 114–15
  Nazi crime archive created by, 205–6, 208, 242
  Nazi-hunting unit joined by, 71
  police job acquired by, 48–49

Aedtner, Alfred *(continued)*:
  police promotion sought by,
    60–61
  post-war difficulties of, 27–28
  retirement of, 188–89, 198,
    199
  Rieger interviewed by, 107–9
  Sommer interviewed by, 114
  Steinacker's office monitored
    by, 138–39
  travel by, 90
  in war, 25, 26–27
  Wiesenthal's relationship with,
    142–43, 144, 199–200
  Zehlendorf archive searched
    by, 126
Aedtner, Eleonore Ackermann,
  28, 48, 100
Aedtner, Harald, 99–101, 189
Aedtner, Lore, 221
Ahmad, Abu, 2
Ahmed, Ali al Hussein, 191
Aktenzeichen XY . . . Ungelöst
  (TV program), 203–4
al-Azhar mosque, 2
Alfred Aedtner: A German Fate
  (documentary), 207–8
Ali, Muhammad, 64
Allied Control Council, 41
Allied Supreme Headquarters, 8
Alsace, 26
Altmann, Klaus, 58, 112
American Counter Intelligence
  Corps (CIC), 17
  Barbie's work for, 57–58
  War Crimes Unit of, 20
American Military Police, 45

Amin, Omar (Johann von Leers),
  112
Anschluss, 9, 12, 31, 215, 244
anti-Semitism, 137, 173–75, 232
Antonio de Mello, Jose, 201
Aqqad, Abbas Mahmoud al-,
  193
Arafat, Yasir, 118
Arajs trial, 156
ARD, 147
Arendt, Hannah, 75
Argentina, 74, 226
Armengol, Ramón Verge, 109
Army, U.S.:
  Modification Board of, 59
  War Crimes Investigating Team
    6836 of, 11–14
Auschwitz, 13, 22, 71, 72, 146,
  147, 206, 219
  Der Spiegel photograph of,
    154
  trials over, 90, 138
Austin, John D., 32
Australia, 220
Austria, 7, 46, 125
  failed Nazi coup in, 31
  fascists vs. Communists
    in, 31
  Germany's annexation of, 9,
    12, 31, 215, 244
  Nazis pursued by, 23
Austrian Ice Hockey Association,
  44–46
Austrian Interior Ministry, 52,
  245
Austrian Legion, 31
Austro-Hungarian Empire, 20

Baader, Andreas, 140
Baader-Meinhof Gang, 106, 139,
    140–41, 145
Bad Dürkheim, 63
Baden-Baden, 76
Baden-Baden, Germany, 3, 61,
    62, 63, 66, 76, 83, 86, 104,
    106–7, 113, 124, 140, 156,
    161, 163, 164, 177, 180–81,
    203, 240
Baden-Württemberg, Germany,
    35, 71, 134, 138, 156, 163,
    218, 222, 241
Bad Nauheim, 44–45, 47, 49, 52,
    56, 86, 174
Balczuhn, Erwin, 181–82
Balfour Declaration, 137
banality of evil, 75
Barbie, Klaus, 57–58, 107, 112
Barsoum, Dr. Mohsen, 232–33
Barth, Birgit, 76–77, 80, 84–85,
    104–5, 222, 246
  in car accident, 95–96
Barth, Georg, 32, 96, 126
Barth, Herta Heim, 30, 32, 110,
    111, 131, 140, 178, 186, 197,
    210
  in car accident, 95–96, 97
  Heim's property managed by,
    86, 103, 124–25, 133, 134,
    156
  Heim's visits to, 76–77, 80
  money transferred to Heim by,
    96–97, 104, 132, 133, 156,
    217
  police questioning of, 85,
    97–98

tax investigation of, 124, 134,
    138–39, 140, 141, 144, 159
Barth, Michael, 140, 142,
    155–56
Bauer, Fritz, 71, 72–73, 74
Bavaria, Germany, 35
Bavarian Christian Social Union,
    176
Baz, Danny, 3–4
"Beach-Bathing Tourism"
    (Heim), 103
Bechtold, Jakob, 53–54, 62, 63
Bechtold, Käthe, 62, 63, 83, 104,
    110, 157, 177
  broken hip of, 177, 178
  Heim visited in Morocco
    by, 91
  loan to Heim from, 177–78
Becker, Arthur A., 11–14, 18
Begin, Menachem, 172
Beihl, Chief Inspector, 97–98
Bendl (investigator), 114–15
Ben-Gurion, David, 74
Berlin:
  Heim's apartment building
    in, *see* Tile-Wardenberg-
    Strasse 28
  Holocaust monument in,
    216
  post-war change in, 123
Berlin Document Center, 39, 127,
    160–61, 168, 200
Berliner Morgenpost, 163, 167
Berlin Interior Ministry, 180–81
Berlin Wall, 83, 123, 214
Bialystok synagogue, 206
Bild, 157

Bild am Sonntag, 230
Bilharz, Theodor, 105
Bindermichl, 19
Bindesbøll, Gottlieb, 151
Black Wall, 71
Böser, Gertrud, 127–30, 225
Böser, Peter, 129, 246
Böser, Waltraut, 127–28, 185–86,
    246
    documentary on, 227–28
    father's past learned by,
        225–26
    journalists' investigation of,
        226–28, 231, 273
Bosnia, 236, 243
Bowie, David, 123
Boys from Brazil, The (film), 201,
    208
Boys from Brazil, The (Levin),
    144
Brandenburg Gate, 124
Brandt, Willy, 72
Braun, Robert, 215, 217, 222
Brazil, 200–201, 226
Briha, 21
Brinkmeier, Jürgen, 160, 163
British Mandate of Palestine,
    135
Brzezinski, Zbigniew, 171
Buback, Siegfried, 139, 140
Buchenwald, 13, 40, 59, 94, 127,
    161
Buediger, Alfred (Heim alias),
    171–72, 192, 235
Buenos Aires, 72, 74
Bund Deutscher Mädel, 157
Bundestag, 148, 154, 176, 177

Busek, Wrazlaw, 163, 183
B.Z., 158

Café König, 63
Cairo, 1–2, 64, 93
    blackouts in, 132
    covert Israeli actions in, 94
    Israeli intelligence in, 111–12
    Muslim population of, 172
    religious revival in, 195–96
Calley, William L., Jr., 135–36
Camp David Accords, 172
Camvaro Company, 118
Canada, 220
Casablanca (film), 91
Ceaușescu, Nicolae, 171
Central Planning Board, 65
Central Registry of War
    Criminals and Security
    Suspects (CROWCASS), 7,
    10, 57
Century of Surgeons, The, 185
Cernay, France, 25
certificate of denazification, 34
Chania, Greece, 32
Charité Hospital, 123
Chelmno, Poland, 219
Chile, 226–28
Chomsky, Marvin J., 146
Christian Democratic Union, 112,
    171
Christian Democrats,
    German, 35
Christmas Amnesty, 32
Claussen, Gustav, 109
Cold War, 4, 21–22, 41, 83

Combat, 112
Communist Party, German, 35
concentration camps, 2–3, 7, 23
Contreras, Joe, 227
Cossacks, 20
Crete, 31, 103, 245
Croatia, 58, 220
Cukurs, Herbert, 111
Czechoslovakia, 7

Dachau, 13, 15, 17, 32, 59
Dalai Lama, 143
Darkness at Noon (Koestler),
    136
Debouche, Carl, 94
Deir Yassin, 135
Demjanjuk, John, 242
Democratic People's Party,
    German, 35
denazification, 34, 35, 40–43
    Germans alienated by, 41–42
Den Gule Cottage, 151
Denson, William, 15–16
deutsche mark, 49
Die Spinne (the Spider), 92
Disbandment Directive No. 5,
    8–9
Doctors Without Consciences
    (documentary), 216
Doma, Ahmed, 232
Doma, Mahmoud, 2, 191–92,
    194, 213, 232, 235, 240
    Heim's death and, 237–39
Doma, Mrs., 196–97
Doma, Sharif, 232
Domestic Security Section, 243

Dorf, Erik, 146–47
Draganović, Krunoslav, 58
Dresdner Bank, 140
Durrell, Lawrence, 132
Dylan, Bob, 119

East Germany, 58, 65–66, 71
East Jerusalem, 219
Eden, Rolf, 123
Egypt:
    agreements with Israel signed
        by, 113, 172
    concentration camps in, 65
    Germans welcomed in, 64–65,
        92–93
    Ministry of Information of,
        112
    Ministry of War of, 65, 93
    rocket regime of, 144
    in Six-Day War, 102, 172, 219
    in Suez Crisis, 93
Egyptian Gazette, 136, 137
Egypt-Israel Peace Treaty, 172
Eichmann, Adolf, 3, 21, 107, 175,
    200, 240
    arrest of, 73–74, 111
    discovery of, 72–73
    escape of, 8, 58
    hanging of, 79, 136
    trial of, 74–75, 90, 218–19, 242
    Wiesenthal's pursuit of, 23, 58,
        60, 74, 103
Eichmann, Nick, 72
8279th General Hospital, 9
Einsatzgruppen, 60
Einsatzkommando Tilsit, 69, 70

Eisele, Hans, 59, 70, 94
Eisenhower, Dwight D., 92
Eissport Klub Engelmann, 30, 44,
   45, 47
El Alamein, 103
El Europeo, 198
el-Kahir, 92
El Minzah, 91
el-Safir, 92
El Salamlek Palace, 121
Ensslin, Gudrun, 140
Eternal Jew, The (exhibition), 60
euthanasia, 23, 37

Fähnleinführer, 24
Fahrmbacher, Wilhelm, 64, 65
Faller, Ernst, 90, 200, 204
Farid, Tarek Hussein, *see* Heim,
   Aribert Ferdinand, Farid
   alias of
Fasold case, 156
Federal Criminal Police, 188
Federal Office for Political
   Education, 148
Final Solution, The
   (documentary), 148
Finland, 36
Fischer, Heinz, 221
Fischer-Schweder, Bernhard,
   68–70
Flakhelfer, 26
Format, 218
Forsyth, Frederick, 143–44
Fouad Street, 119–20
Fragebogen, 36–37, 40, 42–43,
   68–69

France, 36, 140
   Barbie's extradition required
      by, 57–58
   German invasion of, 10
   return of prisoners to, 7
   in Suez Crisis, 93
Franco-German Alliance for
   Youth, 112
Franfurter Rundschau, 161
Frank, Hans, 40
Frankfurter Allgemeine Zeitung,
   120
Franz Ferdinand, Archduke, 30
Free Officers Movement, 64–65
Freikorps, 68
French National Police, 218
French Resistance, 57
Friedberg, Germany, 49
Friedman, Tuviah, 22, 60, 72, 74
Froebel, Klaus, 157
Füllner, Kurt Hermann, 65

Gäde, Joachim, 97, 139–40
Gaggenau nursing home, 221
Galinski, Heinz, 144, 148
Gallner, Rolf, 124–25, 155
Gaza Strip, 219
Geneva Convention, 12
Genscher, Hans-Dietrich, 171
Gerhartz, Ernst-Günther,
   65–66, 70
German Autumn, 140–41
Germany:
   Austria annexed by, 9, 12, 31,
      215, 244
   black market in, 49

collective guilt of, 4–5
currency reform in, 49
division of, 58
five categories of offenders in,
	34–35
France invaded by, 10
guilt accepted by, 241–42
Holocaust weariness in, 147–48
Nazis pursued by, 23
1950s rebuilding in, 4
occupation zones in, 11, 12, 34
POWs of, 8
student demonstrations in,
	106
Gestapo, 65, 69
	false papers issued to officers
		of, 88
	prosecution of, 69
Ghunter, Werner, 184, 188
Globke, Hans, 69, 175
Goebbels, Joseph, 25
Golan Heights, 219
Goldmann, Nahum, 88
Göring, Hermann, 39, 161
Görlitz, Germany, 27
Gorzelezyk, Jakob, 206
Gouverneur, Hector, 184
Grand Mufti, 23
Great Britain, 220
	return of prisoners to, 7
	in Suez Crisis, 93
Green, Gerald, 145
Gusen satellite camp, 115

Haag, Fritz, 25–26, 27–28, 48
Haag, Johann, 28

Habsburg Empire, 30
Haganah, 22
Hahn, Umberto, 183–84, 198, 199
Haifa Institute for the
	Documentation of Nazi War
	Crimes, 60
Hartheim euthanasia facility, 16
HBO, 208
Hebrew University, 219
Heftmann, Max, 244, 245
Heidelberg, Germany, 53–54
Heidelberger Juristenkreis,
	59, 78
Heilbronn, Germany, 42
Heim, Anna, 30, 76, 185–86
Heim, Aribert Christian, 62, 84,
	91, 110, 140
	name changed by, 186
Heim, Aribert Ferdinand:
	accused of killing boy, 174–75
	Aedtner's obsession with,
		106–7
	Alexandria property of, 103,
		105, 120, 213
	appeal of, 170, 173, 180
	arrest warrant issued for,
		55–56, 108, 157, 161
	Aryans treated well by, 50
	at Bad Nauheim sanatorium,
		45, 49
	Baz's alleged evidence on, 3–4
	beachfront property of,
		121–22, 213
	Berlin apartment building
		of, see Tile-Wardenberg-
		Strasse 28
	birth of children of, 62–63

Heim, Aribert Ferdinand
   (*continued*):
   bordello work of, 107–8
   Buediger alias of, 171–72, 192,
      235
   burial of, 237–39
   cancer of, 211
   childhood of, 30–31
   clinical drug trials formed
      by, 76
   as concentration camp
      inspector, 40
   confirmation of death of,
      240–41
   contemplative manner of, 30
   conversion to Islam, 194, 196
   corporal punishment meted
      out by, 46
   custody of children desired by,
      105
   denazification investigation of,
      40–41, 42, 43
   Der Spiegel article on, 145,
      152–53, 154–57, 160, 163,
      196
   description of, 115–16, 165
   as doctor in France, 40–41, 42
   on double standard for former
      Nazis, 135–36
   drafting of, 31
   escape from Austria of, 52
   as "eternal Nazi," 242
   exercise by, 192
   extradition approved for, 56
   Farid alias of, 2–3, 171–72,
      192–94, 196, 213, 232, 235,
      238–39, 241

final illness and death of,
   235–37
fine levied on, 169–70, 180–81
fingerprints of, 184, 207
in flight from Baden-Baden,
   83–85, 156–57, 173, 204, 231
Fragebogen filled out by,
   36–37, 40
in German detention camp,
   29–30, 32–33, 35–38
Gertrud Böser's affair with,
   129
growing fame of, 231
gynecology practice of, 62, 66,
   110, 204
Herta's transfer of money to,
   96–97, 104, 132, 133, 217
human experiments and
   euthanasia by, 14, 51, 108,
   116, 128, 142, 166–67,
   181–82, 200, 245
ice hockey played by, 30, 45–47,
   51, 52, 86, 115–16, 174
illegitimate children of, 80–81,
   129, 185–86
interrogation of, 9–10
investigation of letter of, 164
Kaufmann's accusations
   against, 44, 46, 50
Khazar paper of, 171–72
Kohl's testimony against, 14,
   51–52
large feet of, 115
Magen's case against, 161
marriage of, 54–55
medical article published
   by, 76

Mengele's death followed by, 202

as most wanted Nazi, 3

Nazi file of, 40

at niece's baptism, 32–33

opening of proceedings against, 163

operation on, 210–11

operation on Prague Jew by, 50

papers of, 231–32, 238, 241

passport expiration of, 105

photographs of, 3, 5, 31, 76, 85, 86, 103, 107, 114, 117, 118, 128, 142, 145, 148, 155, 182, 184, 204, 207, 233

photographs taken by, 131, 150, 152, 193

police suspicions about location of, 102–3, 106

Port Said Street move of, 190

as prisoner of Allies, 9–10, 29

propriety of, 63

pseudonym of, 2, 3

reading by, 2, 3, 135, 190–91, 192, 232

in response to anti-Semitism charge, 173–75, 232

reward for, 164, 204, 220

Rieger's relationship with, 107–9, 116–17

in *The Road into Life,* 18

and Rüdiger's education, 110

Rüdiger's transfer of money to, 210, 216–18

Rüdiger's visits to, 118–22, 195–97, 210–14

rumors of death of, 215, 222

scar of, 116, 182

search in Chile for, 226–28

search in Spanish-speaking world for, 184–85

sentence of, 162

in sex talk with niece, 77

skulls collected by, 14, 52, 117, 142

Spanish trip of, 198–99

Steinacker hired as representative of, 78–79, 163–64

Steinacker's meetings with, 133, 134–35

as strict parent, 81–82

as suspicious of strangers, 113

as symbol of Nazi impunity, 154

in Tangier, 91–92, 97

tax investigation of, 124, 133, 134, 159

tenants' protests against, 158–59, 209

testimonials for, 37, 40–41

trial testimony studied by, 172–73

tried in absentia, 166–70, 197

warrant for arrest of, 55–56

wartime service of, 36

wealth of, 216

Wiesenthal's pursuit of, 23, 102–3, 142–43, 173, 174, 183, 231

will of, 2

as worried about past, 45–46

wounded German soldiers treated by, 9

Heim, Friedl Bechtold, 53–56, 76,
91, 110, 133, 140, 178, 217,
222
in custody dispute, 105
divorce papers filed by, 104,
157
education of, 53
family properties looked after
by, 103–4
and Heim's fleeing from
Baden-Baden, 84, 85–86,
156–57
hepatitis B of, 55, 63
marriage difficulties of,
80–81
painting of, 191
pregnancy of, 55
Heim, Hilda, 30, 52, 76, 127, 133,
143, 185, 246
Heim, Josef, 30, 249
paratroopers joined by, 31–32,
245
Heim, Josef Ferdinand, 30, 213
Heim, Leopold, 103
Heim, Peter, 30
Heim, (Rolf) Rüdiger, 91, 105,
160, 222, 223
authors' interview of, 233–34
and Bechtold's broken hip, 177,
178
deviated septum of, 81, 121,
131
education of, 110, 111
father's crimes learned by, 157
father's guilt doubted by, 245
father's papers packed by, 238,
241

father supported by, 178–79,
210, 216–18
interrogation of, 223–24
letters to father from, 131–32
medical school application of,
131, 212
restaurant work of, 150–52, 186
Rh-negative reaction of, 62–63
Rü, 5
strict upbringing of, 81–82,
111
suspicions of father's past held
by, 119, 122
tennis played by, 121, 131, 140,
150, 151
Uhlenbroich's interview of,
230–31
in visits to father in Egypt,
118–22, 195–97, 210–14,
235–37
Heitz (detective), 92
Hermann, Lothar, 72, 73
Hermann, Sylvia, 72
Hesse, Germany, 35
Heuberg concentration camp, 72
Heuser, Georg, 71
Heydrich, Reinhard, 161
Hier, Marvin, 176, 205
Himmler, Heinrich, 12–13, 161
Hitler, Adolf, 2, 20, 175
rise to power of, 24
SA rivals purged by, 68
suicide of, 27
Hitler Youth, 24, 77, 157
Hoffman, Dustin, 144
Hohenasperg, 29
Höhne, Heinz, 145

Holland, 140, 244–45
Holocaust, 3, 4, 22, 93, 136, 142, 243
    Aedtner's videos of, 99–100
    denial of, 242
    German debate on, 148–49, 158
    German weariness of, 147–48
    memorials for, 60, 209, 216
    see also specific camps
Holocaust (TV miniseries), 146–47, 148–49, 154, 158, 159, 169, 177, 206
Holtzman, Elizabeth, 176–77
Hotel Metropol, 143
Hotel Moriah, 187
Howorka, Nikolaus, 108
Human Rights and Special Prosecutions Section, 243
Hungary, 220
Hussein, Saddam, 214
Husseini, Haj Amin al-, 23

Ibiza, 184
IG Farben, 60
Iggy Pop, 123
Interior Ministry of West Berlin, 160
International Criminal Court, 4, 243
International Military Tribunal, 21
International Refugee Organization, 58
Interpol, 183, 188
Interviú, 184

Iraq, 214
Irgun, 135
Iron Cross, 26
Islam, Wahhabi, 196
Israel, 2, 72, 136
    agreement with Egypt signed by, 113, 172
    Cairo infiltrated by intelligence agents of, 111–12
    creation of, 135
    Eichmann captured and hanged by, 73–75, 79, 111
    Holocaust memorial in, 60
    Ministry of Justice of, 73
    in Six-Day War, 102, 172, 219
    in Suez Crisis, 93
Israel, Ancient, 171
Israel Defense Forces, 3, 22

Japan, 4, 11
Jellinek, Wilhelm, 70
Jewish Community of Berlin, 144, 148
Jewish Documentation Center, 176
Jewish Historical Documentation Center, 19, 22
Jones, Edward S., 9, 37
Juan B., 226
June 2 Movement, 141
Justice Department, U.S., 143, 176–77, 243

Kaiser Wilhelm Memorial Church, 123

Kallman, Katharina, 139
Kamhuber, August, 12
Kamil, Hassan Sayed, 93, 94
Kammerer, Ursula, 81, 83–84, 92
Karadžić, Radovan, 243
Karnak Hotel, 214
Kasr el-Madina Hotel, 1–2,
    190–92, 231, 233, 235–37,
    238, 240
Kaufmann, Karl, 3, 44, 46, 114,
    116
  letter to Austrian Ice Hockey
    Association from, 44, 167
  Linz courthouse report on
    Heim by, 50, 232
Khafagy, Nagy, 121, 133, 193,
    211
Khazar Empire, 137, 171–72,
    232
Kiesinger, Kurt Georg, 112
Kingsley, Ben, 208
Klarsfeld, Beate, 112
Klarsfeld, Serge, 112
Kleingünther, Otto, 168
Klemp, Stefan, 228
Knesset, Israeli, 74, 93
Koch, Robert, 105
Kochendorf, 29–30, 35
Koestler, Arthur, 136–37
Kohl, Agnes, 13
Kohl, Helmut, 171
Kohl, Josef, 3, 12–14, 17, 18, 114,
    116, 163
  testimony against Heim by, 14,
    51–52, 168–69
Kostujak, Vladimir, 109
Kraft, Ursula, 37

Kramer, Wilhelm, 49, 56, 86
Kranebitter, Andreas, 245
Kraus, Peter, 77
Krebsbach, Eduard, 16–17
Kristallnacht, 11, 40, 67, 147,
    209
Krupp, 60
Kuchelbacher, Pauline, 174
Kuwait, 214
KZ Mauthausen, 168

Lager 74, 29
Lamprecht, Ilse, 188
Landesbank Berlin, 214, 216,
    217
Landsberg Prison, 59
Lang, Werner Günter, 188
Laternser, Hans, 59, 77
  hired as Heim's representative,
    78–79
Latin America, 64
Latvia, 220
Law for Liberation from
    National Socialism and
    Militarism, 35
League of German Girls, 157
Lebensborn program, 81
Lehi, 135
Lehnert & Landrock, 120
Levetzowstrasse synagogue, 67,
    159, 209
Levin, Ira, 144
Linz, Werner Ernst, 9, 37, 162
Lipschitz, Joachim, 66, 159
Lischka, Kurt, 112
Lithuania, 220

Lotter, Karl, 3, 108, 115–17, 165, 167
  testimony on Heim of, 50–51
Lotz, Wolfgang, 112
Lübecker Nachrichten, 181
Ludolf Krehl Clinic, 54
Luft, Dr., 45, 56
Lufthansa, 140
Luftwaffe, 77
Lugano, Switzerland, 63, 82, 107, 126, 128
Lulu (film), 83

Magen, Rolf-Peter, 160–61, 165, 166, 168, 174
  Bechtold's loan to Heim investigated by, 177–78
Maison Kammerzell, 63
Majdanek, 143
Majdanek trial, 156
Majorca, 103
Mandl, Professor, 174
Marathon Man (film), 144, 201
Marchante, Karmele, 198
Marien Institute, 30
Maršálek, Hans, 115
Martin, Ernst, 16, 114–15, 245
Mauthausen camp, 10, 20, 40, 43, 46, 50, 102, 104, 117, 127, 139, 173
  as Class III, 13
  film produced at, 146–47
  murder of prisoners in, 13–14
  number of casualties of, 155
  operation book of, 16–17

U.S. military trial over, 15–17, 114–15
Maximilian I, Emperor, 186
Mazin, Max, 199
Meco, 93
medical experiments, in Auschwitz, 71
Meir, Golda, 93
Memorial to the Murdered Jews, 216
Mena House, 119
Mengele, Josef, 3, 126, 144, 177
  discovery of grave of, 200–202, 205
  escape of, 8, 58
Mercedes-Benz, 73
Midan Ataba, 120, 172–73
"Midnight Discussions," 148
Milošević, Slobodan, 243
Ministry for Political Liberation, 35
Mladić, Ratko, 243
Molotov-Ribbentrop Pact, 20
Monroe, Marilyn, 83
Montags, 25
Montazah Gardens, 121
Moriarty, Michael, 147
Mossad, 73, 74, 112
  covert Egyptian actions of, 94
  Cukurs executed by, 111
Mound, Gloria, 184
MTP-AG, 93
Mundo, El, 223
Murderers Among Us, The (Wiesenthal), 143
Mürzzuschlag, 50–51

Mussolini, Benito, 92
My Lai massacre, 135–36

Napoleon I, Emperor of the
    French, 64
Nasser, Gamal Abdel, 64, 65,
    92–93, 94, 113, 118, 132
National Bank of Egypt, 2
Nazi Party, Germany, 8
    central card catalog of, 39
    files of, 39–40
    racial theories of, 37
Nazis, Nazism, 2, 31
    Arab allies of, 23
    pressure to discontinue hunt
        for, 58–59
Nazi war crime investigations:
    in Cairo, 111–12
    enormity of task of, 88
    German hostility to, 88–89
    and groups of Nazi helpers, 92
    statute of limitations on,
        148–49, 154, 176, 177
    see also Aedtner, Alfred;
        Wiesenthal, Simon
Neckarsulm, 35–36
Neesemann, Wolfgang, 166, 169
Newsweek, 171, 227
New Testament, 135
New York Times, 136, 147, 219,
    240
New Zealand, 32
Niederschopfheim, Germany, 27
Niedner, Franz, 41
Niemöller, Dr., 96
Nightline (TV program) 201

Nixon, Richard M., 136
Norway, 36
NSV, 37
Nuremberg Major War Criminals
    Trials, 8, 21, 39, 74, 75, 79,
    136, 242

Oberschopfheim, Germany,
    26–27
O'Connor, John J., 147
Odessa, 5, 92
Odessa File, The (Forsyth),
    143–44
Oeller, Helmut, 147
Office of Jewish Affairs, 175
Office of Special Investigations,
    176–77, 243
oil, 196
Old Testament, 135
Olivier, Laurence, 144, 208
Olympic Games, Barcelona, 236,
    237
Olympic Games, Berlin, 31
Operation Barleycorn, 8
Operation Last Chance, 218, 220,
    226
Oranienburg, 51
Organization of Former SS
    Members, 92
Owl, 3–4

PAG Near East, 65
Palestine, 21, 172
Payerl, Johann, 164–65
Peck, Gregory, 144

Peenemünde, 94
Pellet, Blandine, 216, 217, 218, 223, 224, 231
Pernkopf, Eduard, 31
Persil, 34
Pisano, Tano, 150–52, 210, 217, 218, 223–24, 231
Pister, Hermann, 161
Podlaha, Josef, 17
Poland, 7, 20, 31, 146
  partition of, 135
  Soviet claims to territory of, 27
Police Battalion 322, 89, 207
Pöllmann, Karl, 187
Popular Front for the Liberation of Palestine, 140
Posner, Gerald, 200–201
Possekel, Helene, 80, 84, 92
Powolny, Franz, 109
Princip, Gavrilo, 30

Ramleh prison, 79
Raspe, Jan-Carl, 140
Rauff, Walther, 226
Reader's Digest, 189
Rebbe, Walter, 155
Red Army Faction, 106, 139
Red Brigade, 140
Red Cross, 58, 115, 130
Red Devils, 45, 52
Reich Justice Ministry, 39
Reich Main Security Office, 161
Reich Security Central Office, 23
reichsmark, 49

Remington Rand, 69
Revolutionary Cells, 141
Ribbentrop, Joachim von, 73
Richter, Hans, 17
Rieben, Ms., 92
Rieger, Gustav, 107–9, 116–17, 164, 197
Riessersee, 45
Rifai, Abdelmoneim el, 171–72, 194
Rifai, Mrs., 171, 172
Rifai, Tarek el, 171, 194
Rifat, 122, 133, 193
Road into Life, The (Becker), 18
Rodensky, Shmuel, 144
Röhm Putsch, 68
Romanticism, 53
Rommel, Erwin, 112
Roots (TV miniseries), 146
Rosa, Pauline, 21
Rostock, 31, 37
Rückerl, Adalbert, 102
Rundfunk, Bayerischer, 147
Russia, 36
Rwanda, 4, 343
Ryan, Hermine Braunsteiner, 143

SA, 8, 43, 68, 88, 127
Sachsenhausen, 51
Sadat, Anwar el-, 118, 172
Saint-Germain-en-Laye, Treaty of, 30
Sakharov, Andrei, 142
Sanatorium Hahn, 86
Saudi Arabia, 196, 214

Scarabee Hotel, 119–20, 195–97, 211, 237
Schäffner, Inspector, 97
Schauly, Friedrich, 41
Schibukat, Herbert, 45
Schindler's List (film), 216
Schleyer, Hanns Martin, 140
Schmeling, Max, 206
Schmidt, Helmut, 176
Schüle, Erwin, 71, 88–89, 102
Schumann, Jürgen, 140
Schwammberger, Josef, 216
Schwarze Reichswehr, 68
Seconda Sessione delle Udienze Internazionali Sacharov, 142
Second Law for the Conclusion of Denazification, 66, 159–60, 178
Second Vatican Council, 135
Sedlmeier, Hans, 200
Seibel, Richard, 20
Seidenberger Tonwerke, 24
September 11, 2001, terrorist attacks, 216
Seventh Army, U.S., 29
Shinar, Felix, 73
Shin Bet, 74
Siberia, 27
Simon Wiesenthal Center, 143, 144, 176, 205, 219, 240
Sinai Peninsula, 219
Six-Day War, 102, 172, 219
Skorzeny, Otto, 92
Sobibor death camp, 146, 219
Social Democratic Party, Austria, 115

Social Democratic Party, German, 35, 147
Soesman, Ray, 244
Sokolovsky, Vasily, 41
Some Like It Hot (film), 83
Sommer, Rupert, 3, 50, 108, 114
Sophie, Duchess of Hohenberg, 30
Soviet Military Administration (SMAD), 42
Soviet Union, 12, 20
  in Cold War, 4, 21–22, 83
  Egypt aided by, 93
  end of Nazi trials by, 59
Späth, Lothar, 173
Spatzenegger, Hans, 15
Spider (Die Spinne), 92
Spiegel, Der, 88, 92, 120, 149, 207, 222
  Heim article in, 145, 152–53, 154–57, 160, 163, 196
  on Heim's trial, 169
Spielberg, Steven, 216
Sport-Tagblatt, 30
Spruchkammer law, 35, 66, 69, 160, 161, 162, 163, 165, 169, 170, 174, 181, 194
Spruchkammer Neckarsulm, 42–43
SS, 3, 11, 13, 29, 43, 65, 70, 81, 90, 94, 111, 115, 127, 145, 161
  doctors of, 17, 78, 107, 139, 245
  execution of deserters from, 26
  prosecution of officers of, 69

Stalin, Josef, 20, 21
  show trials of, 136
Stalingrad, Battle of, 25
Stark (SS man), 90
Stasi, 217
State Institute for War
    Documentation, 103
State Justice Administrations for
    the Investigation of National
    Socialist Crimes, 71
State Theater, 18
Steinacker, Fritz, 77–79, 172,
    178
  Aedtner's monitoring of,
    138–39
  Heim's appeal filed by, 180
  Heim's custody dispute and,
    105
  Heim's meetings with, 133,
    134–35
  at Heim's trial, 166, 168–69
  Heim's voice recorded by, 134,
    141, 142–43
  hired as Heim's representative,
    78–79, 163–64
  law studied by, 78
  military service of, 77–78
Strauss, Franz Josef, 176
Streep, Meryl, 147
Suez Canal, 93, 113
Suez Crisis, 93
Sunflower, The (Wiesenthal),
    143
Supreme Headquarters, Allied
    Expeditionary Force, 7
Sweden, 140
Switzerland, 125

Tagesspiegel, 158, 160, 183
Tageszeitung, 167–68, 170
Taha, Sheikh, 192
Tangier, Morocco, 91–92, 97
Tatari, Yoash, 207, 208
Taylor, Robert S., 57
Televisión Madrid, 198
Thann, France, 25
Third Army, U.S., 8
Thirteenth Tribe, The (Koestler),
    136–37
"Those Who Shall Never Forget,"
    111
Tile-Wardenberg-Strasse 28,
    66–67, 86, 124–26, 133,
    158–59, 162–63, 173, 180–81,
    209, 213
  Aedtner's investigation of, 124
  damage to, 162–63
  protest over, 158–59, 209
  sale of, 209, 213
  value of, 162
Tiller, Nadja, 83
Time, 171
Tito, Marshal, 171
Treblinka, 219
Tuchen, Lothar, 158
Turkey, 4
Tutu, Desmond, 143

UBAGO, 198
Uhlenbroich, Burkhard, 230–31
Ukraine, 220
Ulm-Wilhelmsburg, 68
  Fischer-Schweder's trial in,
    69–70

Unertl, Franz Xaver, 88
United Arab Republic, 93
United Nations, 74, 119
United States, 125
    in Cold War, 4, 21–22, 83
    former Nazis hired by, 4
    German military personnel in
        custody of, 7–8
United States Holocaust
    Memorial Museum,
    215–16
Unter den Linden, 124
Ustaše, 58
U.S. v. Hans Altfuldisch et al., 15

Vance, Cyrus, 171
Varazdin, 31
Vashem, Yad, 74
Venezuela, 184, 188
Versailles Treaty, 29
Vienna, destruction in, 12
Vietnam War, 135–36
Vogel, Hans-Jochen, 145, 161,
    176
Völkischer Beobachter, 115–16
Volksbank Dreieich, 124
Volkssolidarität, 13
Volkssturm auxiliary, 26–27
Voss, Wilhelm, 65

Waffen-SS, 3, 22, 36, 37, 40, 42,
    161, 174, 196
Wahhabi Islam, 196
Waida, Robert, 189
Waldheim, Kurt, 171, 205

Ware, John, 200–201
Warsaw Ghetto, 147
Wehrmacht, 8, 22, 25, 59, 65,
    112
Weil, Mrs., 95
Weil family, 133
Weinaug, Herta, 37, 91
Weisshaupt, Karl-Heinz, 107
Welsch, Fräulein, 86
Wende, Hannelore, 94
West Bank, 219
Westdeutscher Rundfunk, 148
West Germany, 58, 66, 69, 136
    army of, 154
    economic growth in, 63, 83
    Holocaust memorials in, 209
West Jerusalem, 135
Westner, Gebhard, 109
Wiener Graben stone quarry, 13
Wiesel, Elie, 147, 205
Wiesenthal, Cyla, 19, 21, 222
Wiesenthal, Simon, 3, 19–23, 112,
    161, 198
    Aedtner's relationship with,
        142–43, 144, 199–200
    death of, 222
    Eichmann pursued by, 23, 58,
        60, 74, 103
    and end of prosecution of Nazi
        criminals, 59
    Heim pursued by, 102–3,
        142–43, 173, 174, 183, 231
    legacy of, 243
    in Mauthausen, 142
    Mengele theories of, 01
    movie characters based on,
        144, 201, 208

Nazi reparations desired by, 144–45
press conference of, 102–3
recognition of, 221–22
retirement of, 57, 218
and rumors of Heim's death, 215
statute of limitations on Nazi crimes opposed by, 176
Venezuela trip of, 184, 188
Waldheim scandal and, 205
Wilder, Billy, 83
Wilhelm Droste, 86, 124–25, 144, 155, 159
Woods, James, 147
World Cup, 214
World Jewish Congress, 88, 205

World War I, 20, 30, 67
Wurche, Gottfried, 159

Yad Vashem, 60, 219
Yellow Cottage, 151
Yugoslavia, 7, 128, 243

ZDF, 240
Zimmermann, Eduard, 203–4
Zionist paramilitary group, 135
Zivier, Ernst R., 160
Zoologischer Garten train station, 123
Zuroff, Efraim, 218–20, 226, 228–29, 240, 241

ILLUSTRATION CREDITS

Photo of Mauthausen: BMI/Fotoarchiv der KZ-Gedenkstätte Mauthausen

Photos of Alfred Aedtner: courtesy of the Aedtner family

Photo of Simon Wiesenthal: courtesy of the Simon Wiesenthal Archive, Vienna

Photo of Waltraut Böser: courtesy of Waltraut Böser

Photos of al-Azhar mosque and Kasr el-Madina hotel: Ariana Drehsler

Photos of Heim's briefcase, Egyptian documents, Mahmoud Doma, and elderly Heim in Egypt: courtesy of the authors

Photo of Gaetano Pisano and Blandine Pellet: Joseluis Aznar Muñoz

All other photographs courtesy of the Heim family